LIBERATION THEOLOGY AND SEXUALITY

This book is timely and well-planned and more such books are needed as theologians engaged with the Gospel in Latin America have developed new themes and new challenges. The authors reflect well such type of contemporary liberation theology and the editor is an internationally well-known theologian. Students, teachers and researchers in the field should find this volume invaluable.

Mario I. Aguilar
Director of the Centre for the Study of Religion and Politics
St. Mary's College
University of St. Andrews, UK

Liberation Theology and Sexuality is a book about 'doing Liberation Theology in Latin America' in the Twenty First Century. The style of doing theology remains the same, but this book reflects the work of a new generation of liberation theologians developing a theology that offers a wider and more complex critique of reality, with new perspectives on issues of sexuality, race, gender, culture, globalization and new forms of popular religiosity.

Liberation Theology and Sexuality shows how Christianity in Latin America needs to take into account issues concerning sexuality and poverty, together with traditional religiosity and culture when reflecting on the construction of Christian faith and identity in the continent. For the first time, *Liberation Theology and Sexuality* presents a unique combination of Latin American theologians from more than one generation, reflecting on depth on the ongoing project of the liberation of theology from economic and sexual oppressions in the continent.

¿Se acuerdan, queridos? ¡Qué épocas! Dictadura, miseria, represión y nosotros en la iglesia militante. Nosotros, pensando en Bonhoeffer. Nosotros, leyendo a Gutiérrez. Nosotros, mientras Cardenal leía salmos con los campesinos en Nicaragua. Nosotros haciendo obra en las comunidades de base, releyendo los profetas ... (pero el corazón siempre estaba entre paréntesis; el corazón, en el armario, esperando tiempos mejores: otros corazones, otros amores y otras liberaciones).

Liberation Theology and Sexuality

Edited by

MARCELLA ALTHAUS-REID
University of Edinburgh, UK

ASHGATE

Published by
Ashgate Publishing Limited
Gower House
Croft Road
Aldershot
Hampshire GU11 3HR
England

Ashgate Publishing Company
Suite 420
101 Cherry Street
Burlington, VT 05401-4405
USA

Ashgate website: http://www.ashgate.com

British Library Cataloguing in Publication Data
Liberation theology and sexuality
   1.Homosexuality – Latin America – Religious aspects –
   Christianity 2.Liberation theology 3.Sex – Latin America –
   Religious aspects – Christianity 4.Homosexuality –
   Philosophy 5.Latin America – Religion
   I. Althaus-Reid, Marcella
   261.8'35766'098

Library of Congress Cataloging-in-Publication Data
Liberation theology and sexuality / Marcella Althaus-Reid (ed.).
      p. cm.
   Includes index.
   ISBN 0-7546-5080-4 (hardback : alk. paper)
   1. Homosexuality—Religious aspects—Christianity. 2. Liberation
theology—Latin America.
   I. Althaus-Reid, Marcella.

   BR115.H6L49 2006
   230'.046408664—dc22

                                                                2005031988

ISBN-10: 0 7546 5080 4

Typeset by Tradespools, Chippenham, Wiltshire.
Printed and bound in Great Britain by Antony Rowe Ltd, Chippenham, Wiltshire.

Contents

Acknowledgements   *vii*
The Contributors   *viii*

Introduction   1
Marcella Althaus-Reid

 1 'Let Them Talk …!' Doing Liberation Theology from Latin
    American Closets   5
    Marcella Althaus-Reid

 2 Once Again Liberating Theology? Towards a Latin American
    Liberation Theological Self-Criticism   19
    Otto Maduro

 3 Queer Eye for the Straight Guy: The Making Over of
    Liberation Theology, A Queer Discursive Approach   33
    Ivan Petrella

 4 Oh, Que Sera, Que Sera … A Limping A/Theological
    Thought in Brazil   51
    Claudio Carvalhaes

 5 Commodity Aesthetics and the Erotics of Relationship:
    Challenges of Feminist Hermeneutics of Liberation to
    Market Aesthetics   71
    Nancy Cardoso Pereira

 6 The Prostitutes Also Go into the Kingdom of God: A Queer
    Reading of Mary of Magdala   81
    Martín Hugo Córdova Quero

 7 Liberation Theology, Modernity and Sexual Difference   111
    Frederico Pieper Pires

 8 Liberating Mary, Liberating the Poor   123
    Mario Ribas

 9 Seriously Harmful For Your Health? Religion, Feminism and
    Sexuality in Latin America   137
    Elina Vuola

10 Worship and the Excluded   163
    Jaci Maraschin

11 Love in Times of Dictatorships: Memoirs from a Gay Minister
    from Buenos Aires   179
    Roberto González with Norberto D'Amico

Index   *189*

Acknowledgements

I should like to express my gratitude to people who have inspired me and challenged me with their reflections on Liberation Theology and sexuality over the past few years. First of all, I must mention Professor Jaci Maraschin from the Methodist University of São Paulo, at whose invitation I went to Brazil in 2004 to give a series of lectures to his Department of Pós-Graduaçao em Ciências da Religião. Also, all the women of *Católicas pelo Direito de Decidir* who invited me to give a public lecture to the Pontificia Roman Catholic University of São Paulo, Brazil, in 2004. Second, I would like to mention that important Brazilian Feminist Theology collective which is *Mandrágora*, especially Luiza Tomita and Sandra Duarte de Souza. I should also include Graciela Chamorro, a Paraguayan theologian from the University of Hamburg whose work on sexuality and the Jesuitic missions has been important for my reflections on Latin American Christianity and the politics of sexual identity in theology.

Finally, I would like to dedicate this book to the women of the Buenos Aires Sexual Rights Collective *Ají de Pollo*: Paula Viturro, Lohana Berkins and Mónica D'Uva. *Y la lucha continua, compañeras.*

The Contributors

Marcella Althaus-Reid is an Argentinian theologian. She is a Reader in Theology and Ethics at the School of Divinity, University of Edinburgh, Scotland. She is the Associate Editor of *The Edinburgh Journal of World Christianity*, and is a member of the advisory board of *Concilium*. She has published extensively in the area of Liberation Theology and sexuality. Her books include *Indecent Theology* (London: Routledge, 2000; *La Teología Indecente*, Barcelona: Bellaterra, 2005); *The Queer God* (London: Routledge, 2003); and *From Feminist Theology to Indecent Theology* (London: SCM, 2004).

Claudio Carvalhaes is a Presbyterian minister from Brazil, doing a doctoral programme on Theology and Art at Union Theological Seminary, New York. He has worked with immigrant communities in the United States and currently edits the 'Teología y Cultura' section of the website *Teologia Brasileira* (teologiabrasileira.com.br).

Norberto D'Amico was born in Buenos Aires, Argentina, and has been an active member of the Metropolitan Community Church of Buenos Aires since 1990. Currently, he is the coordinator of the communication programme of the Church, maintaining a web page with information and several religious resources in Spanish.

Roberto González was born in Rosario, Argentina. He was a Salvation Army officer working for several years in Paraguay and Argentina, after which he completed his Bachelor in Divinity degree from Instituto Superior Evongélico de Estudies Teológicos, Buenos Aires, in 1987. Rev González came out as a gay clergyman in 1986 and founded the Metropolitan Community Church in Buenos Aires in 1987, where he was finally ordained as minister in 1995. He is a very well known long-standing activist for sexual and religious human rights and a respected public figure in Argentina. Currently, he is a minister in charge of the Buenos Aires *Iglesia de la Comunidad Metropolitana del Centro*.

Otto Maduro is a Venezuelan philosopher and sociologist of religion, internationally known for his contribution to Liberation Theology. Presently he is the Chair of Church and Society in Drew University, where he also co-chairs with Dr Ada Maria Isasi Diaz the Hispanic Institute of Theology. Otto is the associate editor of several journals, including *Social Compass*;

Cristianismo y Sociedad; *The Journal of Hispano/Latino Theology*; and *Concilium*. His many books include *Judaism, Christianity and Liberation* (Maryknoll: Orbis, 1991); *Mapas para la Fiesta* (Buenos Aires: CNT, 1994); and *The Future of Liberation Theology: Essays in Honor of Gustavo Gutiérrez* (co-edited with Mark Ellis; Maryknoll: Orbis, 1989).

Jaci Maraschin is a Brazilian philosopher of religion and minister of the Episcopal Church of Brazil. He is currently a professor of Religious Studies in the Methodist University of São Paulo, and edits the journal *Margens*. He has published many works of theology and poetry. His publications include *O Espelho e a Transparencia* (Rio de Janeiro: CEDI, 1989); *Rastro de São Mateus* (São Paulo: UMESP, 1998). Professor Maraschin is also author and editor of several worship song books.

Nancy Cardoso Pereira is a Brazilian Methodist minister and theologian, currently working in the Pastoral Committee of the Landless Movement. She is the church assessor on politics and spirituality amongst peasant women in Rio Grande do Sul, and Professor of History in the Porto Alegre Institute. Her numerous publications include *Amantissima Evangelho de Maria* (São Paulo: Olho da Agua, 2002); *Palabras: Se Feitas de Carne* (São Paulo: CDD, 2004); and articles in *RIBLA, Cuadernos de Teología* and *Concilium*. Nancy is a member of the editorial board of *RIBLA* (Latin American Review of Biblical Interpretation).

Ivan Petrella is an Argentinian theologian, currently Assistant Professor of Religious Studies at the University of Miami. He is the author of numerous articles published in *The Journal of Hispanic/Latino Theology* and *Cuadernos de Teología*. He is the author of *The Future of Liberation Theology* (London: Ashgate, 2004) and *Liberation Theology: The New Generation* (Maryknoll: Orbis, 2005).

Frederico Pieper Pires is a Brazilian doctoral candidate, currently finishing a research project on postmodernism and religion at the Methodist University of São Paulo, Brazil. He is a member of the editorial board of *Correlatio*, the Journal of the Paul Tillich Society of the Methodist University of São Paulo. His articles have been published in journals such as *Correlatio* and *Via Teologica*.

Martín Hugo Córdova Quero is an Argentinian Anglican minister and theologian, doing a doctorate at the Church Divinity School of the Pacific, Berkeley University. Before that, he served as a minister in Argentina and in Hawaii. He has published articles and chapters in books, and has contributed to journals, including *Studies in World Christianity*.

Mario Ribas is a Liberation Theologian and the rector of All Saints' Church in Santos, Brazil. He currently lives in South Africa, where he is completing doctoral research on sexuality and post-colonialism at the University of Cape Town. He has published in several journals, including *Theology and Sexuality*. He was one of the speakers at the conference 'Halfway to Lambeth' in Manchester, England, 2003.

Elina Vuola is a researcher at the Institute of Development Studies at Helsinski University and director of a project on women's rights in Nicaragua for the Academy of Finland. She has worked in Costa Rica and Nicaragua. Her publications include *Limits of Liberation: Praxis as Method in Latin American Liberation Theology and Feminist Theology* (Helsinski: Finnish Academy of Science and Letters, 1997; *Teología Feminista, Teología de la Liberación*, Madrid: IEPALA, 2000); *Between the Church and the State: Nicaraguan Women's Reproductive Rights and the Promotion of Human Rights in the Finnish Development Cooperation* (Helsinski: The University Press, 1998).

Introduction

Marcella Althaus-Reid

The doing of a Liberation Theology grounded on issues of sexuality, and specifically in queer theory and sexuality, has been and still is a much-debated issue inside and outside the Church and academic circles in Latin America. Surprisingly, although the discussions have been fierce at times, arguments concerning the legitimacy of doing a theology of liberation grounded on people's own sexual life and struggles are scarce. Historically, liberationists may have considered issues concerning gender and the transgression of heterosexual norms a deviance and distraction from the class struggle. Most of the pioneer theologians of the 1970s, Catholics and Protestants alike, concurred in a naïve Marxist understanding that the social revolution was going to expunge every single area of injustice from our lives, including injustices relating to gender and race. While Liberation Theologians developed ideals of the new family, and the new man and woman who would live in this new society, these ideal pictures did not envisage any substantial changes in the way we understand loving relationships in society. In fact, they did not even consider the traditional patterns of family life and sexuality already present amongst the different Latin American cultures. So far as Liberation Theology was concerned, the Kingdom of God on earth was going to be composed of men who were men, and women who were women, without introducing any hermeneutical suspicion about the construction of gender and sexuality within Christianity itself. The concept of sexuality and gender outside the realm of the private, but as part of a structure of sin, took at least another decade to be developed.

In spite of Liberation Theology being, by definition, a dynamic theology representing an orthopraxis, that is, a Church and a dogma in movement, the fact is that over time Latin American Liberation Theology also developed its own orthodoxy. It is this orthodoxy, or the *guardia vieja teológica* ('theological old guard') responsible for it, that are generally identified by those who claim that Liberation Theology has lost its way. Indeed, the criticism has some force: the *guardia vieja* has lost its way, hermeneutically and thematically. The hermeneutical circle ceased to enquire, to distrust the accommodation of ideological discourse into theology; and the 'issue-based' theology pre-selected and actively banned the issues that were relevant to the people although inconvenient for the churches. Paradoxically, the liberationist orthodoxy, as it exists now, was not necessarily created by a core of

Latin American theologians but rather by those in the West who wanted to canonize the liberationist praxis and discourse from the 1970s. There are reasons for this, including the tendency among North Atlantic Christian scholars to fix the theological agenda according to a colonial perspective which included the nativization of sexual and racial stereotypes. However, as this collection of essays shows, doing 'Liberation Theology and sexuality' is an occasion for Latin American thinkers to bring together issues of theology, culture, sexuality and class analysis.

Interestingly, Liberation Theology and sexuality is one of the more grounded examples of theological praxis. It does not arise from within academia, which originally would not consider these issues to be part of the liberationist agenda: it comes from the people, excluded from Church discourses for centuries in Latin America. Issues of sexuality, and specifically issues pertaining to the struggle for identity and the rights of those who do not conform to heterosexual norms, come from basic ecclesial communities and the urban poor, as well as from academics who have continued doing theology that requires listening to the sexually excluded. There has been, for a long time, a kind of closet Liberation Theology developed at the fringes of the churches that has been closer to popular Latin American spirituality and culture than the orthodox liberationist discourses.

The authenticity of Liberation Theology and sexuality can be ignored but not denied. Moreover, it is not the exclusive domain of second- (or third-) generation liberation theologians: Latin America has had theological pioneers in this area since the 1970s. Two of them have contributed articles in this collection. Jaci Maraschin and Otto Maduro are first-generation liberationists who have pioneered a radical theology of liberation in dialogue with many elements that today might be considered part of a queer theology. In their work, issues concerning the body of the poor, sexuality and traditional religions and culture are combined with political analysis.

As a Latin American sexual theologian, my work in the area of queer studies and Liberation Theology has always been developed in dialogue with compatriots. Doing theology and sexuality is part of a community reflection, and this book is an example of that. This collection of essays not only comes from the reflections of Latin American theologians, but is in part the result of some years of sharing and discussing issues of Liberation Theology and sexuality amongst the contributors, both personally and through the Internet. Informally, we have called our group *La Virtual QTL* ('The Virtual Queer Liberation Theology Group'), a title that suggests a tango ensemble rather than an academic association, no doubt reflecting the presence of several Argentinians within its membership. However that may be, this informal network has produced collective reflections on Liberation Theology and sexual dissidence, while at the same time sharing research and other everyday issues of our lives as academics and/or ministers.

Many of the articles in this book come from members of *La Virtual*: Hugo Córdova Quero, Jaci Maraschin, Mario Ribas, Claudio Carvalhaes, Roberto

González, Norberto D'Amico, and myself. Others are Latin American colleagues whose participation in the exchange of ideas in recent years has been important: Otto Maduro, Ivan Petrella, Nancy Cardoso Pereira and Elina Vuola. This collection of essays is an interaction of more than two generations of Latin American liberationists, nurtured in different political situations, church traditions and even cultural contexts. Taken together, they represent Liberation Theology in motion: dynamic, unsettling, still struggling with orthodoxy while engaging in the broad struggle for justice that includes sexual justice.

Liberationists doing a sexual theology are somehow difficult to classify. They may be considered part of a lesbigay, bisexual/transexual theological movement, and yet they also exhibit the peculiarity of the Latin American way of doing theology. There is almost always an analysis of production, based on Marx, which makes them consider the links between consumerism, desire and production in the present global capitalist expansion. Although liberationists will always be primarily political theologians, issues of culture and popular religiosity are equally important. The use of post-colonial analysis in Liberation Theology reflects the need for a deeper understanding of the sexual identity and spirituality of Latin American people. These issues are also considered within the framework of European Continental philosophy. Moreover, reflection on sexuality has important implications for systematic theology, and pastoral theology and spirituality, two fundamental pillars of Liberation Theology. These essays confront us with twenty-first-century liberationist action and reflection, which come not only from an alliance of struggles for justice, but more decisively, by an alliance in the continuous task of unveiling ideological formations of sexuality, class, gender and race in theology and in Church praxis. At the end of the day, a change in sexuality *per se* would not be a revolution, but a change in the production of sexual epistemologies would help to denounce and transform the roots of many mechanisms of power and control.

It is my hope that this book might signal the beginning of a friendship and wider dialogue between different generations of liberationists, doing a political and sexual theology of liberation. This would enable Christian people of Latin America to continue the struggle for justice and peace by subverting a totalitarian sexual theology that is still responsible for much suffering and oppression amongst our people, amongst our poor in particular.

Chapter 1

'Let Them Talk …!'
Doing Liberation Theology from Latin American Closets

Marcella Althaus-Reid

Lambe lambe
Um beijo seu
Revelaçao

Boca a boca
Um beijo seu
A salvaçao
…
na boca do povo
un beijo seu
revoluçao
…
Deixa que digam!
E so um beijo
De homen com homem
Mulher com mulher
Um beijo qualquer.[1]

Nancy Cardoso Pereira (1998: 116)

In Santiago de Chile in 1992, a group of people marched in the streets of the capital city, to demonstrate against the violation of human rights and the atrocities of the Pinochet regime, which left the country with thousands of murdered and disappeared. Inspired by the *Informe de Verdad y Reconciliacion*[2] (the Chilean Document on Truth and Reconciliation), a group of transvestites, homosexuals, bisexuals and lesbians decided to take the streets of Santiago by storm, to show their solidarity with current human rights organizations. They also wanted to demonstrate the links between a homophobic society and a repressive military one. The march was organized by Chilean citizens and socio-sexual activists, denouncing a terrorist state, while at the same time proclaiming the need for a democracy based on participation and respect for human life in its political, religious, racial and sexual diversity. However, according to press reports from the time, the demonstration received little sympathy from human rights activists in general. Señora Sola Sierra, founder of the *Agrupacion de Familiares de Detenidos-Desaparecidos* (Association of Relatives from Detained-Disappeared People in Chile) was aghast at the 'bunch of faggots' in the streets (Núñez Gonzalez 2004: 23).[3] She considered that a gay, lesbian, bisexual and transvestite group of people demonstrating for human rights belittled and ridiculed the political struggle of the mothers of the disappeared. Thus part of a published letter written by the Chilean writer Pedro Lemebel recalling the occasion reads as follows:

> ... the bunch of faggots (*ramillete de locas*) in the procession had full make up on their faces and used all their finery as if the occasion was a carnival. All the poof art folk were there, parading in *La Alameda*, and shouting 'Justice! Justice! We want justice!' ... Next day, all the newspapers gave plenty space to the homosexual [sic] march, which, with their scandalous behaviour, only helped to obscure the denunciation against [state crimes committed with] impunity.
>
> (Núñez Gonzalez 2004: 26)

It is somehow paradoxical and revealing to find that the name that Lemebel gave to the 'bunch of faggots' in Spanish is a *ramillete de locas*. '*Ramillete*' means a small bunch of flowers; '*locas*' means 'mad women' but also is an adjective given to sexually deviant people, including women and gays transgressing gender and sexual codes. For instance, in Argentina during the dictatorial regime which also cost us at least 30,000 disappeared, *locas* was the name of ridicule given to the Mother of the Disappeared by the press of the regime. The paradox involved in the use of the term *locas* both for queers as for the mothers of Plaza de Mayo thus becomes clear. As the gay, lesbian, bi and transvestite movements in Chile started to organize their political aims, their opponents did not realize that they all faced a surprisingly common struggle. To start with, the regime of the times considered all as deviant. They were abnormal, not only politically, but on grounds of gender and sexuality as well as religiously. They stood up to challenge the regimes of normality imposed by a criminal state informed by some Christian codes of submissiveness. For a fascist mentality in Latin America imposing tight control on people's lives and thoughts during the Cold War, the difference between a mother as a political activist, thus challenging a gender role, and a transvestite asking for human rights was negligible.

It is sad to realize that there was little solidarity between political activists and socio-sexual activists at the time. Perhaps the only solidarity experienced was achieved in the midst of common suffering and persecution because, after all, heterosexuals and queers died together in the jails of the dictatorial regimes of Chile, Uruguay or Argentina.

However, there was also little solidarity on the part of the militant churches, informed by Liberation Theology, with the people who lived in fear and suffered persecutions and violence due to their sexual and gender options.

The brutal military regimes of the 1970s were profoundly heterosexual regimes. That was manifested in their organization and expectations of what elsewhere I have called 'decency': a 'Christian way of life' manifested by the length of women's skirts, approved haircuts for men, and strict gender codes applied across everyday life. Moreover, many human rights activists, sometimes distinguished religious leaders, were subjected to state campaigns that accused them of 'homosexuality'. This was an attempt to undermine their work in the defence of human rights by linking it to disapproved behaviour and illegal activities. But the question we need to ask must be more specific concerning Liberation Theology. We need to consider how it was possible that a highly sophisticated, critical theology, its characteristic feature being the courage that leads religious and lay people to martyrdom, was never able to consider issues of sexual ideology in theology? I personally do not believe that liberationists were blind to issues of sexual ideology in theology. We need to consider the extent of the skills on which Liberation Theology was based: Ricoeurian and Marxist influences on biblical hermeneutics and an ecclesiology inspired by Freirean thought.

In reality, the answer to our question must be complex. First of all, we need to acknowledge that Liberation Theology does not arise from a homogeneous church or doctrinal body. Varying from country to country, the militant churches were made up of a mixture of Roman Catholic dioceses, historical Protestant churches, and also some Pentecostals and Evangelical churches such as the Baptists, particularly in Nicaragua.[4] The Pentecostal Church of God of Buenos Aires, a church informed by issues of social justice, was part of the original group of churches that founded the Latin American Council of Churches (CLAI) in 1982. Therefore, the various militant churches came from organizations with very different sexual and gender codes, as well as different traditions of political participation. For instance, some militant churches, such as the Church of God, did not ordain women, while a church with a long tradition of women's ministerial equality and social action, such as the Salvation Army, abstained from involvement in any form of political theological praxis.

In general, all theological reflection on sexuality and gender, during the early years of Liberation Theology, were done in private. Liberationists were too sophisticated to ignore these issues and, as I shall claim later, there may have been an underground sexual theology in the making. Even the argument that gender and sexuality were ignored because Liberation Theology was done by mostly male, celibate priests, who as a group are notorious for their sexual conflicts, does not make sense. It has been suggested that in Liberation Theology people's issues sooner or later became the focus of theological reflection. One can be tempted to think that the conflicts over celibacy and homosexual desire amongst the priests should have been addressed with the same theological honesty that was required of political reflection.

But what about the people in base communities, for instance? Even if the first generation of (male, celibate priest) theologians did not take those issues

on board, people in the communities may have done so. That may be true in
an idealized understanding of how theologies perform, and specifically
Liberation Theology. Common people do not have ecclesiastical power. They
are not the ones required to rethink the organization of their dioceses or
parishes, or approve the theological programmes to be taught in Latin
American universities or seminaries. They do not publish books or have space
in the media. To unveil political or sexual ideologies in church and theology
requires some power, or alliances of power, to be in place. The natural
alliance of power should have been with the existent movements defending
gays and poor transvestites forced into prostitution and persecuted by the
state, but that did not happen. Freire should perhaps have said that for
change to come about these issues had to become part of the formation of
new priests and ministers, and the ministry needed to be opened up to people
of different genders and sexualities.

Sexuality and Liberationists: Some Arguments

To reflect on the main issues arising from the historical silence of Liberation
Theology on sexuality, we must address a few foundational issues. Briefly, we
need to consider the following points, which should have been part of the
Latin American hermeneutical circle:

1   Issues concerning a post-colonial reflection on indigenous sexual and
    economic cultures. There was a lack of reflection on the process of church
    formation and the sexual evangelization of the Latin American people,
    and how this related to the economic disorganization of the existing
    efficient agricultural structures.
2   The early influence of the work of Enrique Dussel, a distinguished Marxist
    theologian and philosopher of liberation, who homologized capitalist
    desire with gay desire. The hermeneutical work of J. Severino Croatto on
    original sin was connected with Dussel's homophobia.
3   Finally, the development of a type of feminist Liberation Theology which
    was complementary and did not question the ideological formation of
    sexuality. The development of Mariology (and Mariology of Liberation)
    may be related to this.

Evangelization and Sexuality in the Americas

One of the causes of the public theological indifference to issues of sexuality
in Liberation Theology was a serious lack of post-colonial analysis.
Liberationists did not research or reflect in any depth on the sexual
indoctrination which accompanied the so-called evangelization of Latin
America. There is a wealth of archival material and studies in this area,

especially on issues of sexuality and the (hetero)sexual indoctrination relating
to the Jesuits in Latin America.[5] These studies include issues of the sexual
imposition of the new power structure of the Americas made by
Conquistadores and priests, for example in the work done by the Paraguayan
theologian Graciela Chamorro. There has also been specific work done on
issues of the legislation of marriage and education according to the sexual
laws of colonial Latin America. Moreover, there are testimonies of
indigenous people who fiercely struggled against diverse issues such as
Christian prohibitions on marrying certain members of a family, or
monogamy, or marriage itself.

It has been part of the paradox of Liberation Theology in Latin America
that it could not recognize the need to extend the analysis of the formation of
ideological apparatuses beyond the field of political economy into wider
cultural impositions in church and theology. However, love and affectivity as
emotional exchanges occur under frames of ideological construction. The
hegemonic absolutization of Western heterosexual manifestations of love in
Latin American society (such as the legal status of Western marriage) is
highly institutionalized. This goes beyond personal and individual expressions
of love, for it includes also, apart from the traditional theological discourses,
the formation, organization and expectations of Christian institutions, where
love is the point of all convergence of the churches' praxis. Christianity in
Latin America has been a sexual enterprise: it de-legitimized public structures
and interfered in the domestic spaces of affectionate exchanges. Missionaries
used linguistic strategies to enforce their own sexual theologies onto the
natives, for instance the concepts of a fallen nature in women after Eve's sin,
the idea of women as sexual temptresses, and the representation of a virtuous
heterosexual masculinity as Christian.

Graciela Chamorro, in her original book *Teología Guaraní* (2002), has
specifically reflected on the construction of womanhood and manhood
amongst the Jesuit missions in Paraguay, particularly the work of translation
by Ruiz de Montoya, the creator of the Guaraní-Spanish lexicon, which was
systematized in dictionaries, grammar books and catechisms (Chamorro
2002: 31). According to Chamorro, there is a strong (hetero)sexual European
matrix in the reconceptualization of the original Guaraní words for 'man' and
'woman'. Montoya resignified the original indigenous concepts by introducing a qualification of woman as bad, and man as good.[6] The Guaraní Nation
was forced to reconsider their own language with new theological
connotations, thus introducing a whole sexist cosmovision into the everyday
vocabulary of the Americas. Chamorro points out how a Guaraní expression
meaning 'a dishonest man' was translated into Spanish as 'an adulterous
man'. The phrase meaning 'to desire a woman' was linguistically deformed to
mean 'a woman inciting a man to have a carnal relationship with him'. The
pervasiveness and extension of the processes of sexual colonization in Latin
America need to be considered as playing a key part in the theological
enterprise of the Roman Catholic Church. The post-colonial insecurity of

Liberation Theology meant that the liberationists were in denial of their own hermeneutical circle. What happened to the continual assertion that Liberation Theology was to be mediated by social sciences such as anthropology?

Although the theological project can never take us into an ideal return to a pre-colonial Latin America, Liberation Theology needs to reflect on the sexual past of the Church in the continent. The history of the Church in Latin America needs to assume its own sexual responsibility for having produced a symbolic discourse that married divinity to heterosexual structures and systems of power. Moreover, the sexual understanding of the native nations also has important contributions to make to the understanding of exchanges not only of love and divine cosmovisions, but also of labour. Traditional economic institutions such as the Ayni, to mention one, depend on a different idea of affectionate exchanges (Althaus-Reid 2003). Even if Liberation Theology wanted to reflect only on economic issues, it would have been worth paying attention to the understanding of sexuality in the traditions of the Original Nations, today sadly represented by the poorest of the poor in the continent.

Gays and Capitalists: In Search of a Primal Structure of Sin

Early in the 1970s, Enrique Dussel produced a sophisticated political condemnation of non-heterosexuality which gave rise to non-heterosexual desires becoming a part of a theological reflection on structures of sin. Marxist theologians who wanted to condemn sexuality outside structures of heterosexuality reflected not by grounding issues of sexuality, but by producing a theological Marxist discourse. They needed to prove how homosexual affections reproduced political, economic and cultural imperialism. Dussel produced the first liberationist dismissal of non-heterosexual desires, not by condemning homosexuality as part of a *petit bourgeois* evangelical argument (he is too sophisticated for that), but by devising a political space for sexual criticism. Dussel reflected on sexuality as part of what he called a project of 'erotic liberation'. He presented his ideas in his influential books *Para una Etica de Liberación Latinoamericana* (1973) and *Filosofía de la Liberación* (1977).[7]

Paradoxically, Dussel's argument is interesting and it could have been a pioneering base for a non-heterosexual theology of liberation. In brief, his argument, based on Levinas, is as follows. The origin of any liberative praxis starts always by our confrontation with Otherness. It is in the encounter with the Other that we encounter God and have the opportunity to act morally. This liberative praxis is produced by our openness to an alternative order, characterized by a relation opposite to that expected in a capitalist system. This encounter with the Other is in reality, according to Dussel, a 'dis-order', which establishes the fact that a liberative practice needs to be also an illegal

praxis. So Dussel asks, 'Is legality the same as morality?' (Dussel 1973: 76).
He answers that while legality means the mere fulfilment of the law, an unjust
law that preserves a capitalist order as a caretaker watches over prisoners in a
jail, morality means rather the fulfilment of love. He even considers how, in
rejecting the idolatrous call of the capitalist system (which he calls 'Totality'),
a Christian engaged in a liberative praxis needs to go beyond any order and
become part of a chaos or chaotic space which will 'break (oppressive) walls'
(Dussel 1973: 73).

Dussel's argument is clear. The capitalist system is characterized by a
rejection of alternatives and Otherness. The face of the Other, of the poor and
vulnerable in society, is excluded and denied. The Other is reified, reduced to
a thing. There is no possibility to accept difference, and that constitutes the
idolatrous base of capitalism. A capitalist system (especially, we should add,
in the present mode of global expansion) is a project of Sameness, of
totalitarian egoism. For Dussel, 'the Other become the Same' (Dussel 1973:
77). Up to this point, the argument, based on a re-reading of Marx and
Levinas, seems very powerful and liberative: it provides a base for a sexual
liberation theology. The heterosexual system, organized as a 'Totality',
constitutes itself as an idolatry. It reifies the Other, the one who is outside its
project of domination. To stand up against heterosexuality as an ideology is
therefore a liberative praxis, morally good, and necessary illegal. It is illegal
specifically in a theological sense when theology, even Liberation Theology,
presents itself as a Totality.[8]

As we follow Dussel's arguments, we find an important affirmation of the
moral duty of LiberationTheology to unveil the construction of heterosexuality in theology as part of a liberative praxis; not only the Church but God
Godself needs to be liberated from sexual totalitarianism. For Marx, a
morally evil act is one characterized by a praxis of domination and
expropriation which includes the identity of people – and we might add,
their relation with God. However, Dussel's argument is not as liberative as it
reads. Why? The first clue comes with the characterization of the exploited.
Dussel speaks of the need to liberate 'women, sons and the poor' (Dussel
1973: 126). He is of course paraphrasing a biblical phrase ('the widow, the
orphan and the stranger'), but he is doing more than this. Dussel's reference is
to the heterosexual family which, in a capitalist system, he sees creating a
chain of oppression: the husband oppresses the wife; the wife reproduces
patriarchy in the education of the son (Dussel uses the masculine term for
child in Spanish, *hijo*), and the son reproduces the entire totalitarian system.
This is part of the original sin, for Adam and Eve are considered as a family
whose act of disobedience was introduced by a desire of totalitarianism. The
original couple wanted 'to become as gods', establishing the idolatrous ethos
of projects of domination. It is not clear how the original couple associate
gods with domination, since the only God known to them was their creator,
unless we concede that the biblical myth implies that the original couple felt
the oppression of their divine master. However, that is the original sin,

according to Dussel: they took an option for a logic of totality. The key is procreation. For Dussel, patriarchy is the alienation of a family relation. The liberative praxis he proposes abounds in references to mothers and fathers, and sons who will constitute the base of a different citizenship. Curiously, he attacks homosexuality and feminism as 'a negation of sexual diversity' (Dussel 1977: 101). He publicly retreated from his antifeminist position some time ago, but not from of his homophobia, because this is foundational in his scheme. Sexual diversity for Dussel is biological diversity. Therefore, the logic of totality is a gay logic. It is the logic of capitalism, of egoism, of the denial of the liberative praxis of the family and the advent of the new man in the son of that family. Leaving Marx aside, Dussel coincides here with the military dictatorial regime in Argentina which cruelly persecuted him, forcing his family into exile during the 1970s. The military culture was nurtured by the ideal of the new family, ordered by strict gender obligations and prolific producers of obedient children. Against that stood the lifestyle of the terrorist, which was considered immoral; the life of concubinage, not having children, or being promiscuous or divorced – two terms equivalent at the time.

It is not a coincidence, then, that during the 1970s the argument that liberationists used against homosexuality was one from Dussel. Homosexuality was equivalent to egoism, or desire of the 'same'. It was a sin of capitalist societies and only supported by Christians indifferent to the biblical plea of 'the women, the sons and the strangers'.

This argument of original sin as arrogance, or totalitarian pretensions, was also simultaneously developed by J. Severino Croatto, the influential biblicist of liberation. Dussel's ideas became popularized in liberationist circles by Croatto. For the latter, the origin of evilness in the narrative of Genesis 2:4–3:24 lies in the desire to 'overcome limits marked by YHWH God' (Croatto 1986: 221). The liberation argument against homosexuality as a proud or arrogant act, in the sense of 'going beyond limits' was part of Croatto's elaboration on the ethical categories from Genesis, which cluster around what Croatto calls a sin of *desmesura* (literally, 'going beyond measure') (Croatto 1986: 226). That primordial sin covers four excesses: an excess of knowledge, violence, technical and sexual excesses.[9] In all of these there is a fear of dis-order, reminiscent of a Pauline argument. Paradoxically, what liberationists wanted was precisely to dis-order the legitimatization of political and religious ideologies of injustice.

Another liberationist argument of the time, perhaps originating in readings of Dussel, was that homosexuality is an egoist act, wanting to love 'the same' and denying the sacrificial givenness of oneself in a family, orientated to the production of children. Homosexuality was considered as partaking of the capitalist ideological standpoint of domination, or of pleasure without a liberative praxis of love manifested in reproduction. The sexual act is for Dussel a liturgy of liberation, culminating in the advent of the son, as an Other for the couple (Dussel 1977: 102). Both Dussel and Croatto were

Roman Catholic theologians, heavily influenced by the ideology of the family
in Latin America, which acted as a metanarrative of power in their reflections.
The effect of the re-reading of Genesis was influential because it provided
liberationists with a quasi-Marxist rejection of a possible debate on sexuality,
since it took people away from their engagement with the struggle.
Homosexuality was condemned as a sin of arrogance and individuality, an
idea that may well persist to this day in some circles.

Feminist Liberation Theology: Real Women Are Mothers

Apart from a lack of post-colonial reflection and the influence of Dussel and
Croatto, homogenization of gay issues with capitalism, at the level of the
leadership of the militant churches, enlisted other arguments too. There were
speculative arguments considering strategical issues, as churches mimicked
guerrilla groups deciding the shortest and safest route to the next villa. They
were concerned not to diversify the struggle of political liberation into other
fields, or divide the Church on what they thought were minor issues, such as
gender or sexuality. It has been said that sexuality and gender issues
(including domestic violence) were not part of the discussion of a theology
primarily represented by celibate clergymen, but the truth is that celibate
priests have themselves conflictual sexualities and have many problems
related to gender on which to reflect. Had they decided to start by examining
their lives during their seminary years, they might have found inspiration for
theological reflections grounded on sexual conflicts. However, it was easy to
be theologically dishonest. Some liberation theologians could quickly dismiss
women's rights as an issue coming from privileged women in the West, and
gay issues as arising from moral decadence of the West, but in the end the
struggles of both women and gays were seen as politically sinful, along the
lines of the exegeses of Croatto and Dussel. Both heterosexual and gender
dissidents were guilty of the sin of vanity. In the 1970s and early 1980s, the
militant churches considered as vain those who put their energies into
anything that was not the struggle for liberation. There was vanity and
superficiality in the actions of people who did not seem to be committed to
further the political Kingdom of God: they were distractions from the life of
the revolutionary Christian. Women were thus told that, although their cause
was just, there were many fronts on which to struggle and it was not possible
to diversify.

Latin American women, for strategical and cultural reasons, focused on
doing a theology in community, that is a theology which was not against men
and not outside the parameters of heterosexual order and patriarchy. On this
basis, they claimed their right to participate in the process of liberation of
their own communities. Feminist Liberation Theology was a community
theology, not an individualist, egoistic, 'white women' theology. That is, the
ghost of the 'capitalist is gay' (or feminist) argument we have noted above

continued to be very strong and compelling. Behind that was another subject of discussion, namely the question of who were 'real women' in theological discourses, as opposed to academic discourses. Curiously and significantly, there was no corresponding discussion in Liberation Theology on the subject of who are 'real men'. Trained theologians are privileged people, being well educated and often well travelled, perhaps having had studies abroad or attendance at international conferences. The question of how detached they were from Latin American reality became an issue with the advent of women theologians. They were not regarded as 'real women'. In fact, reality was taken to be something else. People who lived in the basic ecclesial communities or participated in the life and work of any of the many militant Catholic parishes or Protestant churches of liberation, were used to negotiating their identities and struggles in relation to a much broader base. The clashes between some academic liberationists and 'real' people at this point are legendary, sadly resulting at times in a process of mutual disqualifications, although both suffered from the contradictions of attitudes towards sexuality that permeated religious life in Latin America. As important as feminist Liberation Theology has been and still is, and considering the fact that Liberation Theology has only survived and continues thanks to the theological praxis of women who, paraphrasing Dussel, fought against the egoistic totality of the liberationist process in terms of gender, their discourse did not advance the debate on sexuality as an ideology. In part, this may have been due to the influence of Mariolatry in the continent. Contributions to the Mariology of Liberation, as important as they may have been at a certain level, helped to confirm the limits of gender and sexual constructions in the Church, rather than to transgress them.

Queers Are Us

The interesting thing is that Liberation Theology failed to recognize something that queers and revolutionaries have in common, that is a resistance to products of historical naturalization processes, such as sexual and class divisions. Such naturalizations, according to Bordieu, have left marks not only on bodies but also on social institutions, including also the Church. When Latin American sexual dissenters intervene in human rights discourses, they intervene not only to claim denied rights but a complete realignment of power in their societies. Liberationists thought that it was possible and desirable to differentiate amongst the multiple inscriptions of power; for instance, class, cultural and religiously constituted institutions of power. Meanwhile, liberationists did not realize the great missed opportunity by not only depriving themselves from extending the grounds of their praxis of solidarity, but also by ignoring and actively opposing what I should like to describe as the 'theological maturity of the closets': the spirituality of the political sexual dissidents, or the spirituality of the *locas*. It is well known that in Liberation Theology, spirituality always precedes action. Decades ago, Gustavo Gutiérrez reflected on the important role of spirituality of liberation in his book *We Drink From Our Own Wells* (London: SCM, 2005). It is true that Liberation Theology's prophetic praxis provided material for a different, richer spirituality, but more than that, without a rich, courageous spirituality to start with, it would not have been possible to face the risks of contesting power during the 1970s and 1980s in Latin America. To talk here of the spirituality of the *locas*, is different from assessing feminist spiritualities. Feminist spirituality of liberation has a different route. While both spiritualities come from a struggle for equality at the beginning and difference later on, *las locas* are queer. Reflecting on the papers produced by the first Latin American Forum, 'Inescapable Bodies',[10] collected in Buenos Aires in 2004, with the participation of socio-sexual activists from different countries and of differing sexual orientations, we are struck by just how spiritual is their discourse. Reading different presentations of matters concerning sexuality, economic exclusion and issues of race, we are confronted with many theological discussions on the churches and the need to rediscover the true face of God beyond sexual ideological frames. The queer theological debate is alive and growing, but is it happening outside the Church? In a way it is tempting to say, yes. We could say that as always, the excluded do theology in exclusion from the centres of power. But it is important to remember that there is a quasi-subterranean tradition in Liberation Theology of those who, since the 1970s, have been doing a theology from sexuality and poverty.

We need to remember here some pioneer names, such as Jaci Maraschin from Brazil, who has been nurturing up to this moment a new generation of Liberation Theologians of a more transgressive type. Maraschin was a pioneer in producing a religious reflection on sexuality, a reflection which merged a political with a sensuous discourse, rediscovering the body of the poor in theology. Another theologian from Brazil who has done very important work in this area is Rubem Alves. Coincidentally, both Maraschin and Alves are poets. Maraschin has published poetry in the context of a re-reading of the Scriptures, as well as songs and liturgies. Alves has reflected since the 1970s on issues of theology and repression, and theology and imagination. Theologians such as Maraschin and Alves did not produce a ghetto type of reflection, but all their work in Liberation Theology has been based on a framework of body theology. For Alves, it was the challenge of the prophet, as someone who announces a new world by imagining it with courage. They were not gay theologians, but they transgressed the limits of a Latin American heterosexual theology.

Today, there is a generation of Liberation Theologians who are producing a rich reflection on issues of sexuality, ideology and culture. Some of their voices are represented in this book. They come from different ecclesiastical and theological traditions, different countries and situations, and they have taken Liberation Theology towards a renewal of its traditional *caminata*. It was encouraging to hear the challenge that Otto Maduro, a pioneer of

Liberation Theology and part of the Latin American founding group, presented to the World Forum on Theology and Liberation in Brazil 2005. Perhaps this is a symbol of what a Theology of Liberation for the twenty-first century is: a theology that embraces the unveiling of sexual ideologies in theology without leaving aside its obstinacy for social justice and peace.

I finish with the story of two groups seeking liberation. Let their convergence be a metaphor of hope for our time. In 1931 a group of anarchists dug a tunnel from a local coal store to the *Punta Carretas* jail in Uruguay, to bring about the escape of political prisoners. The tunnel was closed after the successful escape and lay forgotten for forty years until discovered by other political dissidents. It happened that in 1971 a group of more than a hundred guerrilla activists from the political organization *Tupamaros* planned their escape from the same jail. Digging their tunnel, they found, by coincidence, the old passage left by the anarchists. The *Tupamaros* decided to leave the following message at the crossroads of the two tunnels: 'In this place we had an encounter between two ideologies and a common destiny: freedom.'[11] May this story, which comes from Latin Americans in their struggle for justice, political alternatives and human rights, become the vision of an encounter between the *locas* who challenged Pinochet claiming human rights and the liberationists who sacrificed so much for the Christian duty of all liberationist praxis.

Notes

1 'Lick, lick/ a kiss from you/is a revelation/ Mouth to mouth/ a kiss from you/ is salvation/ On the mouth of the people/ a kiss from you/ is a revolution./ Let them talk!/ I am a kiss/ of a man with another man/of a woman with another woman/ any kind of kiss.' *Beijoqueira* (The Kisser) by Nancy Cardoso Pereira, in 'Mandrágora', *Revista do Núcleo de Etudos Teológicos da Mulher na América Latina*, Universidade Metodista de São Paulo, 1988. My translation.

2 The *Informe de Verdad and Reconciliación*, also known as '*Informe Rettig*' in homage to the judge who was in charge of the investigation of the human rights violations in Chile, was produced in 1992.

3 Núñez González claims that Sra. Sierra changed her views on this later one. See Núñez González, 'Prácticas Políticas y Estratégicas de Alianza del Movimiento GLBTT en Chile' en Paula Viturro, Josefina Fernández and Mónica D'Uva (eds) *Cuerpos Ineludibles. Un Diálogo a partir de las Sexualidades en América Latina* (Buenos Aires: Ají de Pollo, 2004), pp. 26–7.

4 One of the best introductory books to Liberation Theology in Latin America was published by Baptists. Cf Roberto Compton, *La Teología de la Liberación. Una Guía Introductoria* (Casa Bautista: El Paso, 1984).

5 See, for instance, José del Rey Fajardo, *Pedagogía Jesuítica en la Venezuela Hispánica* (Caracas: Academia Nacional de la Historia, 1979). Also Guillermo, *Furlong Historia Social y Cultural del Rio de la Plata* (Buenos Aires: TEA, 1969).

For more references, see Asunción Lavín (ed.) *Sexuality and Marriage in Colonial Latin America* (Nebraska: University of Nebraska Press, 1989).

6   See the study done by Graciela Chamorro concerning the place of 'the word' amongst the Guaraníes, in *Teología Guaraní* (Quito: Abya Yala, 2004). Also, her article 'A Construçao do "Ser Homem" e do "Ser Mulher" durante la Conquista Espiritual', in *Mandrágora* (Universidade Metodista de São Paulo, 2001/2), pp. 30–7.

7   See Enrique Dussel, *Filosofía de la Liberación* (Mexico: EDICOL, 1977). Also, E. Dussel, *Para una Etica de Liberación Latinoamericana II* (Mexico: EDICOL, 1973).

8   I have called this totalitarian system the 'T-Theology'. See Althaus-Reid, *The Queer God* (London: Routledge, 2003), p. 172.

9   Cf Severino Croatto, *Crear y Amar en Libertad. Estudio de Génesis 2:4–3:24* (Buenos Aires: La Aurora, 1986).

10 The papers from the forum were published by Paula Viturro, a well-known lawyer and sexual rights activist, in collaboration with other colleagues, under the title *Cuerpos Ineludibles*.

11 Cf Hernán Palomino, 'Cruce de Destinos e Ideologies. Entrevista con Virginia Martínez'. Online at http://www.otrocampo.com/9/virginiamartinez.html, p. 2.

Chapter 2

Once Again Liberating Theology? Towards a Latin American Liberation Theological Self-Criticism[1]

Otto Maduro

A Daring Theology, Prone to Forget 'Other Others'

During the 1970s, groups of Latin American lay people and clergy started working with underprivileged communities, sharing in the oppression and repression that marked the everyday life of the poor. These Christians, from both Roman Catholic and Protestant congregations, began to do theology in deep connection with the culture, experiences, struggles and insights of the oppressed themselves. This practice gave rise to the movement known as Latin American Liberation Theology (LALT), a movement that found its first public voice in the writings of Latin American theologians such as Gustavo Gutiérrez, Rubem Alves, Leonardo Boff and others.[2] A trait distinguishing it from other critical theologies was precisely its daring position on the practice of theology. Claiming that all theologizing is socially and historically bound to specific faith experiences of concrete communities, LALT denounced and relativized official, predominant theologies as *particular* theologies, that is, each being just one among many other possible theologies, whose appearance and pretence of universal and eternal truth was simply the *particular* pretence typical of those with an experience of privilege and power that gave them both the interest and the capability to deny the historically and socially bound character of their theologizing – and thus to cast their theologies as eternal and universal instead.

As with LALT, almost simultaneously and quite independently from each other, US black theology, as well as feminist theologies, found their own way to express and justify the religious needs of communities which, until then, had been denied a public voice by mechanisms of ecclesiastical control and power.

Every new theology of liberation tends thus to reveal, in a subversive way, one more hitherto hidden particularity of dominant theologies, thus further undermining the pretence of universal truth of official theological systems. In this way, Liberation Theologies continue to render it possible for church leaders and believers to see that 'the emperor has no clothes'. That is, that official, dominant theologies carry the appearance of universal and eternal truth only because those who stand by them have both the interest and the power to legitimate them. The appearance of universal truth in these dominant theologies is thus merely an expression of the particular needs and privileges of the elites in power, usually constituted by adult, urban, heterosexual Christian male scholars, often from affluent North Atlantic families, whose shared, particular interests are thus reflected in their theologies. No wonder that for such dominant theologies, any departure from their own theological understanding is perceived as heretical, mistaken, sinful, or – at best – as a 'marginal theologizing', with a very limited field of interest and applicability.

In this way, every new theology of liberation keeps opening the Pandora's box of theological creativity. Beyond the Liberation Theologies mentioned above, we now have Asian, African and Indigenous theologies; Caribbean, Jewish and Palestinian theologies of liberation; together with ecotheologies and sexual theologies (lesbian, gay, bisexual and transgendered).

Fortunately, some dialogue has indeed developed among these subversive theologies, from the Theology in the Americas encounters in Detroit (1975 and 1980), through the many meetings of the Ecumenical Association of Third World Theologians (EATWOT, from 1976) up to the present time. Calls have been heard since, in those and in many other venues, for all Liberation Theologies and theologians to listen carefully to each other, to humbly learn from those who come from a different experience of oppression, and to actively resist the tendency to raise one's own perspective – in the habit of dominant, official theologies – as the best or the only valid one. However, neglect or even silencing of new and different perspectives is of course commonplace, not least, probably, because Liberation Theologies are subaltern, not hegemonic theologies (since we have not reached yet the utopian, egalitarian 'kindom' of God), and, as such, they tend to accept and reproduce, at least in part, traits typical of dominant Christian orthodoxy. But this happens possibly, too, because of the normal search of all subaltern initiative for legitimacy and respectability – legitimacy and respectability that, once conquered even partially, bring about rewards and privileges (such as employment, publication, career advancement, recognition, remuneration, influence, and other forms of power). The understandable need to avoid some of the risks, threats and dangers looming over Liberation Theologians in many corners of our world might also elicit a certain prudence and discretion, not rarely leading to avoid explicit attention to novel, demanding perspectives in theology.

The temptations of power and fear follow every intellectual pursuit – even more if such pursuit is relatively successful, in whatever sense we understand 'success'. My purpose here is to review our own path in Latin America in order to discern, and critically evaluate, which oppressions, oppressed groups, and struggles against oppression we tend to disregard or to forget in contemporary LALT. At the risk of upsetting some people, I assume that we have the ethical responsibility to, every so often, pause and reflect humbly on the probable loss of sight, avoidances, and neglects that inevitably arise from any particular standpoint – including the standpoint of LALT. My hope is that these reflections will contribute to the emergence of a new and better world where 'other others' will be welcome.

On the Real Life of the Oppressed

Every reality carries a degree of complexity that tends to challenge our initial perceptions and expectations. Individuals as well as communities often find it difficult to see the diversity, change and conflicts in our midst. It is even harder to communicate and analyse critically such complexity, especially when confronted – from a position of disadvantage – by the powers that be. Why would it then be surprising that we avoid seeing, recognizing and critically analysing the incoherencies, weaknesses, diversity and conflicts present both in ourselves and amongst the oppressed people with whom we work and identify ourselves? It is indeed easier to concentrate our attention on the faults of the powerful elites, rather than further complicating our lives by scrutinizing the small- and large-scale complexities in our lives and in the lives of the vulnerable with whom we work.

The oppressed, the poor, are – as human beings that they are – far more diverse, creative and unpredictable than our institutions, theories, leaders and projects (political, economic, cultural or religious) fancy them to be. Sadly, part of the failure of some of our attempts to elicit social and religious change is due precisely to ignoring the creative diversity of our communities, instead of embracing it as a promising, fertile challenge. Maybe this is why we should encourage, among other approaches, a riskier, bolder theological variety, creativity and flexibility than LALT has dared to promote up to the present.

The oppressed, like any other portion of humanity (including those allied to the oppressed), are much more deeply susceptible to the deleterious effects of domination than our theologies (and other theories) of liberation have been willing to recognize. Amongst the poorest of the poor, just as amongst the powerful and the conformist, we find the curse of domestic violence, exploitation and abuse of the weakest, consumerism, individualism, materialism, sexism, homophobia, disregard for the environment, racism, discrimination and intolerance. To pay no heed to such weaknesses and inconsistencies is at least as pernicious as to discount the creativity, diversity and versatility present in the daily lives of the oppressed.

My impression is that, in LALT, we have tended to overlook, forget, and gloss over – with generalizations and oversimplifications – the weighty plurality and complexity of the lives of our oppressed people. We have ignored the various conflicts and contrasts present in the psychological, social, economic, emotional, workplace, racial, sexual, cultural, linguistic, domestic, educational, political and religious dimensions of the lives of the subaltern. We have disregarded how such an array of differences and divergences affects the families, communities, movements, and organizations of our own oppressed people, as well as the initiatives and actions emerging among them.

Why such neglect? Firstly, in order to face oppression with a certain hope of overcoming it, it seems more urgent and useful to elicit consensus among those sharing the struggle rather than stimulating critical self-examination. Focusing our critical glance on our own communities and allies runs the risk of provoking rejection, exclusion, debilitating divisions, new difficulties and higher chances of defeat. After all, it is already difficult and demanding enough to try to analyse the relations of oppression from which the powerful derive their power. Why, then, invest our scarce time and limited energy, while putting the struggle for liberation at risk, in the pursuit of such a dangerous and unpredictable aim?

What saddens me while reflecting on these issues is the observation that Latin America is today further back on the road towards a just and peaceful society than it was during the 1970s. This is in part due, indeed, to the ingenuity, resources and perversity of our elites. There are, however, sufficient grounds to believe that this situation owes much, in addition, to the support of the oppressed and their allies of the dynamics of domination. Support more frequently unwilling than deliberate, perhaps; often due to confusion and fear rather than to selfish choices, possibly; fuelled more by omissions than by an active commitment to injustice, granted – cooperation given without wanting, without knowing, but also often without wanting to know: complicit, therefore.

I would suggest that a real challenge for the future of our continent lies in the recognition, further investigation and critical reflection of the enormous complexity, as well as the richness, of the everyday life of the people whom we claim to serve.

The Persistent Oppression Exerted by the Churches

Since the early 1980s, poverty, unemployment, underemployment, migrations, the unravelling of entire communities and families, drug addiction, AIDS, and the daily violence of the poor against the poor have increased both in Latin America and in the Caribbean. At the same time, we cannot deny any longer that there has been a decline in the influence of both Liberation Theology and the basic ecclesial communities (BECs) – while Pentecostalism and African-Brazilian religions have increased their presence and influence amongst the poor.

It is paradoxical, to be sure, that precisely when they seem most needed, LALT, BECs, the Left, progressive popular movements, and labour unions are rather in decline throughout Latin America and the Caribbean – no doubt in part because of the pace of impoverishment and insecurity in our corner of the globe – although some dim signs of hope have seemed to emerge in recent years in a few nations south of the Rio Grande.

What is lacking, then, in our established churches, both Roman Catholic and Protestant, as well as in LALT, BECs, the Left, progressive popular movements, and labour unions? Why do hundreds of thousands distance themselves from these and embrace, among others, evangelical churches and African-based religions? What do the latter offer to our youth and our poor in the Caribbean and in Latin America that is missing in the former?

I can only suggest hypotheses as part of a fragmentary response. I believe that part of the answer lies in the brutal anti-communist persecution from the 1960s to the 1980s, which assassinated well over half a million people in Latin America, while terrorizing and torturing millions more. Thousands of Christian activists inspired by LALT died under those persecutions. Meanwhile, Pentecostal churches and African-based religions have been offering some dignity, equality and agency that are rare to find in established churches, especially for those marginalized both in church and in society: women, black people, the indigenous, the illiterate, the unemployed, the divorced, single mothers, former prisoners and drug addicts.

While acknowledging the tremendous achievement of putting the Bible in the hands of the poor, encouraging novel readings of the Scriptures, at both a personal and a communitarian level, it must be said that Protestants, Pentecostals and LALT have all developed a certain resistance – similar in this to conservative Catholics – to discussing and critically reflecting on the historical, fragmentary, heterogeneous and contradictory character of the Bible; on the artificial and conflictive formation of the biblical canon, and of its supposed unity and definitiveness. In short, they have avoided any conversation on the partial, partisan, provisional, presumptive and polemic character of the canon and of its interpretations. Instead, a timid paternalism, understood as respect for the believers, bars the possibility for the poor to consider a more open, humble, critical and creative approach to that crucial *and* ambiguous legacy of the European invasion of the Americas which is the Bible.

Isn't it the case that – as with biblical interpretation – theological production, liturgical leadership patterns, preaching, the conceptualization and administration of the sacraments, as well as the management of religious personnel and goods, have all been monopolized almost exclusively by clergy*men*, even in LALT? Be it because of inertia, fear, tactical moves or deep conviction, either proactively or passively, we usually leave unquestioned the monopoly of the production, reproduction, consumption and distribution of religious goods by an elite – a white, urban, male, scholarly and economically secure elite, usually heterosexual as well.

Something similar happens to our understandings of God, Jesus, Mary, the Trinity, holiness, salvation, church, tradition and evangelization: even in LALT, these concepts are still too deeply linked to racist schemes, patriarchal structures, authoritarian relationships, monopolist interests, and official church theologies imposed by Protestant and Roman Catholic empires. There is thus much to do for a theology in search of a radical liberation of our people from all oppressions.

Our Subjectivity, Embodiment and Sexuality

The theological dimension of our own subjectivity, and the reality of our bodies and experience of sexuality, are as crucial for the poor and oppressed of our societies as for anybody else. This dimension has been neglected and even evaded by the majority of Liberation Theologies, inside and outside Latin America. This may reflect the fact that those who have had the most time, preparation, self-esteem, support, captive audience, pre-established networks, as well as channels to publish and spread Liberation Theologies in Latin America, have been mainly clergymen – and, at that, mostly Roman Catholic priests, subject to celibacy, and therefore with all the limitations and pressures inherent in that *particular* religious condition.[3]

If we were to highlight a single aspect where Liberation Theologies need to examine themselves critically from the unique perspective that they birthed – that is, that all theologies are *particular and interested*, marked by the specific location of its producers – precisely in this area of sexuality.

Every human being, from childhood on, evolves within a complex dynamic of desires, needs, images, ghosts, emotions, fears, memories, pleasures and frustrations, as well as prohibitions, difficulties and anticipations. Our physical and social context might respond to our initiatives in different ways; at times more or less consistently; other times in chaotic, startling ways. Different personalities and subjectivities will emerge in relation to those experiential variations. If our environment responds to our movements in a more or less predictable, coherent manner, that will make community consensus more viable. Such stability, however, might be based on fear and pain, tied to the prohibition and punishment of certain relationships, desires and discourses. Women who leave their abusive husbands or who decide to re-marry or to remain single; individuals romantically attracted to people of the same gender; people whose poverty makes for an impossible balance between home and work; children forced by sheer need to prostitute themselves and/or to join the drug traffic. These are usually the first to be sacrificed for the benefit of the consensus and stability of our communities. In this way, the creativity and diversity of our society end up being severely restricted, while submissive, authoritarian, violent and sadomasochistic personalities are encouraged. People's own subjectivities and personalities are thus affected by the responses of our community (by church, schools, families, neighbourhoods) to our emotional needs, our eroticism, our need for a loving touch and sensual pleasure.[4]

But what have liberation theologies done up until now in these decisive areas of our existence, personal and collective, subjective and erotic? Let us be honest: not much, besides *neglecting, avoiding* and *forgetting*.

In these matters, LALT has shown insignificant variance from the official Protestant, Catholic, or Pentecostal voices; or, for that matter, from right-wing ideologies, Islamic or Jewish fundamentalisms, or even, ironically, orthodox Marxism – be this one in power or in the opposition: with significant exceptions, all tend to coincide in avoiding, evading and deriding these crucial dimensions of human existence.

Unfortunately for the oppressed people with whom we do theology, this attitude has at least two negative consequences. First, by not allowing ourselves to critically discern and healthily struggle with our own subjective motivations for doing theology in the service of the underprivileged, we run the risk of ending up *using* the oppressed, rather than serving them – while doing theology in the image and likeness of our own individual or corporate cravings, fears and frustrations. Further, by denying and repressing the rich complexity of our subjectivities, our bodies and our sexualities, we end up reinforcing the internalized structures that sustain authoritarianism, torture, repression, domestic violence and the abuse of the most vulnerable members of our societies. Without wanting, without knowing, without wanting to know. It is therefore urgent and crucial to take a deep look at ourselves, including within our theological production and conversations.

Half of Humanity: Women

We have heard this many times: the majority of the poor are women; the majority of women are poor; and the poorest among the poor are women. It has been said, albeit not as often as it should have been, that women and children are the majority of the victims of violence, both domestic violence and war. It has also been mentioned, but not enough, that women are generally excluded from the decision-making bodies in governmental, economic, educational, religious and political life. Ironically, women are also the majority of the unpaid and low-paid workers, and the bulk of those who do the basic work in the families, schools, hospitals and churches. Most families are headed by women, often alone. And curiously, women are a significantly small minority of those who commit crimes, violent or otherwise.

And yet, the oppressions and contributions specific to women are forgotten, marginalized or silenced by most Liberation Theologies outside of feminist theologies – while feminism is often cast by both conservatives and progressives, religious or secular, as a concern of white, affluent women only, those with nothing better to do with their lives.

Once again, isn't it time already to start an honest, courageous process of self-criticism, concerning the sexist character of most Liberation Theologies throughout the world? Or to be harder and clearer: isn't it time to examine how patriarchal misogyny has contaminated not just official theologies but Liberation Theologies as well? And not only this, but we must also ask ourselves how this has happened, in order to be able to start the difficult task of transforming Liberation Theologies – making them all also feminist theologies, not just in their discourse, but, likewise, in the ways we produce, discuss, communicate and transform our own theologies. And if not now, when?

Interestingly, feminist theologies (using this or other names) are increasingly present, opening paths and orienting movements in Latin America as elsewhere, even without the support of other Liberation Theologies. Part of what we all need to attentively reflect on is precisely what these theologies are capable of grasping, intuiting, and suspecting from their *particular* locations: what is hardly visible from the masculine particularity in a patriarchal Church and society.

For instance, we need to reflect on how feminist theologies perceive divinity: as less exterior, prior, superior, separate and distinct from human lives; as less omnipotent, omniscient, omnipresent and punitive – a more vulnerable, sensitive, caring and gentler divinity. Less Zeus and more Sophia. A way of seeing the divine that allows for a more accepting, loving, positive and optimistic view of humanity. Less as fallen, cursed, sinful – more as vulnerable, interdependent, and in need of healing love. But this entails also a way of understanding the Church: less exclusive and infallible; more open, compassionate and in solidarity; less interested in defining and possessing the ultimate truth; more interested in living lovingly; less obsessed with the drive to convert others to one's own faith; and more inclined to accompanying, dialoguing with, and sharing the lives of the needy and vulnerable in our midst.

In this sense, I think that mission, evangelization, sin, salvation, ethics, God's kindom, as well as political and pastoral projects, all find, in a feminist theological perspective, new possibilities to be rethought, reconceived and resurrected.

Until now, however, many Liberation Theologians seem fearful of confronting such creative possibilities, and we prefer either to remain silent in the face of the feminist challenge, or to hurriedly mention one or two female theologians and colleagues so as to not appear as ignorant, and/or simply state our solidarity with the struggle against sexism.

However, I would like to insist that we should go beyond that: recognizing, criticizing and deconstructing, together with feminist theologians, the ways in which patriarchy, colonialism, racism and other social and historical forms of domination and exploitation have infiltrated our conceptions of God, Jesus, Church, Bible, salvation, the Trinity and evangelization – even in our Liberation Theologies.

Lesbians, Gays and Other *Different* People

Every subaltern, subordinated, oppressed group – even in its rebelliousness and resistance to oppression – tends to partly repeat and imitate the vision of the oppressor. This is what Paulo Freire called the process of internalization of oppression (Freire 1993: 30).

One of the ways in which rebellious people can prove to themselves and to others that they are more decent, moral, and respectable than the elites is by becoming 'more papist than the pope himself', especially in those aspects defined as crucial by the dominant criteria. Thus, we can often find trade unionists and revolutionaries displaying a sexism, an authoritarianism and a racism as strong as those present in the power elites – but coexisting amongst the former with a radical economic and political critique of the latter.

On the other hand, colonial and creole elites often stereotype the oppressed – not just to delegitimize the subaltern, but also to show themselves as superior, as morally obliged to impose themselves over the oppressed – those seen as primitive, almost animal people, who cannot control their sexual appetites: prostitutes, homosexuals and libertines, polygamists, corrupted, obscene and immoral people. Or, at times, as 'less men'. Maybe that is why those who resist economic, political and cultural oppression are often more scrupulous than their own oppressors precisely in that dimension of sexual and gender relations. In order to show the falsity of the stereotypes used against them, and in order to claim a higher moral ground than the elites, the oppressed often adopt, exacerbating them, the dominant criteria of morality and decency, thus reducing morality to the strict observance of certain traditional, dominant patterns regarding sexual relationships, sexual identity, and gender construction.

This tendency is noticeable in many labour, socialist, nationalist and/or revolutionary movements across human history and geography. A similar propensity is observable in liberation movements arising from religious traditions which, during centuries, have condensed sacred duties into purity codes regarding ethnic, bodily, and sexual relations. Restricting morality to a sexual dimension, however, is tantamount to denying ethical import to the remaining aspects of human life. In this way, banks, political institutions, education, science, laws and governmental repression are left outside the ethical debate, as if these were morally neutral territories to be left to the 'experts' already in control of the related institutions. By the same token, sexuality is left in the straitjacket of patriarchy, misogyny and authoritarianism.

Today, the new scapegoats of the dominant morality are gays and lesbians. The current US government, one of the most powerful on earth, has as one of its central themes the prohibition of gay marriages. The position of the papacy coincides with such obsession. Several churches (Anglican, Methodist, and Presbyterian in the first place) seem to be on the brink of splitting over the same issues, and people's positions in relation to homosexuality have become, for many, *the key criterion* to decide who is or who is not a good Christian. And all this, considering that Jesus and the Gospels do not even mention this matter.

What are the theologies of liberation saying about these issues? Apart from some feminist theologies, very few are standing up to defend a lesbigay position, or to criticize the homophobia and heterosexism of our elites and our churches. And even fewer are the Liberation Theologians daring to bring up in a supportive way the growing number of lesbian, gay, transsexual and bisexual (LGBT) Liberation Theologians and Theologies.

However, any courageous Liberation Theology has to take seriously, once and for all, the integral defence of the life of our lesbian, gay, bisexual and transsexual sisters and brothers. Liberation Theologies should enter into an open, sensitive, respectful and continuous dialogue with LGBT theologians and their work. We need to pursue the critical analysis of Christian homophobia, heterosexism and erotophobia from historical, psychological, anthropological, sociological, biblical and properly theological perspectives. We should then propose an open ethic in favour of an abundant, loving and pleasurable life for an ever increasing diversity of ways of living in harmonious communities.

Liberation Theologies cannot continue silencing the cry of our LGBT sisters and brothers demanding their right for a life worth living.

Towards an Ethical-Epistemological Humility and Theological Plurality

I have tried here to give a sympathetic, albeit critical, perspective on the current situation of LALT, evaluating some absences in its development. This assessment is also a critical self-examination, as a person whose life has been deeply intertwined with the first generation of Latin American Liberation Theologians. We continue to forget, neglect and silence *other oppressions* and *other oppressed groups* than those that have been at the centre of our concerns since the late 1960s.

I want to end these reflections by underscoring an idea that somehow is present in everything I have said here.

The reality of which we are part is infinitely rich, complex and dynamic. Our capacity to know, understand, and transform such reality is extremely limited. What we might be able to grasp is in fact just a tiny portion of our surroundings and relation, and its knowledge, at any rate, is partial, partisan, provisory, presumptive and polemic. What we ignore, what we don't know, is practically immeasurable. Nonetheless, our need for clarity and certainty has made us forget these limitations, as we tend to absolutize and universalize our perceptions of reality, while closing our minds to other perspectives on our world.

A humble and courageous theology, conscious of its own limitations and temptations, has the ethical duty to ask itself which are the aspects and new situations arising from our context that we may be forgetting; which experiences and which cries are we blind and deaf to; whom we are overlooking and who might be the possible victims of our particular viewpoints. For these reasons, I want to underline the need for a deep ethical and epistemology humility. We need to recognize the particularity, finitude, fallibility and provisionality of our knowledge, and therefore the duty to revise, doubt, question, rethink and constantly criticize what we know, and how we use our knowledge in terms of people's relationships. In other words, I am referring to the duty to patiently search and attentively listen to people who have different life experiences from ours, who hold other viewpoints and understandings of our reality; especially if we are dealing with people usually considered as irrelevant, absurd or disturbing. It is in the contrast that we shall be able to see the limitations, contradictions, mistakes, incoherencies and holes in our ways of grasping reality.

Perhaps this ethical-epistemological humility will enable us to embrace the plurality of religions, churches and theologies, as a blessing amongst us; to see diversity not as an obstacle to overcome, but as a goal; not as the result of a humanity divided by egoism and oppression, but as an expression of richness and creativity, of our infinite imagination, our multiplicity of experiences and the kaleidoscopic multidimensionality of the human condition. And perhaps, starting from a loving embrace of a religious, ecclesial and theological diversity, we shall be able to see that our task is not to imagine just one possible world. Precisely, much of our problem comes from the ideological need to unify our plural history, cultures, communities, sexualities and ways of being human. Perhaps what we need is to join those who are dreaming of a simultaneous multiplicity of possible worlds, of ways of being human, of organizing our communities, of relating to the divine, of erotically living our sensuality, and of freely expressing our tentative understandings of reality. Perhaps we need more freedom to communicate with others in different ways, to celebrate life, to find structures to procreate and care for new lives, to feel, to believe, to wait, to love, to create, to fight for things, to heal, to reconcile and to dream.

In any case, as a Caribbean person happy about being such, I prefer to embrace the uncertainty of a festive chaos and the centrifugal multiplicity of gods, religions, sexualities, churches and theologies, rather than to submit myself to the grey certainty of *one* established truth, *one* interpretation of *one* Bible, *one* belief in *one* god, *one* religion, *one* church, and *one* Liberation Theology only.[5]

Notes

1 This is an abridged, revised version of a paper presented to the World Forum of Theology and Liberation (Porto Alegre, Brazil, 24 January 2005).
2 I am referring here to the beginning of the movement in terms of publications and sharing of key texts from Gustavo Gutiérrez and other less known names in the West. However, it is important to recognize the deep and complex roots of the theologies of liberation, and never to reduce them to published work which has been accepted in academic circles. That would be an elitist and simplistic perspective. Moreover, many of the ideas from Liberation Theologies can be found in the traditions and praxis from common people which even precede Liberation Theologies, or which developed those reflections simultaneously with Liberation Theologies in Latin America and abroad.
3 In this way it is good also to remember the ones who have facilitated the theological praxis of Latin American priests and ordained ministers. Those have been the manual workers in general, and women in particular: the mothers, daughters, wives and domestic servants. Yet, these are theological protagonists whose voices have been silenced in society.
4 It is unfortunate that there are abuses in the power relationships in our communities in the exploiting of the sexuality of the vulnerable, for instance, the younger, poorer women. To silence people's own sexuality also means what my friend Matilde Moros pointed out in a conversation on this paper, that is, to suppress women's need to denounce and struggle against the destructive subordination of sexuality. That includes the denied pleasure, some taboos and prohibitions, rape and other forms of sexual violence, concealed sexual illnesses, unwanted pregnancies. In all this I should like to ask why different voices such as those of Marcella Althaus-Reid, Tom Hanks or Ivone Gebara are not given more attention in Latin American Liberation Theology?
5 I would like to thank my friends Matilde Moros, Mayra Rivera, Imelda Vega-Centeno and Marcella Althaus-Reid for the important critiques and suggestions each of them made to earlier versions of this essay.

References

Althaus-Reid, Marcella (2004) *Indecent Theology: Theological Perversions in Sex, Gender and Politics*. London: SCM Press.
Boff, Leonardo (1995) *Ecology and Liberation: A New Paradigm*. Maryknoll, NY: Orbis Books.
Boff, Leonardo (1997) *Cry of the Poor, Cry of the Earth*. Maryknoll, NY: Orbis Books.
Freire, Paulo (1993) *Pedagogy of the Oppressed*. London: Penguin.
Gebara, Ivone (1999) *Longing for Running Waters: Ecofeminism and Liberation*. Minneapolis, MN: Fortress Press.
Gebara, Ivone (2002) *Out of the Depths: Women's Experience of Evil and Salvation*. Minneapolis, MN: Fortress Press.
Hanks, Tom (2001) *The Subversive Gospel: A New Testament Commentary of Liberation*. Cleveland, OH: Pilgrim Press.

Musskopf, André Sidnei (2002) *Uma brecha no armário: Propostas para uma teologia gay*. São Leopoldo: Sinodal.

Petrella, Ivan (ed.) (2005) *Latin American Liberation Theology: The Next Generation*. Maryknoll, NY: Orbis Books.

Tamez, Elsa (1989) *Through Her Eyes: Women's Theology from Latin America*. Maryknoll, NY: Orbis Books.

Chapter 3

Queer Eye for the Straight Guy: The Making Over of Liberation Theology, A Queer Discursive Approach

Ivan Petrella

In the United States, Bravo Network's TV show 'Queer Eye for the Straight Guy' is a smash hit. In the show, five queer guys – the fab five – remake the look and the lifestyle of one straight guy. The straight guy is at what could be called a point of reckoning: he might be a struggling artist who finally gets to show his work at an art gallery but has no clue how to organize, behave or even dress for such an event; he might be a dishevelled and discouraged guy in his mid-twenties applying for a new job; he might be a guy who wants to ask his girlfriend to move in and so must show his girl that he is, in fact, not a slob; or he might be a married suburban dad trying to jumpstart his career and marriage with a new look. In every case, however, the straight guy needs a makeover to help him achieve his goal. The fab five give him a new haircut (or get rid of his toupee and shave his head bald), change his wardrobe, redo his apartment, give him pointers on how to cook a romantic meal or throw a party. They give him a new look that is the outward expression of greater self-confidence and self-esteem. The fab five give him the first push on a path that hopefully leads to a better, more fabulous future.

In this chapter, I will play the part of the fab five and Liberation Theology will play the part of the straight guy. I believe that like the straight guy on Bravo, Liberation Theology is at a point of reckoning and would be well served by a queer makeover to better face the future. My argument will develop in two parts. First, I will describe the point of reckoning at which Liberation Theology stands. I will suggest that Liberation Theology faces a contemporary context in which, on the one hand, exclusion is growing at an alarming pace, and, on the other hand, Liberation Theology seems powerless to truly address that exclusion. That powerlessness is shown by the co-option of Liberation Theology's vocabulary by groups that support political and economic policies which are the direct opposite of what Liberation Theologians typically espouse. The co-option, in turn, is made possible by Liberation Theology's inability to develop historical projects to give content to its theological ideals. In a nutshell, therefore, the point of reckoning stems from the following: Liberation Theology claims 'liberation' as its goal but is unable to deliver the goods. Second, I will describe one element of the makeover required. Here, I will draw from queer theory to show that Liberation Theology's approach to the concept of capitalism is itself an obstacle to the avowed goal of liberation. While commentators typically argue that external factors – the fall of socialism, the silencing and condemnation of Liberation Theologians – are the cause of Liberation Theology's decline, I will claim that Liberation Theology's understanding of capitalism is a central, internal, and unacknowledged cause as well. Despite wanting to unmask capitalism as an idol, Liberation Theology actually makes capitalism a god. Liberation Theology, I will suggest, must 'queer' its understanding of capitalism as a first step in addressing contemporary challenges.

The Point of Reckoning

The point of reckoning is composed of two elements. The first element is the new global order that has emerged from the ruins of the Berlin Wall and the subsequent rise of neoliberal market capitalism.[1] This new global order is marked by increasing inequality and exclusion – a growing division between those who are able to participate within its boundaries and those who are excluded from those boundaries. As Ankie Hoogvelt has shown, despite what many apologists for globalization proclaim, the contemporary global economy is not characterized by expansion and incorporation but by involution and rejection.[2] The current order is marked by 'an accelerated withdrawing, a *shrinking* of the global map, rather than an *expanding* phenomenon, and one which expels ever more people from the interactive circle of global capitalism'.[3]

For example, share of developing country participation in world trade has increased by a mere 3.6 per cent from 1953 to 1996. That increase, however, includes Hong Kong, Korea, Taiwan and Singapore – the Asian Tigers – which account for 33 per cent of the developing world's share of trade while representing only 1.5 per cent of its population. In 1995, once you exclude the Asian Tigers, the developing world's share of global trade was only 18.3 per cent, down from the 1950 share of 25.9 per cent, calculated again excluding the Asian Tigers. Latin America's share of world trade in 1995 was 4.8 per cent, down from 10 per cent in 1950. Recorded growth in world trade, therefore, has bypassed rather than integrated the developing world into the global economy. Similarly, the developing world's share of foreign direct investment (FDI) has dwindled. Up to 1960, the developing nations received half the world's total direct investment flows. By 1988/89 that proportion was down to 16.5 per cent, with over half going to different parts of Asia. The 1990s saw a turnaround, with the developing world receiving 38 per cent of FDI by 1997, yet fully one-third of this investment was concentrated in

China's eight coastal provinces and in Beijing. In fact, in the first half of the 1990s, 86 per cent of all FDI went to 30 per cent of the world's population.[4] In addition, the distance in income between the rich and the poor countries continues to grow at a dramatic pace – from 35:1 in 1950, to 44:1 in 1973, to 72:1 in 1992. All this in a context in which the rich industrial nations consume 70 per cent of the world's energy, 75 per cent of its metals, 85 per cent of its wood and 60 per cent of its food, while becoming, proportionally, a smaller part of the global population. So, while the population of the developing world increases, its participation in the global economy and its consumption of the world's resources decreases. Exclusion and irrelevance are the hallmarks of the new global order.[5]

The point of reckoning's second element lies in Liberation Theology's inability to give concrete content to key concepts such as 'liberation' and the 'preferential option for the poor'. This inability is best seen in the co-option of Liberation Theology's basic terminology by opponents. Franz Hinkelammert's essay 'Liberation Theology in the Economic and Social Context of Latin America: Economy and Theology, or the Irrationality of the Rationalized' is the only discussion of this situation by a mainstream liberationist. Hinkelammert takes as his example a speech delivered by Michael Camdessus, then head of the International Monetary Fund, at a congress for French Christian businessmen in 1992. In this speech, Camdessus echoes themes from Liberation Theology. He states (referring to the IMF and businessmen everywhere):

> Our mandate? … It is a text from Isaiah which Jesus explained; it says (Luke 4, 16–23): 'The spirit of the Lord is upon me. He has anointed me in order to announce the good news to the Poor, to proclaim liberation to captives and the return of sight to the blind, to free the oppressed and proclaim the year of grace granted by the Lord.' And Jesus only had one short response: 'Today this message is fulfilled for you that you should listen.' This today is our today and we are part of this grace of God, we who are in charge of the economy (the administrators of a part of it in any case): the alleviation of suffering for our brothers and the procurers of the expansion of their liberty. It is we who have received the Word. This Word can change everything. We know that God is with us in the work of spreading brotherhood.[6]

Camdessus takes concepts central to Liberation Theology – the preferential option for the poor, the Reign of God, liberation – to develop a theology whose practical outcome is God-given support for the very same structural adjustment policies denounced by Liberation Theologians. Hinkelammert draws two crucial consequences. First, 'the fact that these two contrary theologies (the theology of the IMF and Liberation Theology) cannot be distinguished on the level of a clearly theological discussion stands out. At this level Liberation Theology does not visibly distinguish itself from the anti-theology presented by the IMF. The conflict seems to be over the application

of a theology shared by both sides.'[7] Second, 'imperial theology is in
agreement with the preferential option for the poor and with the economic
and social incarnation of God's Kingdom. It presents itself as the only
realistic path for fulfilling those demands ... the option for the poor can no
longer identify any specification and natural affinity for Liberation Theology.
Now, the question is over the realism of the concretization.'[8]

The point of reckoning, made by the new global order and Liberation
Theology's inability to give content to its theological terms, can be defined in
the following fashion. Today there is greater exclusion from access to basic
needs for life than ever, yet Liberation Theology's ability to address that
exclusion has dwindled. It has dwindled because Liberation Theology has no
overarching project to oppose the IMF and other advocates of corporate
globalization. The central challenge Liberation Theology must now face,
therefore, is how to give a vague notion of 'liberation' socio-political and
economic content.[9] Only in this way can Liberation Theology truly tackle the
injustice at the heart of the emerging global order. Indeed, Liberation
Theology was born with the promise of being a theology that would not rest
content with mere talk about liberation, but rather would concretely pursue
liberation in society. The current global context and Liberation Theology's
inability to give concrete content to its theological terms make this challenge
and pursuit even more urgent than it was at Liberation Theology's birth. The
key issue at this point of reckoning, I believe, becomes what practical
political, social and economic content Liberation Theology gives to its
theological terms. There is a need to stress, once again, the interrelationship
between the theological and the constructive political aspects of Liberation
Theology. It is by stressing this connection that Liberation Theology can
distinguish itself from other projects which use the same vocabulary and thus
at face value espouse the same ideals, as well as more forcefully address the
injustice of the global status quo.

In my mind, to succeed in the point of reckoning, Liberation Theology
must recover the intimate link between thinking about ideals and thinking
about institutions once embodied in the notion of a 'historical project', that
is, a halfway term between a developed model of society and a utopia.[10] This
concept, however, has practically disappeared from contemporary Liberation
Theology. The loss of a historical project means, most importantly, the loss of
a particular way of thinking combining an attention to both the religious
ideal and the concretization that might approach that ideal. Generic concepts
such as liberation and capitalism hide as much as they reveal about the way
life chances and social resources may be theoretically approached and
institutionally realized. The focus needs to be on the practical political and
economic mediations of these ideals and concepts; the lack of such mediations
opens up the space for the co-option of the language of Liberation Theology
exemplified previously. In Liberation Theology today, while the critique of
current society is presented in concrete political, economic and sociological
terms, liberation, and thus the constructive part of the liberationist agenda, is

vaguely posited as the overcoming of slavery, a new man, or a new culture of solidarity.[11] The mechanisms by which such abstract goals are to be achieved are thus handed on a platter to Liberation Theology's opponents. And while Liberation Theology struggles to define its ideals in the current context, the new global order steam-rolls on.

The Makeover

With the 'end of history' and the apparent triumph of neoliberal capitalism, the viability of revolutionary change seems to have vanished, but the necessity of such change remains.[12] Of course, Liberation Theology's inability to give content to its own vocabulary stems from a number of external factors and pressures, including the Vatican's condemnation of Liberation Theology's use of Marxism as a social scientific mediation, the silencing and investigation of prominent theologians, as well as the loss of socialism as a viable alternative to capitalism. Here, however, I will argue that a central obstacle to Liberation Theology recovering the ability to develop historical projects lies in its understanding of capitalism. It is at this crucial juncture in my argument that the queer eye comes in. Indeed, resources and lessons from queer theory are central to recovering Liberation Theology for a new time.

I will not attempt a summary of queer theory, nor trace its rich intellectual lineage which includes Freud, Althusser, Saussure, Lacan, Foucault and Butler among others. Instead, I will examine the different ways Liberation Theology has approached the concept of capitalism. The examination will take place through the lens of a book that has greatly influenced my thinking on the relationship between Liberation Theology and capitalism, J. K. Gibson-Graham's *The End of Capitalism as We Know It: A Feminist Critique of Political Economy*. In this work Gibson-Graham attempts to rethink the notion of capitalism by applying insights from queer theory to political economy.[13] As is well known, at the heart of queer theory lies an attack on essentialism[14] – the belief that any apparant complexity can be uncovered to reveal simplicity at its core – and a denaturalizing of identity.[15] Gibson-Graham suggests that in the same way that queer theory argues that there is no core gender, that gender is a cultural fiction constituted, stylized and constrained within ritualized production, capitalism too has no universal or common essence, but is rather the product of multiple and fractured struggles granted unity by a common imagination and grand narrative of expansion and domination. Her project, therefore, seeks to unmask and reveal 'capitalism' as a dominant *discursive practice* rather than the dominant economic model it is usually understood to be. From this perspective, narratives of capitalism on the left – familiar narratives, narratives that paint capitalism as an expansive, monolithic, all-encompassing economic system – actually reinforce the very capitalism they seek to subvert. Let me show this process at work in the three ways Liberation Theology has thought about capitalism.

In its inception, Liberation Theology's understanding of capitalism was taken from the dependency theory espoused by Andre Gunder Frank, as José Míguez Bonino states:

> The major historical shift was the rise of dependency theory. It was a dividing of the waters. When people influenced by the Catholic renewal were confronted with the dependency theory crisis, there was a parting of the ways. Some remained in the modern European renewal and others left to pursue liberation.[16]

Juan Luis Segundo also claims that:

> As is well known by now, Liberation Theology arose as a reaction against the developmentalist theories and models formulated by the United States for Latin America in the decade of the sixties. The developmentalist model was characterized by the fact that it covered over and tried to hide the critical and decisive relationship of dependence versus liberation.[17]

How, then, does Frank view capitalism? He writes:

> ... underdevelopment is the *necessary product* of four centuries of capitalist development and of the internal contradictions of capitalism itself. These contradictions are the expropriation of economic surplus from the many and its appropriation by the few, the polarization of the capitalist system into metropolitan center and peripheral satellites, and the continuity of the fundamental structure of the capitalist system throughout the history of its expansion and transformation, due to the *persistence or re-creation* of these contradictions *everywhere and at all times.*[18]

Notice that for Frank capitalism will necessarily produce underdevelopment in the Third World; there is no escaping this system, a system that encompasses the whole globe. Capitalism's contradictions, as well as their ability to persist and recreate themselves, are spatially omnipresent and untouched by time or history; capitalism is a totality encompassing the whole globe and a unity that stands or falls in one piece. Its essence is understood as a hegemonic totality that is necessarily exploitative. Such a capitalism is by definition a beast immune to step by step reform: 'Therefore, short of liberation from this capitalist structure or the dissolution of the world capitalist system as a whole, the capitalist satellite countries, regions, localities, and sectors are condemned to underdevelopment.'[19] Latin America thus needs to decide between two poles: 'capitalist underdevelopment or socialist revolution'.[20] Small wonder that for Liberation Theologians only a radical revolutionary upheaval would do.

World systems theory provides the second lens, and current lens, through which Liberation Theology has viewed capitalism. World systems theory and dependency theory are siblings, and thus it is not surprising that Liberation Theologians would also incorporate the former into their socio-analytical framework.[21] Currently, in fact, Andre Gunder Frank is a major contributor to the development of world systems theory. Reflecting on his intellectual journey, he offers the following critique of dependency theory and his movement toward a world systems framework:

> First, real dependence exists, of course, and more than ever, despite arguments to the contrary. However, dependency 'theory' and 'policy' have never answered the question of how to eliminate it and how to pursue the chimera of nondependent or independent growth. Second, dependence heterodoxy has nonetheless maintained the orthodoxy that (under)development must refer to and be organized by and through (nation-state) societies, countries, or regions. This orthodox tenet turns out to be wrong. Third, although I turned orthodoxy on its head, I maintained the essence of the thesis that economic growth through capital accumulation equals development. Thereby, the socialist and dependence heterodoxies were caught in the same trap as development orthodoxy, and any real alternative definitions, policy, and praxis of 'development' were precluded. Fourth, in particular, this orthodoxy incorporated the patriarchal gender structure of society as a matter of course.[22]

Note points two and three: the demotion of the nation state and regional economies in favour of the capitalist world system as the unit of analysis, and the rejection of national socialism as an alternative mode of economic and social organization. These two moves have the effect of discursively strengthening the capitalism that Liberation Theology struggles against by expanding the scope of capitalist dominance beyond that postulated by Frank's earlier dependency theory. Within dependency theory, socialism was the solution; within world systems theory, socialism as conceived by dependency theory remains part of the problem. Within dependency theory, a national solution to underdevelopment was deemed possible; within world systems theory, national solutions are rendered ineffectual by capitalism's global scope. For dependency theory, national projects of socialist liberation were the path to take. For world systems theory, only a global alternative will do.

The expansion of capitalist dominance is evident in world systems theory's founding father, Immanuel Wallerstein. According to Wallerstein, the current capitalist world system possesses four main traits. First, the capitalist world economy is a distinctive reality in world history, with its own laws and dynamics; its fundamental law being the need for capital accumulation.[23] Second, capitalism necessarily increases inequality: 'the so-called "widening gap" is not an anomaly but a continuing basic mechanism of the operation of the world economy'.[24] Capitalism, as was the case in dependency theory, possesses laws and dynamics that make it necessarily exploitative. Third, Wallerstein argues that all facets of the social and political organization of territorial units, even states, derive from their position in the world system.[25]

So, for example, 'the development of the capitalist world-economy has
involved the creation of all the major institutions of the modern world:
classes, ethnic/national groups, households – and the "states." All of these
structures postdate, not antedate capitalism; all are consequence, not cause.'[26]
Capitalism, within this conception, defines all of global society since the
sixteenth century. It is all-encompassing; nothing lies beyond its scope.
Finally, for Wallerstein capitalism and socialism as they have existed in
history are really opposite sides of the same coin. Both are the product of a
soon to be defunct Western civilization obsessed with economic growth.[27]

World systems theory exacerbates the problems found in Liberation
Theology's use of dependency theory. In both, capitalism is a total system
that encompasses the whole globe; capitalism is defined by laws internal –
never external – to its being, and capitalism is seen as the real subject of
history to the point that all other structures are its creation. Yet within world
systems theory capitalism is even more daunting than dependency theory's
version of the beast. Dependency theory at least had a model – socialism,
however flawed – that it viewed as a possible alternative. Its link to the state
as a unit of analysis allowed for envisioning a national solution to the
problem posed by dependency. Here countries could escape the periphery and
achieve autonomy through a socialist revolution. World systems theory,
instead, collapses the dichotomy capitalism/socialism into an absolute
rejection of Western civilization that, however, remains abstractly defined
as capitalist through and through. It represents the most extreme version of
an understanding of capitalism as an all-encompassing, monolithic totality.
Nothing lies beyond its grasp. So, for example, Franz Hinkelammert claims
that in the current global context:

> we face not only a crisis of capitalism but a crisis of the foundational basis of
> modernity ... The crisis of capitalism has been transformed into a crisis of
> Western civilization itself ... Now, instead of the polarization capitalism/
> socialism, there emerges another, which is capitalism/life, capitalism/survival of
> humankind. Only that now capitalism has a wider meaning ... It means Western
> civilization, modernity and the belief in universal institutional systems that can
> homogenize all human relations. For this reason, the crisis includes socialism as
> well, as it emerged in the socialist societies of the Soviet tradition.[28]

For Hinkelammert, therefore, Liberation Theology must overcome not just
an economic system but Western civilization as a whole. Not even the
revolutionary overcoming of society's economic structure suffices. Collapsing
capitalism into Western civilization as a whole has the further effect of giving
capitalism power over our very being. Capitalism begins to define our
ontology. According to Ignacio Ellacuría, capitalism displays:

> an almost irresistible pull toward a profound dehumanization as an intrinsic part of
> the real dynamics of the capitalist system: abusive and/or superficial and alienating

ways of seeking one's own security and happiness by means of private accumulation, of consumption, and of entertainment; submission to the laws of the consumer market promoted by advertising in every kind of activity, including the cultural; and a manifest lack of solidarity in the individual, the family, and the state with other individuals, families, or states.[29]

Capitalism's ability to possess our very being is taken to the extreme in the following statement from Boff. For him:

> the dominant system today, which is the capitalist system ... has developed its own ways of collectively designing and constructing human subjectivity ... The capitalist and mercantile systems have succeeded in penetrating into every part of the personal and collective human mind. They have managed to decide the individual's way of life, the development of the emotions, the way in which an individual relates to his or her neighbors or strangers, a particular mode of love or friendship, and, indeed, the whole gamut of life and death.[30]

Capitalism is everywhere and is responsible for everything. Within this conception it is practically impossible to find a place to anchor the construction of new historical projects; even envisioning a means of negative resistance is a close to impossible task.

Borrowing a term from Gibson-Graham, I call the third way Liberation Theology approaches capitalism, the 'undertheorizing' of capitalism. Like world systems theory, this approach is current. To undertheorize capitalism is to use the concept without developing the social theoretic background that specifies its meaning and implications. In Liberation Theology, the failure to fully theorize capitalism reproduces by default the same picture of capitalism as a unified, all-encompassing and necessarily exploitative system found in dependency theory and world systems theory. Take Gustavo Gutiérrez, a Liberation Theologian who has distanced himself from dependency theory in particular, and the use of social and political theories such as Marxism in general. Jung Mo Sung notes that Gutiérrez has abandoned his once incisive take on socioeconomic issues for a much vaguer discourse.[31] He cites a passage from Gutiérrez's *The God of Life* as an example:

> Jesus goes to the root of the matter: all dependence on money must be rooted out. It is not enough to throw off foreign political domination; one must also break away from the oppression that arose from attachment to money and the possibilities it creates of exploiting others. Return the money to Caesar, Jesus is telling them, and you yourselves will be free of the power exercised by wealth, by mammon; then you will be able to worship the true God and give God what belongs to God.[32]

Sung, however, counters:

to say that money universally victimizes the dispossessed ... to propose freedom
from money as an evangelical solution for our social problems may sound poetic
but it remains nonetheless ineffective. If 'to be a Christian today means to worry
about where the poor will sleep,' as Gutierrez states, that requires, for example, the
need to build new houses. There is, therefore, a need for investments and thus for
money. It is not enough to simply say 'freedom from money,' it is necessary to
articulate that subjective liberty with the objective need we have for money, for
social investment and as a means of exchange.[33]

Insofar as Gutiérrez exhibits an undertheorized approach to capitalism in
particular and economic issues in general, he may have abandoned
dependency theory, but he has not abandoned a notion of capitalism as
something that must be rejected completely. Even without dependency theory
as the explicit theoretical lens, the same underlying understanding of
capitalism remains.

As long as capitalism is undertheorized and thus not consciously rethought
in a different mode it retains its systemic, necessarily exploitative, all-
encompassing quality. In this undertheorizing, capitalism is often invoked
rather than analysed and is portrayed as an inescapable radical evil. The
following examples may seem trivial, but they represent undertheorized
modes of thinking that reproduce by default an image of capitalism that
paralyses the imagination of historical projects. Take Leonardo Boff stating,
in a short commentary on the Lord's Prayer, that the petition to deliver us
from evil should be translated as 'deliver us from the evil one'. Boff adds: 'He
has a name; he is the capitalism of private property and the capitalism of the
state.'[34] Another example is Hinkelammert's claim that 'the world which now
appears and announces itself is a world where there is only "one lord" and
"master," where there is only one system ... There is no place of asylum ...
The empire is everywhere. It has total power and knows it.'[35] Capitalism
appears metaphorically as an all-encompassing and absolute empire that
cannot be escaped. Take also his statement that 'today we are before a system
of domination which includes even our souls, and which tries to suffocate
even the very capacity for critical thinking'.[36] Here capitalism becomes the
devil itself; nothing, not even our souls, lies beyond its scope. The terms
'market' or 'globalization' are also catch phrases – capitalism's alter egos –
depicting entities marching toward world domination or as already
triumphant. So Pablo Richard can write that 'it is not possible to live *outside*
the system, since globalization integrates everything, but it is possible to live
against the spirit of the system'.[37] In this case, the main trait of this opponent
is that it remains vaguely defined as a 'system' which is impossible to escape.
Capitalism, moreover, seems to completely control the deployment of
political power itself: 'For *el pueblo* [the people] (the popular sectors, social
movements at the base) political power has become impossible (the system
does not allow for the orientation of political power in benefit of popular
interest), political power become *irrelevant* (since everything is determined by

market logic and it is impossible to govern against that logic).'[38] Given the enemy's awesome scope and power, the only possible resistance becomes a vague shift in attitude that leaves the actual structures of oppression untouched.

Conclusion

Elsewhere I have developed the constructive implications of this argument, here let me focus on unpacking the basis of the critique.[39] My queer discursive approach to the examination of Liberation Theology and capitalism operates under the assumption that social theories are not neutral mirrors of reality; they shape and thus also facilitate and constrain modes of acting in society. Because there is no neutral theory, no God's eye view from which to analyse society, social theories do not just represent reality, they also construct reality. As Gibson-Graham argues, one must pay attention to the 'performativity of social representations – in other words, the ways in which they are implicated in the worlds they ostensibly represent'.[40] Every construction necessarily closes off some perspectives as it opens up others. An approach that focuses on social representations and the way they shape, facilitate and constrain modes of acting thus pays careful attention to the metaphors used to describe phenomena. It realizes that the adoption of a social theory – the selection of metaphors one uses as a roadmap to our environment – is inevitably a political act in that they are constitutive of the worlds we inhabit. What really matters, therefore, is how different theories make sense of the world and move people to act in different directions. In a nutshell, to develop historical projects, Liberation Theology must become aware that our descriptions add to the world.

From this standpoint, Liberation Theology's approach to capitalism reveals itself as a straitjacket that must be escaped. The very way Liberation Theology theorizes capitalism makes radical structural change a virtual impossibility; Liberation Theology's approach to capitalism blocks rather than opens avenues for change. In this framework there seems to be no middle space between revolution and local activism; to aspire for the former is to hope for too much, while to rest satisfied with the latter is to fail to hope enough. Indeed, in the movement from dependency theory to world systems theory and undertheorizing, capitalism takes up more and more space, becomes more and more all-encompassing, ever more powerful. What makes the need for an alternative understanding of capitalism urgent is that Liberation Theology often depicts capitalism not just as an economic system but also as the defining element of all of society, Western civilization as a whole, and life itself. Combating such a capitalism is a gargantuan task, no avenue of escape comes to sight. The idea of capitalism as an all-pervasive indivisible totality, encompassing the nation, the globe, and even the inner recesses of the human heart, cannot but suffocate the emergence of new historical projects. The causes of Liberation Theology's inability to fully meet the challenge posed by the contemporary global order, therefore, are not just external, they are internal as well.

There is no small irony in this end result of Liberation Theology's approach to, and critique of, capitalism. If I am correct, then the socio-analytic tools that were to further liberation have become the shackles that bind the theologian. This irony, however, is lost on Liberation Theologians. Take Jon Sobrino:

> The experience of God and witness to a just life becomes ever clearer in Latin America because structural injustice is there given explicit or implicit theological sanction. The presently prevailing structures – a capitalism of dependence and national security, whatever their forms – function as real deities with divine characteristics and their own cult. They are deities because they claim attributes that belong to God alone: ultimacy, definitiveness, and inviolability. They have their own cult because they demand the daily sacrifices of the masses and the violent sacrifice of any who resist them.[41]

The irony lies in the fact that Liberation Theologians' own analysis of capitalism reinforces the latter's idolatric tendencies; instead of unmasking idolatry, Liberation Theology inadvertently ends up reinforcing it. Sobrino *et al.* are blind to the fact that their own discourse on capitalism – an economic system or Western civilization of awesome force, that shapes all other aspects of our lives, and that can only be resisted but not changed unless it were to collapse of its own accord – further infuses capitalism with the very same aura of ultimacy, definitiveness and inviolability they bemoan. The best way to combat the idolatrous nature of capitalism, therefore, is to rid it of its systemic, all-powerful, all-encompassing, quasi-divine quality. The task is to show that the idol is an idol; that it is made of clay. Only then can room be made for the development of new historical projects. By queering capitalism, Liberation Theology can open up a space for the imagination of alternative historical projects and thus recover the bite of its critique.

Notes

1   In a nutshell, neoliberal market capitalism is characterized by the retreat of the state, extensive deregulation at the national level (the flexibilization of labour serves as one example) and the international level (exemplified by the push for free financial flows), as well as the rollback of networks of social protection. The new global order is a process that helps to extend and consolidate the hegemony of this type of capitalism worldwide.

2   See Ankie Hoogvelt, *Globalization and the Postcolonial World: The New Political Economy of Development* (Baltimore: The Johns Hopkins University Press, 1997). The following discussion draws from her excellent discussion of global economic trends on pages 67–93.

3   Hoogvelt, *Globalization and the Postcolonial World*, p. 70.

4   Hoogvelt here relies on and cites Hirst and Thompson who conclude, 'this means that between a half and two thirds of the world was virtually written off the map as far as the benefits from this form of investment was concerned.' Paul Hirst and Graham Thompson, *Globalization in Question* (London: Polity Press, 1995), p. 74; cited in Hoogvelt, *Globalization and the Postcolonial World*, p. 79.

5   As Manuel Castells explains: 'The more economic growth depends on high value added inputs and expansion in the core markets, then the less relevant become those economies which offer limited, difficult markets and primary commodities that are either being replaced by new materials or devalued with respect to their overall contribution to the production process. With the absolute costs of labor becoming less and less important as a competitive factor ... many countries and regions face a process of rapid deterioration that could lead to destructive reactions. Within the framework of the new informational economy, a significant part of the world population is shifting from a structural position of exploitation to a structural position of irrelevance.' Manuel Castells, 'The Informational Economy and the New International Division of Labor', in *The New Global Economy in the Information Age*, ed. M. Carnoy, M. Castells, Cohen S. S., and F. H. Cardoso (New York: Pennsylvania State University Press, 1993), p. 37; cited in Hoogvelt, *Globalization and the Postcolonial World*, p. 92.

   This is an irrelevance unless those parts of the world can become a dumping ground for the toxic byproducts of the rich countries industrial development. For a remarkable statement of the argument that it would be more efficient to dump highly polluting industries and waste on the poorest nations, see Larry Summer's comments when head of the World Bank in an internal Bank memo, 12 December 1991, commenting on the 1992 edition of the Bank's *Global Economic Perspectives*. In a nutshell, Summers argues that it makes perfect economic sense to dump 'a load of toxic waste in the lowest wage country'. It makes perfect economic sense because an inhabitant of, say, the US, produces more income and consumes more products than an inhabitant of the 'lowest wage country'. The potential loss of global income and productivity caused by ill health and/or death resulting from pollution in rich countries is thus far greater than in poor countries. For a fascinating discussion of World Bank culture, see Susan George and Fabrizio Sabelli, *Faith and Credit: The World Bank's Secular Empire* (Boulder, CO: Westview Press, 1994). Chapter 5 deals with Summers (currently president of Harvard University) and the memo.

6   Cited in Franz Hinkelammert, 'Liberation Theology in the Economic and Social Context of Latin America: Economy and Theology, or the Irrationality of the Rationalized', in *Liberation Theologies, Postmodernity, and the Americas*, edited by David Batstone, Eduardo Mendieta, Lois Ann Lorenzten, and Dwight N. Hopkins (New York: Routledge, 1997), p. 40.

7   Hinkelammert, 'Liberation Theology in the Economic and Social Context of Latin America', p. 44.

8   Hinkelammert, 'Liberation Theology in the Economic and Social Context of Latin America', pp. 44–45.

9   For my book-length take on Liberation Theology's present and future, see Ivan Petrella, *The Future of Liberation Theology: An Argument and Manifesto* (Aldershot, England: Ashgate, 2004). This essay draws from one chapter of the book. For other recent books, see John Burdick, *Legacies of Liberation: The*

Progressive Catholic Church in Brazil (Aldershot, England: Ashgate, 2004); Marcella Althaus-Reid, *The Queer God* (New York: Routledge, 2003); Daniel M. Bell Jr, *Liberation Theology After the End of History: The Refusal to Cease Suffering* (London: Routledge, 2001) and Marcella Althaus-Reid, *Indecent Theology: Theological Perversions in Sex, Gender and Politics* (New York: Routledge, 2000). To my mind, the most important assessment of Latin American Liberation Theology from within a mainstream liberationist perspective remains Jung Mo Sung, *Economía: Tema Ausente en la Teología de la Liberación* (San Jose, Costa Rica: DEI, 1994).

10   For a classic discussion of the notion of a historical project within Liberation Theology, see José Míguez Bonino, *Doing Theology in a Revolutionary Situation*, edited by William H. Lazareth, Confrontation Books (Philadelphia: Fortress Press, 1975) especially pp. 38–41.

11   Sung, *Economía: Tema Ausente en la Teología de la Liberación*, p. 96.

12   For the idea of an 'end of history', see Francis Fukuyama, *The End of History and the Last Man* (New York: Free Press, 1992) and Francis Fukuyama, 'The End of History', *The National Interest*, Summer (1989): 3–18.

13   J. K. Gibson-Graham, *The End of Capitalism as We Knew It: A Feminist Critique of Political Economy* (Cambridge: Blackwell Publishers, 1996). J. K. Gibson-Graham is the pen name of Julie Graham and Katherine Gibson; for simplicity's sake I refer to them throughout as a unified 'she' rather than 'they'.

14   Cf. Althaus-Reid, The Queer God, ch. 1.

15   Works on queer theory, essentialism and identity abound. I have found most helpful the following: Judith Butler, 'Against Proper Objects', *Differences: A Journal of Feminist Cultural Studies*, 6 (Summer-Fall 1994): 1–24, Judith Butler, 'Against Proper Objects', Judith Butler, *Bodies That Matter: On the Discursive Limits of 'Sex'* (New York: Routledge, 1993), Judith Butler, *Gender Trouble: Feminism and the Subversion of Identity* (New York: Routledge, 1990); Eve Kosofsky Sedgwick, *Tendencies* (Durham: Duke University Press, 1993), Eve Kosofsky Sedgwick, *Epistemology of the Closet* (Berkeley and Los Angeles: University of California Press, 1990); the essays in Michael Warner (ed.), *Fear of a Queer Planet* (Minneapolis: University of Minnesota Press, 1993) and Diana Fuss, *Essentially Speaking: Feminism, Nature, and Difference* (New York: Routledge, 1989). Marcella Althaus-Reid's work is the most important bridging of queer theory and Latin American Liberation Theology. See Althaus-Reid, *The Queer God* and *Indecent Theology*.

16   Cited in Christian Smith, *The Emergence of Liberation Theology: Radical Religion and Social Movement Theory* (Chicago: The University of Chicago Press, 1991), p. 258, from a 1987 interview with Bonino.

17   Juan Luis Segundo, *The Liberation of Theology* (Maryknoll: Orbis Books, 1985), p. 37.

18   Andre Gunder Frank, *Capitalism and Underdevelopment in Latin America: Historical Studies of Chile and Brazil* (New York: Monthly Review Press, 1967), p. 3; italics added.

19   Frank, *Capitalism and Underdevelopment*, p. 11.

20   Cited in Cristobal Kay, *Latin American Theories of Development and Underdevelopment* (New York: Routledge, 1989), p. 162.

21 They share a common heritage that includes Marxism, Lenin's theory of imperialism and Latin American structuralism; indeed, dependency theory itself is the major influence in world systems theory's development.

22 Andre Gunder Frank, 'Latin American Development Theories Revisited: A Participant Review', *Latin American Perspectives* 19, no. 73 (Spring 1992): 136.

23 Will Hout, *Capitalism and the Third World: Development, Dependence and the World System* (Hants, England: Edward Elgar Publishing Limited, 1993), p. 114.

24 Immanuel Wallerstein, *The Capitalist World Economy: Essays* (Cambridge: Cambridge University Press, 1979), p. 73; cited in Hout, *Capitalism and the Third World*, p. 115.

25 Hout, *Capitalism and the Third World*, pp. 114–15.

26 Immanuel Wallerstein, *The Politics of the World-Economy: The States, the Movements, and the Civilizations* (Cambridge: Cambridge University Press, 1984), p. 29; cited in Hout, *Capitalism and the Third World*, p. 115.

27 On this, see especially Immanuel Wallerstein, *After Liberalism* (New York: The New Press, 1995). For the main liberationist work developing this idea, see Franz Hinkelammert, *Critica a la Razon Utopica* (San Jose: DEI, 1990).

28 Franz Hinkelammert, 'Capitalismo y Socialismo: La Posibilidad de Alternativas', *Pasos* 48 (julio-agosto 1993): 14.

29 Ignacio Ellacuría, 'Utopia and Prophecy in Latin America', in *Mysterium Liberationis: Fundamental Concepts of Liberation Theology*, ed. Ignacio Ellacuría and Jon Sobrino (Maryknoll, NY: Orbis Books, 1993), p. 298.

30 Leonardo Boff, *Ecology and Liberation: A New Paradigm* (New York: Orbis Books, 1995), pp. 33–34.

31 Sung, *Economía: Tema Ausente en la Teología de la Liberación*, p. 97.

32 Gustavo Gutiérrez, *The God of Life* (Maryknoll, NY: Orbis Books, 1991), p. 60; cited in Sung, *Economía: Tema Ausente en la Teología de la Liberación*, p. 98.

33 Sung, *Economía: Tema Ausente en la Teología de la Liberación*, p. 98; translation my own.

34 Cited in Iain Maclean, *Opting for Democracy: Liberation Theology and the Struggle for Democracy in Brazil* (New York: Peter Lang, 1999), p. 142.

35 Franz Hinkelammert, 'Changes in the Relationships Between Third World and First World Countries', in *Spirituality of the Third World*, ed. K. C. Abraham and Bernadette Mbuy-Beya (Maryknoll, NY: Orbis, 1994), pp. 10–11; cited in Bell Jr, *Liberation Theology After the End of History*, p. 67.

36 Franz Hinkelammert, 'Determinación y Autoconstitución del Sujeto: Las Leyes Que Se Imponen a Espaldas de los Actores y el Orden por el Desorden', *Pasos* 64 (marzo–abril 1993): 18.

37 Pablo Richard, 'El Futuro de la Iglesia de los Pobres: Identidad y Resistencia en el Sistema de Globalización Neo-Liberal', *Pasos* 65 (mayo–junio 1996): 31; italics in original.

38 Pablo Richard, 'Teología de la Solidaridad en el Contexto Actual de Economía Neoliberal de Mercado', in *El Huracan de la Globalización*, ed. Franz Hinkelammert (San Jose, Costa Rica: DEI, 1999), p. 233, italics in original.

39 See Petrella, *The Future of Liberation Theology*.

40 Gibson-Graham, *The End of Capitalism*, p. ix.

41 Jon Sobrino, *The True Church and the Poor*, translated by Matthew J. O'Connell (Maryknoll, New York: Orbis, 1984), p. 166.

References

Althaus-Reid, M. (2000) *Indecent Theology: Theological Perversions in Sex, Gender and Politics*. New York: Routledge.

Althaus-Reid, M. (2003) *The Queer God*. New York: Routledge.

Bell Jr, D. M. (2001) *Liberation Theology After the End of History: The Refusal to Cease Suffering*. London: Routledge.

Boff, L. (1995) *Ecology and Liberation: A New Paradigm*. New York: Orbis Books.

Bonino, J. M. (1975) *Doing Theology in a Revolutionary Situation*, ed. W. H. Lazareth. Confrontation Books. Philadelphia: Fortress Press.

Burdick, J. (2004) *Legacies of Liberation: The Progressive Catholic Church in Brazil*. Aldershot, England: Ashgate.

Butler, J. (1990) *Gender Trouble: Feminism and the Subversion of Identity*. New York: Routledge.

Butler, J. (1993) *Bodies that Matter: On the Discursive Limits of 'Sex'*. New York: Routledge.

Butler, J. (1994) Against Proper Objects, *Differences: A Journal of Feminist Cultural Studies*, 6 (Summer-Fall): 1–24.

Castells, M. (1993) The Informational Economy and the New International Division of Labor, in *The New Global Economy in the Information Age*, ed. M. Carnoy, M. Castells, Cohen S. S., and F. Cardoso. New York: Pennsylvania State University Press.

Ellacuría, I. (1993) Utopia and Prophecy in Latin America, in *Mysterium Liberationis: Fundamental Concepts of Liberation Theology*, ed. I. Ellacuría and J. Sobrino, pp. 289–327. Maryknoll, NY: Orbis Books.

Frank, A. G. (1967) *Capitalism and Underdevelopment in Latin America: Historical Studies of Chile and Brazil*. New York: Monthly Review Press.

Frank, A. G. (1992) Latin American Development Theories Revisited: A Participant Review, *Latin American Perspectives*, 19 (73), Spring: 125–39.

Fukuyama, F. (1989) The End of History, *The National Interest*, Summer: 3–18.

Fukuyama, F. (1992) *The End of History and the Last Man*. New York: Free Press.

Fuss, D. (1989) *Essentially Speaking: Feminism, Nature, and Difference*. New York: Routledge.

George, S., and F. Sabelli (1994) *Faith and Credit: The World Bank's Secular Empire*. Boulder, CO: Westview Press.

Gibson-Graham, J. (1996) *The End of Capitalism as We Knew It: A Feminist Critique of Political Economy*. Cambridge: Blackwell Publishers.

Gutiérrez, G. (1991) *The God of Life*. Maryknoll, NY: Orbis Books.

Hinkelammert, F. (1990) *Critica a la razon utopica*. San Jose: DEI.

Hinkelammert, F. (1993a) Capitalismo y Socialismo: La Posibilidad de Alternativas, *Pasos*, 48 (julio–agosto): 10–15.

Hinkelammert, F. (1993b) Determinación y Autoconstitución del Sujeto: Las Leyes que se Imponen a Espaldas de los Actores y el Orden por el Desorden, *Pasos*, 64 (marzo–abril): 18–31.

Hinkelammert, F. (1994) Changes in the Relationships Between Third World and First World Countries, in *Spirituality of the Third World*, ed. K. Abraham and B. Mbuy-Beya. Maryknoll, NY: Orbis.

Hinkelammert, F. (1997) Liberation Theology in the Economic and Social Context of Latin America: Economy and Theology, or the Irrationality of the Rationalized, in *Liberation Theologies, Postmodernity, and the Americas*, ed. D. Batstone, E. Mendieta, L. A. Lorenzten, and D. N. Hopkins, pp. 25–52. New York: Routledge.

Hirst, P., and G. Thompson (1995) *Globalization in Question*. London: Polity Press.

Hoogvelt, A. (1997) *Globalization and the Postcolonial World: The New Political Economy of Development*. Baltimore: The Johns Hopkins University Press.

Hout, W. (1993) *Capitalism and the Third World: Development, Dependence and the World System*. Hants, England: Edward Elgar Publishing Limited.

Kay, C. (1989) *Latin American Theories of Development and Underdevelopment*. New York: Routledge.

Kosofsky Sedgwick, E. (1990) *Epistemology of the Closet*. Berkeley and Los Angeles: University of California Press.

Kosofsky Sedgwick, E. (1993) *Tendencies*. Durham: Duke University Press.

Maclean, I. (1999) *Opting for Democracy: Liberation Theology and the Struggle for Democracy in Brazil*. New York: Peter Lang.

Petrella, I. (2004) *The Future of Liberation Theology: An Argument and Manifesto*. Aldershot, England: Ashgate.

Richard, P. (1996) El Futuro de la Iglesia de los Pobres: Identidad y Resistencia en el Sistema de Globalización Neo-Liberal, *Pasos*, 65 (mayo–junio): 9–16.

Richard, P. (1999) Teología de la solidaridad en el contexto actual de economía neoliberal de mercado, in *El huracan de la globalización*, ed. F. Hinkelammert, pp. 223–38. San Jose, Costa Rica: DEI.

Segundo, J. L. (1985) *The Liberation of Theology*. Maryknoll, New York: Orbis Books.

Smith, C. (1991) *The Emergence of Liberation Theology: Radical Religion and Social Movement Theory*. Chicago: The University of Chicago Press.

Sobrino, J. (1984) *The True Church and the Poor*, trans. M. J. O'Connell. Maryknoll, New York: Orbis.

Sung, J. M. (1994) *Economía: Tema Ausente en la Teología de la Liberación*. San Jose, Costa Rica: DEI.

Wallerstein, I. (1979) *The Capitalist World Economy: Essays*. Cambridge: Cambridge University Press.

Wallerstein, I. (1984) *The Politics of the World-Economy: The States, the Movements, and the Civilizations*. Cambridge: Cambridge University Press.

Wallerstein, I. (1995) *After Liberalism*. New York: The New Press.

Warner, M. (ed.) (1993) *Fear of a Queer Planet*. Minneapolis: University of Minnesota Press.

Chapter 4

Oh, Que Sera, Que Sera … [1]
A Limping A/Theological Thought in Brazil

Claudio Carvalhaes

Nobody drives those whom God has perverted/led astray.[2]

Raduam Assar (2001: 8)

Either by accident, destiny, the angel of God or *fortuna*, I was named Claudio, an improper name, a name that limps, that faults, that errs. The story of my *quasi* transgression started at the baptismal font when I was named by a Presbyterian minister who baptized me in a church in São Paulo in the name of the Father, the Son and the Holy Ghost. These names were others to me, offered and imposed with the promise of a blessing, of a belonging and also with the unnamed assurance that I would have to deal with these *other names*, and so many others, for the rest of my life. Without knowing, and being unable to remember, I became a hybrid of these names and other names from the past and from the future. I am haunted by so many names and yet, I cannot name *the* name that is unnameable.

There is a story in the Bible about a man who fought with the angel of God and started to limp. His original name was Jacob, but by way of a new beginning he had his name changed by the angel of God to Israel. In his fight with the angel, a fight of names, he was touched in his thigh and started to limp. From the valley of Jabbok he was thrown into another beginning, with a new name, and had to deal with what he thought he was and what he had to become. Jacob/Israel survived the angel of God and was marked by a sign. Limping, he got to Peniel. Nobody saw it, nobody really knows what happened there, but after this encounter he could never walk straight again. Something happened in that place: 'And as he passed over Peniel the sun rose upon him, and he halted upon his thigh.'[3]

By calling names, returning to new beginnings, and searching for the angel of God, this article tries to perform an unfinished rehearsal of a recent history of theology in Brazil, attempting to engage Liberation Theology with postmodern ways of thinking and not thinking of God. I advocate here not Vattimo's 'weak thought' but a transgressive 'limping thought'. A limping thought has yet to be thought, but it has its contours in many names from abroad and from within Brazil. The Brazilian names that will be indexed later in this essay may be unknown to most of its readers. A limping theological thought tries to slip away from the ontotheological structures of theological discourse and offers a Brazilian taste to its production.

In order to find traces of the angel of God, the limping thought has to be considered over and against the colonial enterprise and the enlightenment that clearly defined who and what we are. Since colonialist times, after we were 'discovered', Latin America and other colonized countries became the other, an Other over against which the colonizer might maintain itself as Same. This project was and still is so intense that even in Brazil, throughout our history, some of our most brilliant thinkers could not help but create our identities and describe ourselves within the framework of a kind of syncretism and hybridism that was paradoxically an intrinsic part of the exclusion set forth within modernity's project of purity and homogeneity.

In this way, a limping thought tries to find ways of transgressing our own definitions and opens up possibilities of critique by disseminating other ways of thinking about God. It does this, continually rooting itself in the intense poverty, exclusion and violence seen in Brazil. In this process we find ourselves not naming the conceptually stable God of metaphysics but naming a name that cannot properly be named in this place of poverty and exploitation.

The religious project of modernity was the continuous and progressive production of meaning. Theological endeavours in Latin America tried to do just that. Liberation Theology was itself a product of modernity. However, this meaning machine has come to a point where its centre can no longer hold. Religious representations of reality have not been able to fix points as they used to do, and even the utopias that fed the liberationists have lost their power. The question now should be not how to reveal the hidden teleological sense of a nonsensical place like Latin America, but rather whether there is any possibility of making meaning at all within structures of absurdity. It is no longer acceptable to justify – even if by means of a transformative vision – a representational system that maintains 50 per cent of the population of Brazil below the poverty line. Considering the complexity of social conditions in Latin America, any thought that tries to unsettle the hegemonic representations of reality under which Liberation Theology still operates will need ceaselessly to cross religious, economic, social, psychoanalytic, historical, and sexual vectors of identity. Herein would lie the transgressions of a limping a/Liberation Theology.

A limping a/theological thought comes from and reaches toward the impossible visit of someone or something, an *arrivant* that we do not know. This a/theology takes place between the valley of Jabbok and Peniel, never able to reach its destination and see God face to face. The maps that promised to take us to Peniel have failed. Our condition is one in which, as Heidegger teaches us, the gods have fled and left us wondering and longing for their presence. This is our paradox: we live between the longing for what we have lost (and ultimately never knew) and the hope for what we have not yet met. Between Jabbok and Peniel, we can neither say that we have met the angel of God nor that we have not met. Derrida describes this *arrivant*:

> The absolute *arrivant* does not yet have a name or an identity. It is not an invader or an occupier, nor is it a colonizer, even if it can also become one. This is why I call it simply the *arrivant*, and not someone or something that arrives, a subject, a person, an individual, or a living thing, even less one of the migrants I just mentioned. It is not even a foreigner as a member of a foreign, determined community. Since the *arrivant* does not have any identity yet, its place of arrival is also de-identified: one does not yet know or one no longer knows which is the country, the place, the nation, the family, the language, and the home in general that welcomes the absolute *arrivant*. This absolute *arrivant* as such is, however, not an intruder, an invader, or a colonizer, because the invasion presupposes some self-identity for the aggressor and for the victim. Nor is the *arrivant* a legislator or the discoverer of a promised land. As disarmed as a newly born child, it no more commands than is commanded by the memory of some originary event where the archaic is bound with the *final* extremity, with the finality par excellence of the *telos* or the *eskhaton*. It even exceeds the order of any *determinable* promise. Now the border that is ultimately most difficult to delineate, because it is always already crossed, lies in the fact that the absolute *arrivant* makes possible everything to which I have just said it cannot be reduced, starting with the humanity of man, which some would be inclined to recognize in all that erases, in the *arrivant*, the characteristic of (cultural, social, or national) belonging and even metaphysical determination (ego, person, subject, consciousness, and so on).[4]

This *arrivant* might also be the angel of God. However, the angel of God is slippery and confuses our certainties, unsettling our most tightly held beliefs and eluding us with its shining glory. The angel of God holds us wandering in the desert in order to look for it, in a path that has erased all traces, leaving only a thin line of hope. We always wonder about this encounter and keep trying to guess how it might have been, what it would be like. Questions that have no answers place us even deeper into the placeless place of their *mazing grace*,[5] a labyrinthine space of transgressive possibilities for the impossible.

The angel of God wanders in Latin America but we are not sure exactly where. For some, the angel has gone a long time ago, never to appear again. For others, the angel is still here, somewhere, somehow, somewhat. Where is the angel? Would the angel be visiting prisons, following kids on the streets, helping abused women to survive their husbands, living in the *favelas*, controlling the narcotraffic, watching people shooting and killing each other without purpose or reason? Would the angel be living in the mansions of the rich or in the cocaine used by their daughters and sons? Would the angel be in the Prozac creating psalms of comfort or in the phallic controlling system of a society made for men? Perhaps the angel of God might be transgressing rules without consideration for the Other, or transgressing boundaries of identities and sexual behaviour to open space for the excluded ones. Would the angel be transgressing rules, placating waves of furious religious and secular beliefs, be they Christian or psychoanalytic, and changing the landscape of the rights and wrongs of our laws? Perhaps, the angel might be crossing the paths of those who go beyond their possibilities and wrestling with them to give them the strength to live into new names and experimental identities – even if at the cost of limping.

The Angel of God in Brazil

The angel of God, the angel of life and death, is always unclear, morphing from interpretation to interpretation. For some, the angel of God came to Latin America with Spanish and Portuguese conquerors in 1492, delivering us by their guns into the hands of the Roman Catholic defenders of God, Reason, and the explanation of the order of things. Following this deliverance, as adopted sons and daughters of European civilizations, we have tried to accommodate Cartesian and Christian *ratio* within our exotic ways of being and thinking. Faced with rational mechanisms of cultural imposition, namely guns, Latin America was supposed to learn to think like Europe, the cradle of civilization. As underdeveloped and uncivilized, we were to learn, for instance, that we had to cover our shameful and sinful bodies. Before the conquerors, we used to play in the fields of *Pacha Mama* (the Earth goddess of the Incas) without clothes, moving about life with our poor beliefs and uncivilized manners. After them, we started to play in the fields of the Lord and struggled to become the same. Without knowing why or how, like George Orwell's book *Nineteen Eighty-four*, we were finally able to see four fingers on a hand that showed us five.

The conquerors switched our temporality. Even today, people in Brazil say that Brazil is the country of the future. We are not a country of the present because we have not reached the point we should have as civilized people. By switching our temporality, the conquerors controlled the power of exploitation and also of interpretation. Those who hold the future are always waiting. As a Negro spiritual says: 'We are the one who've been waiting for ...' Those who hold the present are always determining how and what things are.

During the process of the Portuguese colonization, the angel of God also came with the African slaves and their religions from Africa. They were forced to work for the white Europeans and were killed if they did not do the jobs given to them. Besides working, the African women were sexually abused and took care of the children of the white men.

Brazil, the last country to outlaw slavery, is now filled with so-called 'cordial racism', which expresses itself daily against the African Brazilian people, who compose a majority of the nation's population.

In the eighteenth century, the angel of God started to arrive with the Protestant missionaries and their faith against the Roman Catholic Church. In the recent past Pentecostals and neo-Pentecostals have grown by leaps and bounds, conquering every corner of Brazil with their gospel of prosperity. Brazil is known as the largest Catholic country in the world, yet this is now starkly challenged by the rapid growth of its Pentecostal and neo-Pentecostal movements.

A product of all these angelic visitations, Brazil has typically been understood as a hybrid of cultures and a cordial syncretic religious place. Immigrants have settled in Brazil from all around the world: Brazil has welcomed Germans, Dutch, British, Japanese, Italians, Spanish, Turkish, Lebanese, Chinese, Koreans and many others into its manifold. However, this process of openness to others and blending it all up within the Brazilian melting pot reiterates colonial processes of exclusion characterized by enticed assimilation. It is only now that new studies are challenging Brazilian inclusion.[6]

It is clear by now that the angel of God – at least as we have imagined *him* – has never accepted any hybridism or any blurring of identities that might transgress the Christian status quo. Any suspicion of transgressive thought, sexuality or behaviour would be labelled as disorder, marginal and consequently dangerous to the wellbeing of society. The universal logic of faith, mathematics, law, culture, sexuality, democracy, forgiveness, economy and politics had already been worked out by the colonizers, and has subsequently been internalized and redeployed by Latin America as the only way to inhabit the civilized world.

The Angel of God and Protestant Theology in Brazil

If we take the ontotheological route, it is easy to find the angel of God in Brazil. Both liberals and conservatives are able to explain the existence, and worse, the love of God within the misery of any *favela*[7] in Brazil. Afterwards, it is not a difficult enterprise since God is always there, as a given, prior to any language, structure or ground. What happens theologically within Protestantism in Brazil is therefore similar to what happens in the Protestant arena in United States.

On the side of the conservative theologians, everything can be explained by the presence of inner sin. It is our sinful nature that keeps people from knowing God and consequently knowing a better life. Once Jesus lovingly takes the hearts and minds of those that have not yet met God, and gives them salvation, life will be abundant and people will rise up within the social structure. The world is thus structured for these thinkers within a dualism between good and evil, God and Satan, which explains every single event in social and private histories. The liberals accuse them of giving too much attention to the spiritual side of the Christian message, forgetting the daily and concrete life of oppression lived by the people.

From the liberal side, including Liberation Theologies, the problem lies in social sin. The structures of society themselves are sinful, which means that to realize the kingdom of God, we must first overcome the unjust structures that keep people from living a decent life. The mission of Christianity is to live an ethical life that will 'speak the truth to power' and bring justice to everybody. The liberal Christian ethic is simple: whatever is unjust is not God's. Whatever is just, fair or good is named as God's action in the world. The conservatives accuse them of putting too much stress on the material side, enforcing social and not personal categories of the gospel and not paying attention to people's inner need of salvation and their risk of eternal condemnation.

There is a third group that tries to find a mid-point between conservative and liberal theologies, the evangelicals. They criticize both sides and say they take the best of each theology, creating a so-called 'integral Christianity' that does not forget the spiritual side of the human being which needs personal salvation from God, while fighting social injustices and being active within social and political movements. Both conservatives and liberals criticize the evangelicals for not taking either side consistently.

A limping a/liberation theological thought relies on none of these possibilities. It comes from within the theological movement and tries to fissure and disrupt its hegemonic metaphysical and ontotheological two-column structures with not-yet-thought possibilities.

Colonization and Liberation Theology

Because of the internalizing mechanisms of colonization, theology in Latin America is a by-product of the Enlightenment. European metaphysics and ontotheological thought therefore ground all of Latin America's liberationist metanarratives. They are structured in a given ground, in an *a priori*, a self-existent origin, *causa-sui*. This origin holds the essence of all the existing and non existing things and consequently the truth to be uncovered and revealed. Its universality, priority and exteriority mark the metaphysical truth. Universality that is applied to the human knowledge as category; priority because the reality is structured in binary terms and there is always a term that is hierarchically higher than the other; exteriority because every truth is the representation of an original essence. Liberation Theology used the same referents, the same principles as the European metaphysicians, thereby creating new approaches to the same old theology.

Many years later, more precisely in the nineteenth century, the Reformation movement set its feet in Brazil for good and, even though they said that we could read the Bible, they taught us that there were specific ways to read and interpret it. Both Roman Catholics and Protestants translated their own theological canons; from Aristotle to Thomas Aquinas to Karl Rahner; from Augustine to Calvin to Karl Barth, respectively. Theology became a matter of learning, memorizing and regurgitating the thought of Europeans and North Americans. It was in the 1960s that the angel of God arrived with a new promise: Liberation Theology, the map to travel from Jabbok to Peniel. It was a time when Latin American thinkers and theologians started to become alienated from thought forms imposed on them by strangers. They recognized that what was imported to theology had nothing to do with the reality lived by the people of Latin America. As a result, after meetings and movements, they started what we now know today as Liberation Theology. Using the thought of Karl Marx for the most part to read and analyse the brutal and unfair reality of Latin America, and devising a methodology based on orthopraxis rather than an orthodoxa, this theological movement was able not only to speak out loud about the sufferings and misery of the people of Latin America denouncing their abject situation, but also to attempt to re-read the entire theological tradition. Of course, Liberation Theology posed a considerable threat to the Catholic Church and as a consequence, thinkers and priests such as Leonardo Boff and Archbishop Oscar Romero were silenced by the Church, some even killed by political parties.

Liberation Theology has given us many wonderful gifts. It has placed Latin America on the map of international theology, it has exposed some of the injustices of the world, and it has helped and empowered social movements, sparking changes throughout Latin America and in the wider world. It has empowered countless struggles and has drawn attention to the difficulties of the poor in general. It has also challenged theological thought with the assertion that God is on the side of the poor. It has even shaken the hierarchical structure of the Roman Catholic Church. Moreover, it has forced us to recognize that our thoughts cannot be so abstract and out of touch with what goes on in the world, especially among the poor.[8] It has reminded us that the economic system in place in the world operates by means of the exclusion of those who cannot produce what the system wants.

Yet as Liberation Theology tried to become grounded and let the poor be the subject of their own history, there was a tendency towards the idealization of those poor. At the same time, the theological locus gradually reverted to the offices of the theologians. For instance, the poor could never write a book called *Mysterius Liberationis.*[9] Moreover, there was an aesthetization of the poor that added a certain glamour to poverty. The 'organic intellectuals', a term used by Antonio Gramsci to define those thinkers who are engaged in transforming reality, forgot that they were not living in the conditions they saw and deplored, and could not really access this situation. Since the poor were the subject of their own history, Liberation Theology propagated and worked passionately for a dream of justice, a utopia in which the poor would see the realm of God concretely, historically. Unfortunately, the utopia never materialized. Of those who believed it, some were burned out and left the dream altogether. Among those who stayed, a sense of being in limbo filled their hearts and a more prudent form of speech replaced their radical optimism.

Forty years have passed since the first publication of *A Theology of Liberation: History, Politics and Salvation*[10] by Gustavo Gutiérrez, and it seems that Liberation Theology, as it was, has come to an end. Even though different Liberation Theologies still advocate their lasting importance, since not much in the world has changed (and this is true) the methodological sources of Liberation Theology have become outdated, and Liberation Theology itself has become a piece of history within Western theological thought.

I believe that the greatest contribution of Liberation Theology has been to bring to a place of prominence the annoying and challenging presence of the poor. The poor had been mostly forgotten by the dominant European theological discourses that emerged after (and in spite of) Saint Francis. It was Liberation Theology that placed them back at the centre of the theological stage, saying that unless we discuss the nagging and burdensome presence of the poor, we cannot be faithful to the gospel of Jesus Christ. What is needed now for Liberation Theology is to let its seed die in order to be born again, to disfigure itself through serious engagement in relations that perhaps have not been thought or permitted before. Unless Liberation Theology engages with postmodernism, poststructuralism, post-colonialism and queer studies, it will not be able to resurrect its new disfigured self from the ashes of its beautiful history.

In Latin America, we used to be told by others how to define and interpret the world. The 'This *is*' never belonged to us because the 'this *I*' belonged to those who regulated the production of meaning. 'This *is*' always names certain facts, given truths and that inexorable correspondence between the possible event and its narration. Resistant to all this, the limping thought cannot say clearly what are the facts since it cannot create this correspondence any more. Thus, it does not hurry to be on time or to regurgitate the words pronounced in Europe or North America as theology did for a long time, but wants to annoy these theological and non-theological discourses with new performances, creativeness, hospitality, happiness, friendship, bodily/sexual approaches and warm hearts. In order to have an A/Latin American theological discourse engaged with poststructural and post-colonial thought, it is necessary to engage, even at this late stage, with the new discussions of postmodern discourses.

A Limping A/Theological Thought

A limping thought that I am advocating is a process undertaken by those who always arrive late at any event. A limping thought plays with rigorous rules but never complies with them, never satisfies the procedures, never fulfils its obligations, and never adjusts itself to the proper way of thinking. A limping thought tries to dismantle the certainties of the present since the present is always the past when it arrives and the future has always yet to come. It tries always to recognize that 'this *is*' always comes with a reminder. 'This *is*' belongs to those who see clearly and persevere in controlling the vision-truth of the present, those who live mostly in Peniel and tell everybody what the face of God looks like. A limping thought sees neither the truth nor the angel of God and can only offer parasitic, supplementary and derivative, performative assertions. Since it might be driven by shadows, it 'sees things imperfectly as in a poor mirror ... (and) all that I know now is partial and incomplete'.[11] It realizes that reality is always opaque and that we can't see anything clearly.

Tangential to every dogma, a limping theologian relates to Mark C. Taylor's figure of the 'a/theologian'.[12] In order to write about God, the theologian needs to go through this process of fighting with the angel of God and become a limping person. In this fight, the a/theologian loses her/his powerful tools to understand God, he/she gives up the arrogance of saying what God *is*, acknowledges his/her intentions, discovers that Peniel is like Derrida's *Khora*,[13] an unnamable place where one can/not meet God and from where one can neither arrive nor leave. As Mark Taylor affirms: 'To break the tyranny of immediacy, it is necessary to figure the "vanishing point of God" otherwise.'[14] The performative process of writing and *liturgizing* God follows a limping process, a process in which the writer loses the pace, the rhythm and the track and never gets to where she/he was supposed to be. He/she arrives late at Peniel and wonders how God's face might have looked. This late arrival irreducibly runs after the sacred, trying to get to Peniel on time, and that is the hope we carry since this improbable angel of God is always calling us, sometimes from the past, sometimes from the future. We long for a presence that never was, but a presence nonetheless. Its presence is revealed by its absence, a sort of *déjà vu*. I limp because of this encounter, an encounter that disfigured me even though I have never met this angel. The angel of God appears by its effacement:

> The 'trace of effacement' is the 'visual operator of disappearance' through which the impossibility of presenting both presence and presentation is 'presented' ... In different terms, disfiguring figures the unfigurable in and through the faults, fissures, cracks, and tears of figures.[15]

The way to be a liberation a/theologian in Brazil involves negotiations of how the a/theologian figures and de-figures the sacred, which is already disfigured. Thus, a limping thought might be used here as a tool to deconstruct the theological discourse in Latin America. Being aware of the dangers of practising mimetic theology, we ought to re-create a new *anthropophagic movement* that eats theology up and creates a space in which neither the indigenous nor the foreigner should be placed at ease. Trying to find ways into a new anthropophagism, deconstruction should bring about what was left out, dismantling binary structures, evoking possibilities to disrupt ontotheological thought, always hoping to trace the untraceable, to name the unnameable and disrupt dogmas and truths that promise security but give only violence.

The *anthropophagic movement* was created in São Paulo in 1922 by the poet Oswald de Andrade and other thinkers at the famous 'Week of Modern Art'. They were against xenophobic feelings, but they proposed a new way of creating Brazilian thought: it should be neither afraid of foreign influences but integrate them all, devour them all and eat them all up by adding what is part of our own contribution to the world, our happiness. At a certain point of the manifesto he says: 'We were never catechized. We made carnival ... The spirit refuses to give life to the spirit without the body. Happiness is the final proof.' When I mention a new anthropophagism I am looking for ways to explode Brazilian modernism from within and use a limping thought to create ways of thinking and living in Brazil, Latin America and the world. The new anthropophagism should add the transgressive thought of what disarrays, of what disturbs, of what errs, of what has no bounds, of what tears apart, always destroying and disfiguring itself.

A new anthropophagism does not desire God outside of our bodies. The desire of God is not a spiritual longing, if what we call spiritual has no body. This desire has to do with concrete bodies with emptied stomachs, with illnesses that are not controlled or cannot be healed, with bodies discarded by government programmes, with bodies abused and battered, enslaved bodies, disfigured bodies, bodies not fully observed, bodies that burn in desire. Moreover, the desire of God has to do with lack, with the emptiness of our skin, with our search for other bodies, transgressing the norms of what is allowed or permitted as we construe fragmentary notions of love. Our desire for God has to do with the rubbing of our skin, with the kisses we give, the caresses we receive, with the orgasms we have.

A limping thought wants to point to repressive elements within the structure of thought, trying to remember what was left out, shocking the powers that take hold through dogmas, hierarchy and higher knowledge. It moves through a parasitic process that never ends and it has no place from which it starts or to which it arrives. It wants to fissure and disconnect from within theology its pretensions of truth and universal unsaid intentions. It wants to affirm a groundless ground and a life of an impossible faith lived on the edge, always risking itself. It intends to translate an original that has no origin and is irreducible to definitions.

A limping thought, a sort of a/theology, knows it can never get to a proper understanding or to a safer place. A limping thought knows its presuppositions but is aware of its own constructions, limitations and indefinite meanings. A limping thought cannot associate thought and knowledge with truth. It resists the competition of truth between groups, even the marginal ones, all of whom can only create and sustain mutual violence.

Limping theology cannot avoid its own mistakes and knows that it can never attain the truth. It wanders in the desert tackling errant issues. In Mark C. Taylor's words:

The erring a/theologian is driven to consider and reconsider errant notions: transgression, subversion, mastery, utility, consumption, domination, narcissism, nihilism, possession, uncanniness, repetition, tropes, writing, dissemination, dispossession, expropriation, impropriety, anonymity, spending, sacrifice, death, desire, delight, wandering, aberrance, carnival, comedy, superficiality, carnality, duplicity, shiftiness, undecidability, and spinning. In view of these preoccupations, it should be clear that erring thought is neither properly theological nor nontheological, theistic nor atheistic, religious nor secular, believing nor non believing. A/theology represents the liminal thinking of marginal thinkers.[16]

Popular songs can help us to move forward in this, provoking limping a/theological thought. Regarding our mistakes, Kid Abelha, a Brazilian rock band, sings this song, *Nada Sei (Apnéia)*:

> I know nothing from this life
> I live without knowing
> Never knew and never will
> I just live without knowing
> What place is mine
> That I could give away
> Which place contains me
> That could stop me
> I am mistaken, I am errant
> Always wandering, always wondering
> Until I have time

Losing what Lyotard called the sense of the 'metanarratives', or overarching beliefs, a limping theology arrives at a crossroads where neither immanence nor transcendence alone offers solace. Even though transcendence is all around, we can never know where. This undecidibility creates a community that fights against homogenization, that surpasses the limits of any prescription, that erodes the traditional. Michael Strysick says:

> It may be most apt to suggest that our current moment is concerned with how unbearably intractable the traditional has become. This concentration has taken the form of considering the relationship to the Other. Indeed, in *The Unawoable Community*, Blanchot declares that the ethics of community has to do with 'an infinite attention to the Other' (1988: 43). The challenge is to act ethically outside the limiting prescriptions of traditional community.[17]

This community is like that which another Brazilian group called *Tribalistas* sings in their song of the same name:

> The *tribalistas* don't want to be sure anymore
> They don't want to have certainties, wisdom or religion
> The *tribalistas* don't want to argue anymore

They don't get into any argument about doctrine or gossip
Tribalism has arrived at the pillar of construction

Kicking God and embracing natives' faith
One day I was a chimp
But now I walk with two feet

The *tribalistas* long for the future
They use sunglasses and overuse their eye drops
They are tourists like you and your neighbor
Within the placenta of the little blue planet

Tribalism is an anti movement
That will disintegrate in the next moment
Tribalism should be and must be whatever you want
Nothing is required besides being who you are
Tribalism has arrived ...

Kicking God and embracing natives' faith
Kicking God and embracing natives' faith

This is a community that disintegrates, representations of God that we want to throw away in an endless search for the roots of an unknown origin. A limping a/theology rests in this un-restful place, the *hymen*, the *double bind*, to use Derrida's words or the *aboutness* of Taylor. In this space we might be able to think the sacred in relation to the irreducible difference, which might be what Mark Taylor meant when he coined the term *altarity*.[18] What moves the limping theologian seems to be the unending and dazzling attempt to know the secret, to see what might be already gone but that still haunts us, to find possible ways for what will be always impossible. In this 'traffic of interpretations',[19] there should be joy, there should be samba, there should be carnival, but there is no trust in any correspondence between what we say and what it might mean. There will be struggle, there will be pain, there will be unwanted attempts to avoid the Other, but there would not be final regulation, final destiny, or final and/or perpetual meaning, rather a responsible and at the same time random toss of the dice, hoping for better. There will always be hope while we have our traditional musical instruments: *um tamborim, um cavaquinho e uma cuica* (a drum, a ukulele and a small friction drum).

This theological endeavour is marked by inter-textuality, working within the context of any performance, by the metonymic creation of our discourses, by over-exposition of images and by the re-placing of countless re-presentations, making it impossible for the limping theologian to decide what is proper and what is not. While we wait for what is yet to come, we celebrate what haunts us through a *mazing grace* that is like carnival, astonishing, glorious, repetitive and haunting.

Where might the angel of God be present nowadays? To find *him* within and without the exploded frames of a limping thought, one should try constantly and unceasingly to realize where *he* should be and with what materials *he* has been constructed. What is it that haunts and fascinates us? What should the angel of God be like? One of the best Brazilian songwriters, Chico Buarque, might help us here in his song *O que sera, que sera* (Oh, what shall it be?):

What shall it be?
That has been muttered in the alcoves
That has been whispered in lyrics and songs
That has been planned in the shadows
That is in every mind and every mouth
For they are lighting candles in every alley
And shouting in the market
That for sure lives in the natural

What shall it be?
That has no certainties and never will
That has no way to mend and never will
That is unmeasurable

What shall it be?
That lives in the minds of the lovers
That the most delirious poets sing
That the drunken prophets swear
That might be in the pilgrimage of the crippled
That might be in the fantasy of the unhappy
That might be in the everyday of the whores
In the planing of the bandits and of the needy
In every sense, what shall it be
What has no decency and never will
What has no censorship and never will
What makes no sense

Names that Transgresses – Sources for a Limping A/Theological Thought

A limping theological thought dislocates, disconnects and disfigures the order of things and it does so not for the sake of dislocation itself but to open up other ways of thinking, of living, of knowing and not knowing. It opens space for the new and for hetero, blurring the inside with the outside without homogenizing them. The post-secular critique of the modern rationalization of the religious space has created a possibility to blend and to contaminate fields of knowledge. I will name Brazilian names from different fields of knowledge, hoping to create a new provisory index to be added to the sources of a limping a/theology.

Within the Brazilian culture, there are thinkers, artists and poets who can help us to transgress the limits of the secular and the sacred. They might be angels of God helping us to use a limping thought. The names mentioned below come to us as spectres, ghosts that most of the readers do not know, haunting us with their ghostly features. They offer suggestions, senses of responsibilities, justice, passion and traces of unforeseeable futures that remain open. Their spectrality haunts both me and my work. By naming them here, I open the confined box into which many of them have been placed; their work and thought were located in camps of academic isolation and exile that the globalization process has created.

Some of these names are 'moderns', some 'postmoderns'. Some names are drowning in rivers of forgetfulness and inutility; names that do not count as proper names; names that perform in language other than English; names that are thinking and writing with Brazilian accents; names that limp. These should be names locating me by the river in Jabbok and names that take me closer to Peniel; names to be criticized and challenged; names that make me dance and cry, that haunt me and call me from within and beyond a *Khôra*. These transgressive names, some more, some less, open possibilities for the impossible to appear.

Current Names for a A/Limping Liberation Theology

Rubem Alves

Alves is a theologian and a poet. He challenged realism through his own poetical language and helped generations of students of theology to think of religion as a human attempt to find God. He is also a psychoanalyst and does theology without doing theology, writing poems and small stories.

Jaci Maraschin

Jaci Maraschin is an artist who for some time did theology. He is a liturgist, a pianist and a poet. He influenced and set the tone of liturgical studies in Brazil, associating it with art and aesthetics, going from modern to postmodern approaches within the field. He has also worked on sexuality and the sacred, affirming the body as a central locus for any religious thought. He has abandoned theology and is now writing about postmodern approaches to religion. Both Rubem Alves and Jaci Maraschin loosened up the beliefs and the fixed structures of theology, influencing three generations of students of theology by giving them tools to go beyond the limits of the theological field.

Ivone Gebara

It is easy to do theology in the United States when one has *ink* to write. *Ink* means money, wonderful libraries, resources and sabbaticals to think and produce without having to worry about daily struggles to survive or to help others to survive. Ivone Gebara works with the poor women in the northeast part of Brazil and has transgressed some boundaries within the Catholic Church. While she does her intellectual work, she has street kids come to her lap and has to abandon her computer constantly to help the women who live around her house. Her theological thinking is on the edge between immanence and transcendence – always worked out in the light, and shadow, of the poor.

Clarice Lispector

A Ukrainian writer and poet who came to live in Brazil when she was two years old, she was herself a mark of a hybridism that could never be accommodated. Her literature is powerful like a magic potion. Her writings expand the women's imaginary and helped the Brazilian chauvinist culture to learn more about women. As another Brazilian writer, Otto Lara Resende, describes her transgressive art: 'You must be aware with Clarice. She does not do literature, she does witchcraft.'[20]

Garrincha

After Pelé, Garrincha was considered one of the best soccer players in the world. His dribbles made history in soccer. People use to go to the stadium only to see him playing. He turned soccer games into masterpieces. This angel of God had curved legs, 'the left one was bent inwards and the right was six centimeters shorter and curved outwards – he made some of the most beautiful soccer performances ever'.[21] He was able to make people smile with their eyes and mouths open, dribbling as he performed his dribbles.

Bispo do Rosário

Bispo do Rosário lived in an asylum for 50 years. Until his death in 1989, his art was almost completely unknown, since Bispo refused to be separated from the works he produced. He had never intended to be an artist. After being visited by angels one day, he received the mission to 'follow the voice of God that had told him he should reconstruct the world and present it to him on his death'.[22] He transgressed purity in art and created his work out of garbage, trash, embroidery, bedclothes, old linen, pieces of scrap iron junk, and all kinds of other leftovers. His work was exhibited in many countries including Holland, Italy, Germany and France. His limping art shows the *mazing grace* of God.

Aleijadinho

It was around 1730 that Antonio Maria Francisco, or Aleijadinho, was born in Vila Rica, Minas Gerais, Brazil. A son of an African slave mother and a white carpenter, Aleijadinho changed both Brazilian art and history. He assisted the revolutionaries in their movement of insurrection against Portugal while creating and sculpting figures of saints, doors, altars and constructing whole churches. In the church built for black people in his town, he sculpted his mother's face and placed her at the centre of the church. He used to retell the stories of the gospels by using revolutionary figures and the history of the revolution alongside the biblical figures of Jesus, the prophets and the apostles. Due to an unknown illness, his body started to become deformed and crippled until he could not use his hands anymore and had to sculpt with tools attached to his arm. One cannot recount the history of Brazil without taking time to learn about Aleijadinho. Upsetting and going beyond both artistic movements (Barroco and Rococo) and religious faith, he was passionate about his country. His work blurs faith with politics in an unsettling way.

Patricia Galvão-Pagu

Pagu was a political activist and a writer, one of the most combative Brazilian feminists around the decade of the 1920s. She was part of the second wave of the anthropophagic movement in São Paulo and worked on many levels, transgressing the values of Brazilian society. Educated in Freudian and Marxist thought, she wrote frequently about sexuality, economic disparities and class conflict, never accepting the values of bourgeois society, relativizing its fixed codes of morality. She criticizes the modernist movement of 1922, advocating a further revolution and satirizing bourgeois feminism. She worked mainly with poor women who were drawn into prostitution when they accepted the promises of their bosses for better conditions. She was persecuted because of her convictions and was the first woman arrested in Brazil for political reasons.[23] Limping theological thought in Latin America could learn a great deal from this revolutionary and transgressive thinker and political activist. Antonio Risério ends his consideration of Pagu by describing her as 'a revolutionary in art, in politics and in her way of living her life'.[24]

Joãozinho Trinta

Trinta is one of the most creative minds in Brazil. He creates artistic and cultural events throughout the country, including one of the most dazzling events in the world, the carnival. He creates, produces and innovates within the samba schools. Joãozinho Trinta has transgressed moral behaviour and cemented artistic and cultural ideas. Rejecting the glamorization of the poor by the so-called 'organic intellectuals', Trinta famously said, 'People like luxury. Only intellectuals like misery.'

Walter Moreira Salles Junior

Walter Salles is a film director and has depicted Brazil and Latin America in beautiful, if sometimes painful images. His work includes films such as *Central Station*, *Behind the Sun*, and *The Motorcycle Diaries*. In them, he captures some of what we can call the Brazilian and Latin American soul in a way that helps the viewer to be part of these piercing landscapes, full of promises of unbelievable and yet possible lives. He uses his films to expand the limits of life itself and believes that imagination can help overcome violence.[25]

Chico Buarque de Hollanda

Maybe this songwriter/singer/poet/writer is the best source for an understanding of recent Brazilian history. He enacts the Brazilian soul wearing multiple guises, and in all of them Chico performs powerfully and graciously. His work gets closer to what we feel we might be, including the things we hate and the things we love. He gives contours to our passions, our frustrations and our uttermost desires. He might be the most complete yet provisory translation of 180 million Brazilians.

Marcella Althaus-Reid

Althaus-Reid is the only non-Brazilian theologian on this list. The reason I am including her is because she has pointed out new directions for Liberation Theology which no one has seen before. Her work has provoked a revolution not only within Liberation Theology but also in theological studies as a whole, with her perversions, indecent theology and queer God. From within the broad scope of Liberation Theology, touching the nerve of the inequality and injustice lived by Latin American people, especially women, she denounces the pretensions of heterosexual theologians to produce an asexual theology and shows us the damaging results of such an enterprise. In her work, she transgresses the field of theology, blending Liberation Theology, post-colonialism, gender studies, economic and social exclusion, political instances and queer theories, creating ruptures and fissures in theological discourses, and producing a quite dazzling result.

A Limping Conclusion

I end, if there is any end to theological reflections, with my own limping. I am not my name but a legion of names. What drives me, a heterosexual man, is a furious 'idea-feeling'[26] that has tired me out since my early days in my parents' home. From the metaphysical influence of theology in my upbringing, this idea-feeling links God with love, a God so often linked with injustice. This connection makes me feel outraged about the idea of a so-called loving God, if God, who lives in absolute reclusion and silence for so long. As much as one finds reasons and solutions to explain this void between a loving God and the obscene poverty of my people, it seems impossible for me not to say that this metaphysical God has no place anymore in the lives of those who still stubbornly struggle to believe.

I worked in a small church within a *favela* on the outskirts of São Paulo for two years. During this time, after seeing more than I should, I lost my faith. I could live with paradoxes and contradictions, but seeing vividly how my people were suffering and seeing even more vividly how the withdrawal of God in silence and muteness played out in this situation, I could not handle this metaphysical God anymore. Something was taken from me forever. Nonetheless, the poor people that used to crowd that rented garage in our regular services gave me something else: I do not know exactly what. It might be this something that I have no idea what it is or was that I pursue now in this limping a/theological thinking. I cannot help but search like a nomad, wandering in the desert for what haunts me in my days and my nights. The angel of God fluctuates around me, scaring and fascinating me but I can neither see nor name *him*. I do not even know if this *something*, which we may call sacred or God, exists. However, I cannot deny it. Perhaps I will know it some day. Who knows? (*Oh, que sera, que sera?*)

Notes

1 *Oh, que sera, que sera* (Oh, what shall it be?) is the title of a famous song written by the Brazilian songwriter and singer Chico Buarque de Holanda (1976). It is said that most Brazilian (and Latin American) people know this song by heart.
2 In Portuguese, *Ninguém dirige aquele que Deus extravia*. Cf Raduam Nassar, *Um Copo de Cólera* (São Paulo: Companhia das Letras, 2001).
3 Genesis 32: 30–31. King James version.
4 Jacques Derrida, *Aporias*, trans. Thomas Dutoit (California: Stanford University Press, 1994), pp. 34–35.
5 Mark C. Taylor, *Erring, A Postmodern A/Theology* (Chicago and London: Chicago University Press, 1984).
6 Benjamin Abdala Junior (ed.) *Margens da Cultura. Mestiçagem, Hibridismo e Outras Misturas* (São Paulo: Editora Boitempo Editorial, 2004).
7 *Favelas* is the Portuguese name for shanty-towns.
8 Today, poverty has increased and the situation of the poor is much worse than in the decades of the 1960s and 1970s. Now Brazil and Latin America in general are facing AIDS and the social exclusion of a growing number of people who are outside the market system of productivity, such as the children of the streets.

9   Cf. Sobrino, J. and Ellacuria, I. (eds) *Mysterium Liberationis: Fundamental Concepts of Liberation Theology* (Maryknoll, NY: Orbis Books, 1993). See also Marcella Althaus-Reid's critique related to my point in her book *Indecent Theology. Theological Perversions in Sex, Gender and Politics* (London and New York: Routledge, 2000), pp. 31, 33.

10   Cf. Gustavo Gutiérrez, *A Theology of Liberation: History, Politics and Salvation* (Maryknoll, NY: Orbis Books 1988).

11   I Corinthians 13:12. New Living Translation Bible.

12   Cf. Mark C. Taylor, *Erring, A Postmodern A/Theology.*

13   *Khôra/Chora* is a word borrowed from Plato's Timaeus by Jacques Derrida and Julia Kristeva. See Julia Kristeva, *Desire in Language: A Semiotic Approach to Literature and Art*, trans. Thomas Gora, eds. Alice Jardine, and Leon S. Roudiez (New York: Columbia University Press, 1980); Jacques Derrida, *Khôra* (São Paulo: Papirus, 1995).

14   Mark C. Taylor, *Disfiguring. Art, Architecture, Religion* (Chicago and London: The University of Chicago Press, 1992), p. 312.

15   Ibid., pp. 7–8.

16   Mark C. Taylor, *Erring, A Postmodern A/Theology*, p. 12.

17   Michael Strysick, 'Community' in *Encyclopedia of Postmodernism*, ed. Victor E. Taylor and Charles Winquist (London and New York: Routledge, 2001), p. 58.

18   Mark C. Taylor, *Altarity* (Chicago and London: The University of Chicago Press, 1987).

19   John D. Caputo, *On Religion, Thinking in Action* (London and New York: Routledge, 2001).

20   http://www.releituras.com/clispector_bio.asp

21   http://usr.solar.com.br/~juliocba/garrincha.htm

22   http://www.thekitchen.org/MovieCatalog/Titles/OBispo.html

23   Antonio Risério, *Pagu: Vida-Obra ObraVida, Obra* in http://www.aleitamento.org.br/meninas/pagu.htm

24   Ibid.

25   Read his complete interview at http://www.filmmonthly.com/Profiles/Articles/WSalles/WSalles.html

26   This expression was created by the Brazilian poet Carlos Drummond de Andrade (1902–1987). De Andrade is known for poems reflecting the impossibility of life, such as *No Meio do Caminho* and *José*.

Chapter 5

Commodity Aesthetics and the Erotics of Relationship: Challenges of Feminist Hermeneutics of Liberation to Market Aesthetics

Nancy Cardoso Pereira

Translation from the Portuguese by Dr Thia Cooper

It doesn't matter if consumption is real or if it only exists in the imagination: objects of desire turn themselves into pieces of worship.

Robert Kurtz (1997)[1]

The great problem is that Christianity still remains in the Western hegemonic model. The fear of confronting the market and its religion is the impasse that reveals our cowardice today.

It is that the churches have already lost too much, have already retreated too far, and now try to keep themselves in equilibrium with the contemporary powers' difficult manoeuvrings. Christianity, as part of the Western civilizing project, after motivating and justifying the movements and strategies of universality, superiority, priority and finality, is seeing itself surpassed in power, weakened in its real influence on the destinies of humanity, and robbed of control over its religious and theological imagining. Hegemonic Christianity lost its share of power, and now negotiates slices of influence, creating a collection of conditions that justifies a systematic and chronic deafness.

The Western world and its economic rationality have the idolatrous pretension to fully realize all human and natural potentialities – through science – and to fully satisfy all necessities and desires – through the market.[2] Globalized capitalism takes possession of sacred discourse and presents itself as the great realizer of human history. In the name of this rationality, sacrifices are demanded, as a form of adjustment necessary to guarantee the totality of the model. Globalized capitalism is an economic religion that does not allow non-believers or dissidents.

Susan George (of the Trans National Institute), in her book *Faith and Credit*, makes an approximation between the missionary and evangelistic models of Christianity and financial capitalism's strategies of control over the markets that makes explicit the incestuous relations between capitalism and Christianity, leaving no doubt as to the interdependence of these systems.

The churches identify the limits and systemic horrors of capitalism but do not identify their pertinence to this system, which makes the unmasking and anti-idolatrous critique of the market and of globalized capitalism impractical. In this sense, the churches' answers and alternatives to the economic, cultural and ecological disaster limit themselves to reformist and charitable programmes that do not situate the churches amongst the protagonists in the struggle for a new economic and social order.

Without self-criticism and the overcoming of the sacrificial christological and ecclesiological models, the action of the churches ends up reinforcing the market's inevitability and its demand for exclusion that generates poverty, alienation and violence, principally against women and children.

It is so difficult to identify an idol when it has our face! It is so difficult to confront a shadow when it charms me! It is so impossible to do theology and to feel the dizziness of desires! It is so complicated to give up the One and the First, to give up being classical and universal in order to try one's luck with the minority religions of the majorities! It is so difficult to unmask the game of producing divinities without anticipating the nudity of the king, the father, the lord.

Of the Alienated Body: The Ethical and the Religious

Silent and careful in confronting the market and its religion, the churches exercise their slice of power in the field of ethics, as a consolation prize for the loss of hegemony over the sacred in the political and economic arenas. The commitment of the churches to the defence of life in questions of reproductive and population rights makes the role that the market and globalized capital reserves for the churches explicit. They respond to the necessity to keep control over reproductive processes, insisting on a heavy and blaming discourse, investing resources, trafficking in influence with national governments, and aggressively lobbying in the international spaces of discussion. Such aggressiveness and zeal on the part of the churches is not matched in the confronting of political and economic questions.

It becomes necessary to evaluate the old yet current discussion over reproductive rights, in particular in the Third World. Here the churches have not had any desire to listen and to dialogue: they insist on repeating themselves, saying the same thing over and over. There is no real flow of conversation with the struggle and movements organized by women in the churches and in society. The churches demand a supra-historical stability for themselves that does not allow itself to be influenced or motivated by extreme suffering and measureless sacrifices.

There are three million clandestine abortions per year in Brazil. At least five women die in that country each day from such abortions. They die from abandonment and fear. They die because they dare to decide. They die from the reduction of ethical arguments. They die from the exchanges of power and influence between the state and the churches. As if there is not already enough hunger, unemployment, illness and desperation to survive.

They die from this narrow and repressive moral discourse, incapable of dialoguing with the concrete experiences of women. They die from that discourse disguised in the public policies of the state. The church says that it is a sin. The state says that it is a crime.

Three million women take the risk to make the decision: for themselves and for the community where they live. These women take the risk to live a personal and communitarian ethic that surpasses the authority of the masculine hierarchy of the churches. They establish an ethic that comes from the experiences and options of women.

We need a theology and movements for women that deal with economic and ethical questions, as a fundamental contribution to the re-signification of the processes of production and reproduction of material and symbolic life. The relations between population, the environment, natural resources, and the development model need to be investigated and articulated from the motivations and commitments of the movements and from feminist reflections, so that they can overcome the hesitations and dislikes that continue to keep these urgent matters under the control of politicians and theologians busy with sustaining capital and patriarchy.

Commodity Aesthetics and its Religion

Things: lined up in order on shelves. Categories and types. Substances and their reverence. Wrappings. Qualities and quantities: value. Coat racks hanging between exchange-value and use-value. *Are you hungry for this?* asks the market as if it knows my native language ... indecipherable by me. I push the trolley that identifies me in the consumer market and I agonize over the offered forms of necessity and desire.

So, it is that, in the logic of the market exchange, relations assume money as the language of value without needing to rely any more on the language of necessity. An abstraction is realized! No one sees, but the whole world experiences: *the miracle of transubstantiation.*

> The exchange value, trapped in the body of a commodity, yearns to be rescued and released into monetary form.
>
> (Haug 1996: 30)

The miracle happens when the person is realized as a consumer. In the act of consumption, *commodities and money kiss each other* and profit promises to bring together all of society, one day, in the perfect market. Or not: it is interesting that profit and value reproduce themselves and fulfil themselves.

It is at the same time a complex and simple operation, too sensual and totally metaphysical. It is a question of realities, things, substances, objects, these and those that, touched by the language of value, transform themselves into the subjectivity of necessities. Material and concrete realities are dispossessed of their everyday value and use, by assuming the metaphysics of the exchange value.

> The lust for money is the reason why, under capitalist production, the commodity is created in the image of the consumer's desires. Later on this image, divorced from its commodity is the subject of advertising promotion.
>
> (Haug 1996: 35)

Lust. Love. Image. Desire. Seduction. They do not seem to be proper words for an economic discussion ... however, they are those that perhaps express better the process of mythmaking of commodity aesthetics.

Marx says that the commodity *is in love with* money and *ogles it with its price casting wooing glances* (Marx, in Haug 1996: 30) and identifies a certain *angelic malice* in the speculation of money (Marx 1985: 163). He affirms that *money is not just an object of the passion* of enrichment, *money is the passion itself* (Marx 1996: 214).

If the metaphors of the loving discourse will be able to be understood as a stylistic resource for industrial capitalism, limiting itself to the field of rhetoric, the analyses of globalized market capitalism can identify in this semantic field a vital hermeneutical key.

The commodity desires to be consumed, needs to be chosen, bought; for this, it needs to make itself loved, desirable, it needs to divine desire or to invent it, offering an aesthetic stimulus. It is necessary to induce a new form of pleasure always subject to maintaining the capacity for the reproduction of capital itself.

Marx introduces two women: Ms Ethics and Ms Religion (Marx 1985: 19). These two women are completely obsolete and unnecessary with respect to economic laws: the ethic of the political economy is profit and it subordinates the two women to its logic in an efficient system of alienation.

Erotic Alienation – the Body Makes Itself a Fetish

In the arena of the market economy, alienation has to be understood not only as a lack but also as an abundance of promises. Alienation is not an absence, but is a promise of presence. Alienation is not a negation of the body, but an expropriation of sensuality and the erotic to the service of the appropriation of the product. The alienation of the materialities of work for the existential consolidation of consumption. Things and bodies lose their immediate materiality in order to become mediated through the consumption of commodities. The body makes itself a commodity. In this way, fetishism functions as well in economic discourse as in porno-erotic language.

Work is made invisible in the glamorizing of physicality and of the erotic. The body of the working classes, transformed into a commodity itself, alienates itself in an eroticized consumption that swings between desire and realization. In the invisibility and impracticality of the experience of work as a humanizing and creative cultural event, the market empties the place of production in order to provoke praise in the arena of consumption, without allowing questions about reproductive and distributive relations.

The market, having localized the fundamental movement in the base of consumption and denying the conflict between capital and work, specifies the distribution of riches, making the democratization of consumption impractical. The dynamic between promise and realization, desire and possession, feeds on sensuality in order to maintain the modes of reproduction and control over capital.

According to Hugo Assmann, in the realms of human behaviour, that which some see as just the existence and workings of dynamic systems that are partially self-regulatory,[3] is seen by feminists to be a reinvention of the historical mechanisms of domination. It would not be possible to call the market a self-regulating mechanism because the reflexive term continues to express a particularity (of class, gender and ethnicity) that presupposes itself to be universal or global.

Eroticising Theology to Confront the Market-God

Alienation and fetishism are not inventions of capitalism and patriarchy: they need to be understood at the level of the creation of myths, of cults, of spells, or magical rituals to maintain both their gods (capital/father) and their tricks. Religion has always been an expression and reproduction of economic situations and of the social relations of power. The feminist theologian perceives in this hinge between the loving and sensual discourse and the religious discourse, not a collection of comparisons of stylistic resources, but a space of analysis and fundamental critique of the relations between capital-market-patriarchy.

In the same way, it shows it is necessary to identify and critique the imagined duality of Marxist thinking divided between the two unnecessary women and the representations of the feminist imagining of the great seductress in the relations of consumption. It becomes necessary to see again the imagined – old and new – in the search for a sustainable and egalitarian economic system. They articulate themselves as a necessary means of unveiling the institutional laws that regulate the world economies (never! self-regulated) and their metaphysical appearance, to suspect and to deconstruct these imagined laws that nurture alienation and the fetish of capital and patriarchy.

The making aesthetic of commodities confers a measure of divinity to money and to the market, guaranteeing the metaphysical foundation for bourgeois culture and their rituals and cults that demand the production of self-legitimization and the constant reification of the necessities of those who are dominated. This aesthetic production, that takes possession of the body, of its creative, inventive, sensual and erotic capacity, co-opts the Christian theologians, their exegeses and hermeneutics, their sacrifices and mechanisms of postponement with missionary language about the supposed non-existence of class conflict and the market's inevitability in fully realizing human life.

The ethical contribution of feminism is in the insistence that the personal is political, the daily is the historical, reproduction is productive, production is distributive, and consumption is creative. This reversibility of the senses and their relations confronts any metaphysical political model of the alienation of daily relations and the fetishization of desires and necessities. There is no mechanism outside history, neither in the past nor in the future, that is capable of concretizing egalitarian relations.

To insist on working with the body, daily life, and its relations as a vital place of the construction and circulation of power and social and theological significance,[4] feminist theology wants to make the commercialization of bodies and commodity aesthetics impractical. In this sense, and in a particular way, the Bible and theology stop being a self-referencing identity in sociological and historical-critical methods and become on familiar terms with the dizziness of the plurality of paradigms: class, gender, ethnicity, ecology. It is these simultaneous experiences and their irreducible differences that makes any attempted idolizing of the commercialization of the body and of commodity aesthetics impossible.

To make visible the hermeneutical character of political and economic relations and to disclose the mechanisms of the construction of idols and self-regulating rituals, they demand a theology capable of giving up any self-regulating invisible hand (whether it be dogmatic or exegetical) in order to register definitively in the field of cultural creation, the aesthetic of memories, the hermeneutic of liberation. God knows: *your measure of people. Dare to: Be the bow and arrow, the string and the sigh.* As in the poem of Octávio Paz:

> The bodies, face to face with fierce stars,
> are made of the same substance as the sun.
> What we call love or death, liberty
> Or destiny,
> Is it not called catastrophe, is it not called
> Massacre?
> Where are the borders between a tremor and an earthquake,
> Eruption and cohabitation?
> . . .
> Imagination is the spur of desire,
> Its realm is inescapable and as infinite as

Boredom,
Its opposite and its twin.
Dare to:
Be the bow and arrow, the string and the sigh.
The sound is explosive. Snap. Come back to being the sun.

(Paz 1999: 120)

Spurs of Desire: Dare to Read the Bible

I choose my materials of imagination and desire without needing to explain
too much to myself: I work with the cracks of biblical literature no more as
destiny or necessity, not acknowledging any border between a tremor and an
earthquake in the body of my personal history and in the under-evangelized
body of Latin America. They are strange and familiar narratives: docile
prisoners of the altars and academies of theology, savage and mythical in the
hesitant and magical use of popular reading. I redo the reading and I invent
opposites: I chew the established narratives with teeth of explosive desires and
I deny all educated forms of participation in the Western, bourgeois and
Christian system of images. When the verb becomes a commodity and
perpetuates itself between us ... it is necessary to seize it again as raw meat,
to negate its exchange-value, to confront its image-value and to glue itself
again to the sweaty skin of the poor men and women, painful and orgasmic,
blessed and damned. I read in the plural feminine, illuminated through the
most delicate brutality of the dispute for bodies and their desires.

The small texts that follow are at the same time a draft of an unfinished
programme and of a theological treatise that does not want to be either a
treatise or solely theological. They are trajectories cultivated in texts and
advisory bodies and, reunited like this, only prove its opposite: what I would
really like would be to make a song.

For an Aesthetic of Desire Without Guilt (Genesis 3):

Eve, the first. The woman of great open eyes that saw beyond what the
divinity and the man would have settled between themselves. Eve, woman of
the apple of her eye. She sees and desires. The tree. The fruit. Between the
look and the desire she creates her own body, she invents another hunger and
launches herself from hand to mouth. Pure eroticism shaping the meat and
projecting alternatives. The tree? Good enough to eat from! Pleasant ...
pleasant to the eyes; tasty in the mouth she would have divined. Desirable for
giving understanding. The body that projects itself in gestures, clay of desire,
invents the world erotically. Produces understanding. To stretch the arms, to
seize with the hands and to put in the mouth. It consumes the thing which her
desire created. The eyes open. They are nude. Examined and put face to face,

Eve and the man divide themselves in guilt and get furious with the ethic that dictates the law without shivers of desire. The creative word subordinates the inventive desire.

The creative work curses the playful and curious body. There was fear and punishment, the first final day of creation.

For an Aesthetic of Work and its Desires (Song of Songs):

The Lover. The woman of great mouth and open legs who took ownership beyond what the divinity and the man would have settled between themselves. She, woman of the apple of her eye, her mouth, her breasts, her hands, her sex, her work, her love. She lives and desires. The man. The earth. The fruit. Between the look and the desire she creates her own body, she invents more than one hunger and launches herself the wrong way down the one way street of the mechanisms of control over the earth, the vineyard, the city, the woman's body, the family. Pure eroticism modelling the meat and projecting alternatives. The man? Good enough to be eaten from! Pleasant to the eyes: the image of the desire to stop wanting. The fruit of liberated work would have divined itself to be tasty in the mouth, in the skin of the loved shepherd/ man. To have an orgasm on the tip of one's tongue: poetry is orgasm, the shadow of desire that invents the world erotically. Produces understanding. To stretch the arms, to weed, to work, to prune, to pick, to load, to gather together, to separate ... to work the world and her forces as one who goes to bed with someone. It consumes the thing which her desire/work created. The legs open. They are nude. Entranced and tired, the Lover and the lover divide in sleep and make themselves comfortable on the bed of the mother and her shivers of desire. The creative word falls in love with the inventive desire. The creative work blesses the playful and curious body. There was orgasm and pleasure, another day of work and the creation of creation.

For an Aesthetic of Ownership and its Erotics (Ruth):

Ruth, the other. The woman of great curved shoulders that desired beyond what the divinity and the men had settled between themselves. Ruth, the apple of the eye of the woman: Naomi. She sees and works. The earth. The rest. Between production and the surplus she creates her own body, she invents another hunger and launches her entire body into the vineyard, into the life of the man, the owner of the earth. Pure eroticism that moistens the meat and projects itself in the clothing of alternatives. The man? Of age. Good enough to let eat. The earth. Pleasant to the eyes. She would have divined that she makes herself tasty in the mouth of the man. The desire that constructed understanding. The body that projects itself in gestures, the festival of desire, invents the world, ownership, the father, and the family erotically. It consumes the thing which her desire created. The eyes open. They are nude. Scared and excited, Ruth says goodbye to the man before it is morning. He confronts guilt and the ethic of the law with the shivers of desire. The creative desire subordinates the passionless law. The manual work blesses the earth in the embrace of women. There was earth and child in that day of recreation.

For a Distributive Ethic and its Pleasures (II Kings 4: 1–7):

Widow, the latest. The woman of a great open mouth that desired more than what the divinity, the spouse and the creditor would have settled between themselves. The widow, mother of the apples of her eye. She sees and screams. A son. The other. Between the debt and the slavery she makes her own body, she invents another hunger, and launches herself greedy and hungry toward jugs and containers. Pure eroticism modelling the hours and projecting alternatives. The oil? Good enough to see pouring out. Marvellous ... from one jug to another; she would have divined a miracle in life. A miracle giving understanding. The body that moves itself between the neighbours and their containers, clay of desire, she invents the world, the life of the sons erotically. Produces understanding. To stretch the arms and to meet others, to fill life with meaning and oil. The children consume the thing which her desire created. The eyes open. They are saved. Liberated and taken care of, she and the sons learn to consume miracles distributed from hand to hand without the shivers of the law. The creative word meets the communitarian work. The inventive desire blesses the tired and glorious body. There was abundance and peace, that day of salvation.

For Liberated Reproductive Relations and the Pleasure of Deciding:

Mary, the Virgin. The mother of great open ears that heard more than what the god, the father and the man would have settled between themselves. Mary, woman of the labyrinth of hearing. She hears and desires. The son. The fruit. Between the hearing and the desire she creates her own body, she invents space for one more and launches herself from mother and mouth:

> *The Spirit of God is upon me ... because I anoint myself saying: yes! to announce the good news to women, to liberate those without choices, to heal those aborted and to proclaim the times of decision (between Isaiah and Luke).*

Pure eroticism modelling the womb and projecting alternatives. The son? Good enough to be desired. Pleasant ... intense in the insides, she would have divined. Desirable for giving understanding. The body that projects itself in the womb, the clay of desire, invents the world erotically. Produces understanding. To stretch the arms, to nestle the child and to offer the breast. He sucks the thing which her desire created. The eyes open. They are nude. Well-ventured and satisfied, Mary and the son join in the shivers of desire of the gospel. The creative word invites the inventive desire of fishermen and prostitutes. The reproductive work blesses the playful and long-suffering body. There was a cross and punishment, the last and first day of salvation.

Notes

1 Robert Kurtz, 'A Estetizacao da Crise. No Capitalismo, o Objetos do Desejo transforman en pecas de Culto'. *Cuaderno Mais!*, Folha de Sao Paulo, 23 November 1997.
2 Cf. Jung Mo Sung, 'Novas Formas de Legitimaçao da Economia', *Koinonia*, ReLat 273, available online http://www.koinonia/or/relat.
3 H. Asmann, cited in Mo Sung, op cit.
4 Cf. *Points for a Feminist Hermeneutic of Liberation, Ribla* 25, Vozes, Petrópolis, pp. 5–10.

References

George, S. and Sabelli, F. (1994) *Faith Credit. The World Bank's Secular Empire.* Middlesex: Penguin Books.
Haug, W. (1996) *Critique of Commodity Aesthetics.* São Paulo: UNESP.
Marx, Karl (1985) *A Contribution to the Critique of Political Economy.* São Paulo: Victor Civita.
Marx, Karl (1986) *Economic and Philosophical Manuscripts of 1844.* São Paulo: Victor Civita.
Paz, Octavio (1999) *Um Mais Além Erótico: Sade.* São Paulo: Mandarim.

Chapter 6

The Prostitutes Also Go into the Kingdom of God: A Queer Reading of Mary of Magdala[1]

Martín Hugo Córdova Quero

Truly I tell you, the tax collectors and the prostitutes are going into the kingdom of God ahead of you.

Jesus (Gospel of Matthew 21:31)

On In/Decent Theology/ies

Normal. Correct. Honest. Saint. Orthodox ... Labels of decency.
Abnormal. Incorrect. Dishonest. Sinner. Heterodox ... Labels of indecency.

All of them are binaries; *positive/negative* oppositions that queer theorists call 'the *either/or* thinking'.[2] Theology has historically invested huge amounts of energy into fitting the *decent* patterns of societies (supported by the so-called *orthodoxy*) and condemning those that are considered *indecent* (related to those classified as *heterodox*). But the result is almost always fractured discourses that remain unresolved. Mary of Magdala is one of those *unresolved fractures* in the decent discourse of Christianity. As with many human beings[3] around the world, in past or present times, she has been historically trapped in binary thinking. She is *either* sinner *or* saint; *either* decent *or* indecent. Binary thinking does not allow for further alternatives.

What underlies those binaries is the abstract ideal of *normalcy*, which also privileges a particular conception of the body, setting up the *differen(ce)t* as *deviant*.[4] Historically, the Enlightenment developed the concept of *normalcy* through which some *Western* societies have been privileged as *the* measure of normalcy, giving meaning to reality, colonizing and labelling all other cultures and societies.[5] Sexuality, as well as all other dimensions of human life, has suffered the consequences of this notion of normalcy. Mary of Magdala has usually been seen through these lenses. The process of *normalization* is based on several facets: *labelling, dehumanizing, demonizing,*

81

exoticizing, stigmatizing,[6] and *silencing*.[7] Michel Foucault calls this *the normalizing gaze*.[8]

What is at the base of this process of normalization is a hetero-patriarchal binary thinking that sets humanity within a masculine/feminine straight sexuality (*good*), while all other experiences and practices of sexuality (*bad*) are to be condemned in order to maintain its *hegemony*.[9] In this way the notions of *decency* and *indecency* control the behaviour of human beings in society.

As historically in the case of Mary of Magdala, experiences seen as deviant need to either disappear or be normalized. Language – spoken and unspoken as well as body language – is an important instrument for the process of normalization. Bodies are the *geography* where this normalization is tested by predominant heterosexualism in society.[10] Religion is not far away from this process since it is also based on language. Furthermore, this makes evident that every *theology* is, in fact, *ideology*; ultimately there is no such thing as *innocent theology*. Every theology represents an ideology that permeates its paradigm and its hermeneutical circle, moulding its productions. Language also defines *identities*. Therefore, an *indecent/queer* theology is not innocent at all. It stands for subversiveness in recovering a *body-paradigm* that denounces the incoherencies and the decencies of traditional/classical theology. This implies the disruption of oppressive grammars, which have inscribed bodies in accordance with ideologies that delegitimize gender and the performance of sexualities.[11] The implication is to abandon the idea of fixed identities and to consider beings as performances of be/coming.[12] Mary has been trapped also in the dynamics of fixed identities. She has been imprisoned.

In her book *Indecent Theology: Sexual Perversions in Gender and Theology*, Marcella Althaus-Reid recovers the issue of language and *subjectivity* in relation to power and uses an original image to find a solution: *women's theology without underwear*. Althaus-Reid relates language to the production of narratives and discourses that are the paradigms for social constructions and which regulate performances of human beings in society, whether sexually, economically or politically. She connects these human productions with the discourses and images we have produced about God, Christ and the Virgin Mary. The main distortion of these narratives and discourses should be done at the level of sexuality and economics; theology has to accept this challenge. This is the core of Althaus-Reid's *Indecent Theology*, as she herself expresses:

> [This] paradigm is an indecent paradigm, because it undresses and uncovers sexuality and economy at the same time. Not only do we need an Indecent Theology which can reach the core of theological constructions, insofar as they are rooted in sexual constructions, for the sake of understanding our sexuality, we also need it because theological truths are currencies dispensed and acquired in theological economic markets.[13]

The case for an indecent/queer reading of Mary of Magdala allows us to see different aspects of this personage. Up until now she is trapped in decent readings from binary thinking, which commodify power at the intersections of economic, social and political arenas. We need to *undress* those readings in order to denounce their mechanisms of submission functioning at those intersections.[14] To move beyond the binary thinking is an act of resistance as well as an act of liberation to open up spaces for be/coming.[15] The subversion in this process of uncovering comes from recovering the body and sexuality as two important core elements in a fully Christological/Incarnational theology. In the end, what every reading about Mary of Magdala evidences is the denial of body and sexuality in order to impose on her a normalization that could make her decent.

It is a fact that in reading after reading, Mary of Magdala still remains a mysterious woman. From portrayals in apostolic times and early Christianity, in Scriptures and traditions, through medieval piety and artistic representations in shrines, paintings and plays,[16] up to contemporary portraits in films and literature,[17] she remains a fascinating mystery. I here attempt to dig into that mystery to unveil alternatives to classical readings on Mary, especially since her life has been deliberately occluded and censored throughout the centuries by male-stream Bible reading.[18] The classical Christian tradition and the heterodox writings offer us different pictures of her. Modern feminist readings have brought the issue back as a subject of research, yet certain matters remain unresolved. Although, since the advent of feminist readings, more attention has been drawn to Mary, who really is she? Are the feminist attempts to make her a decent woman another game of hetero-patriarchalism? Jesus said that prostitutes would be amongst the first to enter the Kingdom of God. Could this be applied to her? Can she still remain a saint if she actually was engaged in prostitution?

This chapter, then, seeks to undress these issues of decency/indecency and sainthood/sinfulness/prostitution gathered around the personage of Mary of Magdala. It also emphasizes the thesis offered by Althaus-Reid that every theology needs a sexual deconstruction in order to uncover assumptions of in/decency.[19] In this respect, some tools provided by queer theory are useful. In exploring the personage Mary of Magdala from this standpoint, I shall attempt to show how sexuality plays an important part in such a mysterious character. Of course, in queering either past events or personages, we also risk looking at them through anachronic lenses.[20] Nonetheless, we need to take the risk in order to unpack the significance of Mary for the Christian faith.

In Search of the Historical Mary

As a mysterious character, Mary of Magdala has always motivated the imagination of popular cultures as well as enlightened scholars. In his recent book *The Da Vinci Code*,[21] Dan Brown posits a creative plot to introduce her to modern times: she was the wife of Jesus. Apart from this shocking statement of Brown's creativity, the book also includes murders and conspiracies as well as secret codes, which are clues to find and solve the last mystery of this suspense novel. The astonishing secret, revealed at the end of the book, is related to the last location of the body of Mary of Magdala as well as two millennia of documents that prove the data about her marriage to Jesus and her pregnancy with the heir of Jesus. In the course of the story Harvard symbologist Robert Langdon and French cryptologist Sophie Neveu decipher the information left by the Louvre Museum's curator Jacques Sauniere, who wrote the initial information on his body before being murdered.

The story evolves over centuries of careful dedication to protecting the secret of Mary of Magdala carried on by a secret society of medieval knights called 'the Knight Templars'. The task of the society has been to transfer the body of Mary to France and guarantee their secret until it can be unveiled on the Last Day. Therefore, she stands as the icon for the truth about Jesus and the whole of Christianity. Due to this, the Vatican and Opus Dei conspire not to let that secret be unveiled. Furthermore, they represent orthodox Christianity that fights against pagan cults that worship the Goddess, the feminine deity of nature, of whom Mary is the icon.

Beyond the cobbling together of historical data with theories from biblical and theological research, the value of Brown's story is to provoke the artistic imagination to preserve the mysterious halo around Mary. *The Da Vinci Code* became a bestseller while also arousing suspicion in some people that the information contained in the book could actually be true. We still need to remember the subtitle of the book: *A Novel*. That is precisely what the whole book is, a novel written in a way that can easily be taken as true. Nonetheless, key to the story's success is the clever mix of scholarly research with imagination. But it still does not help answer the question: *Who was Mary of Magdala?* I fear that there is no single answer. Through two millennia, the meagre amount of information that we possess about her has been edited several times, interpreted through different lenses and filtered with particular motifs.

Can we know something about the historical Mary by looking at her place of origin? She is known in the Gospels with the toponym (place name) of her provenance: Magdala. Several scholars have tried to learn more details about this city. The research of Carmen Bernabe Ubieta,[22] Marianne Sawicki[23] and Richard A. Horsley[24] help us in this section to do so.

Magdala is known in ancient literature by several names: Dalmanutha,[25] Magdal Sebayah, Magdal Nunnyah, Magadan[26] and Taricheae.[27] From recent research we know that this city was at the shore of Gennesaret Lake, about four miles north of Tiberias.[28] It was the centre of reunion for rebel Jews in times of occupation under the Roman Empire and a centre for Hasmonean leaders. It was also victim of the most ruthless slaughter and enslavement of thousands of people by Cassius' occupation in 52 BCE.[29]

Being a Judean was the same as being Hasmonean, a sociopolitic and religious group. The Hasmoneans held political and economic hegemony over the Southern Temple-state. About a century before Jesus' time they imposed that hegemony over the northern territories, taking over Galilee by force from the Seleucid Empire.[30] Judeans were not Galileans. Besides, Hasmoneans were nationalists and against Roman occupation; they were opposed to Herodians, who collaborated with the Roman Empire.

The city was on the route for exchange of products between Rome and its colonized territories[31] and was more important in this capacity than Capernaum. Its economy was based on fishing and agriculture. The excavations of Franciscan archeologists V. Corbo and S. Loffreda between 1971 and 1978 have shown the wealthy state of this city, due to its trade of products with other cities. Some scholars estimate its population at about 15,000 or even 25,000 inhabitants, while others prefer to estimate it as fewer than 10,000 because major cities like Sepphoris and Tiberias (two rival royal capitals) would probably have had a combined population of 15,000.[32] Magdala's society was made up mainly of wealthy peasants and landowners, a fact criticized by rabbinic teachers, who saw this as a relaxation of religious commitments. These teachers also saw wealth as the cause of the city's destruction in the third century CE.

Magdala/Taricheae, as well as cities like Sepphoris and Tiberias, were 'typical Hellenistic-Roman urban institutions that made a city a *polis*: courts, theater, palace, colonnaded streets, city walls, markets, archives, bank, amphitheater, aqueduct, stadium'.[33]

Given this context, Mary's wealth could have come from different sources. There is no doubt that Mary supported economically the ministry of Jesus, but there is no evidence in the Gospels to tell us where her wealth came from. The Gospel of Luke explains:

> ... [The women were] Mary, called Magdalene, from whom seven demons had gone out, and Joanna, the wife of Herod's steward Chuza, and Susanna, and many others, who provided for them [Jesus and his disciples] out of their resources.[34]

In this verse, the Lukan community tells us about the importance of the economic contribution of these women who supported Jesus and all his disciples. They also offer to us a list of wealthy women. The fact that in this list, as well as other lists, Mary of Magdala is mentioned, and always in the first place, indicates her social importance.[35]

These are the only conclusions we can arrive at by looking at her place of origin and the biblical data together with the information uncovered by modern scholarship. Therefore, what we can say about the historical Mary remains in the territory of academic speculation. A similar process occurs with what I identify as the three portrayals of Mary of Magdala.

Three Different Portrayals of Mary of Magdala

From Sinner *to* Saint: *The Classical Christian Tradition*

Traditional theology has portrayed Mary of Magdala as a prostitute, a repented sinner saved by Jesus. Then she appears as the crying woman at the feet of Jesus. Her sinful past was rapidly left aside in order to make a decent and subordinate woman, given the impossibility of erasing her importance for the early Christian communities. We do not know exactly when this became a tradition. According to feminist theologian Mary Thompson, whose research I will follow in this section, the composite of Mary of Magdala with the sinful woman[36] was already in place by the fourth century and was fully developed in the sixth century. The first datum can be traced as early as the writing of Ephraim the Syrian (306–373 CE) especially if the phrase, 'Mary, called Magdalene, from whom seven demons had gone out',[37] is interpreted as a sinful condition.[38] Ephraim says:

> Mary by the oil showed forth the mystery of his mortality, who by his teaching mortified the concupiscence of her flesh. Thus, the sinful woman by the flood of her tears in full assurance was rewarded with remission of sins from beside his feet . . .[39]

Later, Gregory the Great (540–640 CE) enhanced this line of interpretation, completing a more elaborate picture of the sinner Mary. Thompson quotes:

> [Mary of Magdala,] [w]ho, at this time with the other Mary, saw the Lord after his resurrection, and drawing near, embraced his feet. Lord, I ask, what hands are these that grasp your feet before my eyes? That woman, who was a sinner in society; those hands, which were stained with evil have touched his feet who is at the Father's right hand above the angels. Let us consider, if we can, what might be the very heart of that heavenly devotion, and the woman who had been immersed in the depth of the abyss, through her own fault, was so cleansed through grace in a flight of love.[40]

In this quotation Thompson sees the definite debasement for the ongoing classical Christian tradition about Mary in Western Christianity. Neither Thompson nor other feminist theologians can indicate if that was a new argument developed by patristic authors or if they have echoed a tradition already present in popular Christianity, perhaps even originating from apostolic times. The lack of sources in this respect does not allow us to solve this tension. What has reached our times is this notion of Mary, the sinful woman understood as a *prostitute*. Remembered as the crying woman, she became an archetype for those who repent and seek salvation in Jesus.

Therefore, Mary became a decent woman by rejecting her life understood in relation to prostitution. This normalization of Mary from her *sinful* life into *sainthood* is understood in Christianity as *metanoia* (conversion). In the background, it implies the co-option of Greco-Roman cultures by Judeo-Christian morality. But historians tell us about a contrasting picture between Greco-Roman and Judeo-Christian moralities in relation to prostitution.

In Greece, and later in the Roman Empire, prostitution was a valid institution whose place in society was even legally sanctioned. Judaism, and later Christianity, saw prostitution as an evil condition, morally regrettable. Of course, even in Greece and Rome women prostitutes were different from wives, but the difference was related to their function within the organization of society: it was not a moral distinction. A fact to remember is that modern notions on prostitution, as well as wifehood, cannot be applied anachronistically to Greek or Roman societies. In Roman culture, women in general were considered as unequal to men until the first century CE, when a new morality arose giving wives a status of equality to men in the marriage contract. In other words, women were still unequal but, because of their marriage, were *granted* the privilege to participate in equal status with their husbands,[41] who held the power to do so. Wives conducted some business with the permission of their husbands and, when widowed, they could continue with the business only if the will of their late husbands sanctioned this.

We need to recall that Judeo-Christian morality had not yet permeated the Roman Empire, a situation that would not occur until Christianity became the official religion. Concubines also had a role in Roman society. A man of social status, then, had a variety of contacts with women; a *wife* to procreate children and obtain legal heirs for his patrimony; *concubines* living in the same house, with whom he would also have children; and he would finally enjoy the pleasures of sexuality with *prostitutes*[42] and *slaves* (both female and male). Prostitutes were very important in the entertainment of parties and banquets. A nobleman would contract them to recite poetry, play the flute and even to discuss philosophy with male guests.[43] These women were clever and with some education; some even came from noble families themselves.[44] While some prostitutes became famous through their participation in the political life of Roman society,[45] others enjoyed a wealthy lifestyle without the tutelage of a man.

Given this context, Mary, in a city such as Magdala in the midst of the Roman Empire trade network, could have inherited her patrimony either as the widow of an important trader or from working as a prostitute, which was perfectly acceptable in Roman society. Therefore, the question that still remains is: *What if Mary of Magdala was in fact a former prostitute?* Can she still be the first and main witness of the resurrection? It is suspicious that early Christian tradition was able to defeat the strong leadership of Mary by pointing to a moral issue read in a narrow Judeo-Christian view. That reading disempowered her as an apostle, giving her a place seen as appropriate to women: the crying figure pleading for salvation. What underlies this move is an increasing understanding of sexual renunciation as a way to participate in the new life as a Christian. This is at the bottom of the classical Christian understanding of Mary. She leaves a life dedicated to the exercise of human sexuality and dedicates herself completely to the service of Jesus as a new woman, overcoming corporeal needs. She is accepted into the company of the Kingdom by disembodying herself. Thus it was that, as in the case of Mary the mother of Jesus, she became a model for all Christian women. Whether historical or not, Mary's past in prostitution made her vulnerable to a different bondage after her *conversion*: she was required to be controlled and normalized as a decent woman. Surely through that discursive technology she would became an icon for all Christian women.

What is important to acknowledge is that, in its origins, this understanding came just at the same time that Roman society was changing to a new paradigm of morality and ethics, very similar to Stoic and Christian traditions.[46] The understanding of Mary in the sixth century would not be possible without this development in the history of Roman culture and society, as well as its interrelation with the increasing status of Christianity. Christian theologians used her as an icon to fight social customs deeply rooted in Greek and Roman societies. By proposing her conversion, Mary came to a life of *holiness* that embraced a strong *sexual discipline*. In doing this the classical Christian tradition, paradoxically, came closer to the patterns of sexual renunciation and denial of the body required by heterodox writings.

From Sinful Woman *to* Virtuous Leader: *Heterodox Writings*

Though heterodox writings offer differing visions of Mary of Magdala, it is possible to define a profile distinct from that presented in the classical Christian tradition. If the traditional Mary is the crying woman pleading for mercy at the feet of Jesus, the heterodox traditions portray her as a virtuous leader and apostle, especially in the Gnostic writings.[47] Her image in the heterodox writings is also underlined by two main understandings of the submission of body and sexuality basically coming from two distinct Gnostic groups: a) an implicit sexual renunciation, manifested especially in the case of the Encratites;[48] and b) the absorption of the female into the masculine, especially as manifested in Valentinian circles.[49] Although too much effort has been expended either to avoid or to overemphasize the romantic liaison between Mary of Magdala and Jesus, the two understandings previously mentioned are the main – but not the only – manifestations of heterodox movements.

The *Gospel of Mary* suggests that Mary of Magdala had received from Jesus teachings that the rest of the disciples had not. The Gospel is a dialogue between some of the disciples (Peter, Andrew and Levi) and Mary of Magdala. The tension between Mary of Magdala and Peter is as notorious as that found in the heterodox writings. After challenging the validity of Mary's teachings, Peter is confronted by Levi, who defends Mary. He says:

Peter you have always been hot tempered. Now I see you contending against the woman like the adversaries. But if the Savior made her worthy, who are you indeed to reject her? Surely the Savior knows her very well. That is why He loved her more than us. Rather let us be ashamed and put on the perfect Man [*andros*], and separate as He commanded us and preach the gospel, not laying down any other rule or other law beyond what the Savior said.[50]

It is clear in this quotation that Mary of Magdala is very important among the apostles, especially since she teaches them the words of Jesus. Now she was seen as a leader through basically embracing the understandings of sexuality that the heterodox communities were also following. I will follow Brown for this section.

Sexual renunciation: undoing the works of women   According to Brown, the Encratites[51] saw sexuality as something negative. They believed that the victory of Christ over death could be complete when sexuality has ceased.[52] The major expression of halting sexuality was to remain single and to avoid procreation. The phrase 'to stop the works of women', or stopping procreation, illustrates the ideas of the Encratites of bringing the 'present age' to an end. To cease in procreating would stop the course of humanity. This was seen as the possibility to bring the age of Christ or Kingdom to manifestation.[53]

The *Dialog of the Savior* reflects this idea:

The Lord said, 'Pray in the place where there is no woman.'
Matthew said, 'Pray in the place where there is no woman,' he tells us, meaning *'Destroy the works of womanhood,' not because there is any other manner of birth, but because they will cease giving birth.*
Mary said, 'They will never be obliterated.'
The Lord said, 'Who knows that they will not dissolve and ... *[2 lines missing]*?'
Judas said to Matthew, *'The works of womanhood will dissolve* [...] the governors will [...]. Thus will we become prepared for them.'[54]

In this quotation all the problematic about body and sexuality in the Encratite theology was summed up. The author is right, there is no other way of giving birth than through the womb of woman. But in order to procreate, the action is necessary, which, for the Encratites, enforced the bondage of Christianity to this present age and delayed the coming of the age of Christ.

The solution was to cease sexual activity, to renounce it in order to attain salvation. Clement of Alexandria invoked the same idea in the words of Jesus according to the Encratites: 'They say that the Savior himself said: "I came to undo the works of women," meaning by this "female," sexual desire, and by "work," birth and corruption of death.'[55]

Regarding the *Dialog of the Savior* and analysing the case of Mary of Magdala in relation to sexuality, Elaine Pagels summarizes:

> [...] [T]he target is not woman, but the power of sexuality ... Mary Magdalene, praised as 'the woman who knew the All,' stands among three disciples who receive Jesus' commands. She, along with Judas and Matthew rejects the 'works of femaleness' that is, apparently, the activities of intercourse and procreation.[56]

Here lay the most important triumph of Encratite theology, to put this idea in the mouth of Jesus and of Mary of Magdala. That is the most powerful legitimation. For Mary, it implied the co-option into a system that denied not only her sexuality but also her body.

Absorption of the female into the male: the androgynous The second understanding about the submission of the body and sexuality comes from the absorption of the female into the male. In these writings women enter a process through which they become *virtuous*. The Gospel of Thomas is notorious regarding this. Peter is regretting that Mary is present among the apostles because she is a woman. Jesus defends her by replying to Peter:

> Simon Peter said to them, 'Let Mary leave us, for women are not worthy of life.' Jesus said, 'I myself shall lead her *in order to make her male, so that she too may become a living spirit resembling you males.* For every woman who will make herself male will enter the Kingdom of Heaven.'[57]

The term 'virtuous' has in its root in *vir* [male]. To say that a woman has to be made male is a way to affirm that that woman has transcended the limits of her sex.[58] Diana Rocco Tedesco explains that from the first to the fifth centuries this *vir* implicitly carried the notion of *virilization* of women. According to historians and theologians, the Gospel of Thomas is not saying *masculinization* but virilization, that is returning and transcending her own sex in order to return to the *androgynous*.[59] What is judged to be bad is the dualism, the separation between men and women; the ideal is the return to the androgynous being, which is possible through the process of virilization. The kingdom of dualism and separation was not good; it was necessary to reunite the opposites.[60] The female has to be absorbed by the male and, in that process, both become one, a one that is androgynous.

If Rocco Tedesco is correct and the virilization, or *androgynization*, of women and men is a way to escape dualism, it could be possible to see this process as a way of blurring the distinction between them and opening up a space for fluidity in human sexuality. Nonetheless, the line between the co-option of the female by the male, and normalizing the female in the image of an androgynous being that resembles very much the male, is very labile.

What is important to remember is that in the heterodox writings, Mary appears as the apostle among the apostles, almost resembling Jesus. Why does she almost always appear as the counterpart of the male Jesus or of the male apostles? Rocco Tedesco offers an answer to this. She brings in the concept of *sizigia*,[61] or partnership, coming from Valentinian philosophy, in order to explain why Mary is brought into these writings in relation to Jesus, especially through the seeking of deep knowledge. Complementarity with Jesus is at the basis of the election of Mary of Magdala.[62] It cannot be denied that a relationship between her and Jesus of Nazareth already existed. According to the Gospels, she was part of the group of women who supported Jesus in his ministry and she was among the women who visited the empty tomb on the day of Jesus' resurrection. She was an important personage in the Gospels. Because of that relationship, heterodox theologians were led to see the position with different eyes: the functions of the androgyne archetype were underlined in order to transcend the separation between Mary (female) and Jesus (male), to reach the full knowledge of the divine through their relationship, which is the emergence of the androgynous. Brown accords with this when he states that:

> Gnostic circles treasured those incidents in the Gospels that had described the close relations of Christ with the women of His circle, and most especially Mary Magdalen [*sic*.] For a second-century writer, such anecdotes were an image of the sweet and irresistible absorption of the woman, the perpetual inferior other, into her guiding principle, the male.[63]

Filoramo, in his explanation of the androgyne archetype, argues similarly in relation to the Divine: the 'contemplation of the male principle in the "female" mirror'.[64] At the same time, Filoramo concludes that this process is a result of patriarchalist mentality:

> The female function is essentially generative, and generation inevitably means a progressive ontological impoverishment. Therefore the female element is the cause, however indirect, of the creation of the world and of humankind. By itself, however, it is incapable of aspiring to the heights. The process of salvation, in this sense, is essentially male; a process, as it were, of masculinization. The final equilibrium re-established in the bosom of the archetypal Androgyne will therefore be an equilibrium in which the male is destined to triumph. Indeed, this was inevitable in a society still profoundly patriarchal, which had not experienced the boldness of modern feminism.[65]

Therefore, according to this statement, the salvation of Mary of Magdala is based on a maleness act; she is, as every woman in the eyes of Valentinian theology, destined to be absorbed by maleness in order to reach the perfect state of androgyny.

In summary, underlying both understandings is what queer theory denounces as the mechanisms of decency, intent on denying the body and sexuality. Mary, praised as a prominent leader, had to scarify her sexuality in order to be counted as the main apostle among the apostles. Disembodying herself even more by renouncing her gender, she was normalized.

Paradoxically, some centuries later, feminist readings will require the same from Mary in order to free her from hetero-patriarchal bondage.

From Indecent *to* Decent: *The Feminist Reading*

Feminist theologians also deny Mary of Magdala's body and her sexuality. They completely reject her sinful past ascribed to her by classical Christian tradition. Instead, they bring forward the possible connection of Mary with the trade between the rich inhabitants of Magdala and other cities in the Roman Empire. Furthermore, feminist theologians state that Mary's ancestry should be sought within the Hasmonean leaders in the community of Magdala. In this sense, the economic and social independence of this woman is verified by the fact that the Gospels portray Mary as known by her city of origin and not by any man who ruled over her, for example as Joanna the wife of Chuza or Mary the wife of Clopas. If Mary was a trader in Mediterranean society in the times of Jesus,[66] her ability for leadership should be well recognized by the Christian community. This socioeconomic status would allow her – as well as other aristocratic women who followed Jesus – to protect him from rivals as well as support his ministry economically. As has previously been mentioned, the Gospel of Luke offers this datum as the important aspect of Mary among the disciples who follow Jesus.

In following this line of thought offered by feminist readings, the traditional understanding of Mary as a converted prostitute fails and becomes unsustainable, although some of the explanations that feminist scholars argue in order to overcome this interpretation fall short in apprehending its complexity.[67] The fact that the classical Christian tradition still considers as Mary nothing other than a repentant prostitute obscures and occludes the fact that she could have been recognized as a prominent disciple and leader of the early Christian community. According to feminist theologians, the vision of Mary as a prostitute was the male projection over her rather than the Gospels' message. The Gospel of John reveals another understanding of her. John pays attention to her as the first witness of the resurrection, especially in the pericope of 20:11–18 known as *The Christophany to Mary of Magdala.*

Nonetheless, what feminist theologians clearly avoid is the sexual aspect of Mary. The negotiations of power and sexuality lead to a very uneven result: in order to be recognized as an apostle, the personage Mary of Magdala has to sacrifice her sexuality. The recognition from feminist theologians of her as a female leader does not necessarily mean that she is *sexualized* as a leader. Furthermore, it is possible to do a feminist reading of her in a way that is completely functional along the hetero-patriarchal matrix. Again, at the basis of this process language remains as a very important mechanism in producing this gap; what is *said* and what is *not-being-said* because of the former *saying* moulds identities and affects gender and performances of sexuality. Mary is the best example in this respect because, while some feminist theologians emphasize her as apostle, leader, prophet, or pastor, they end up denying her sexuality by imposing onto her those categories traditionally understood as characteristic of male offices. In other words, in making her perfectly suitable to male structures, she becomes an icon for all women and men to fit suitably into hetero-patriarchal understandings of performances, whether these might be ecclesiastical ministry or gender and sexuality. This has indeed non-innocent consequences: in gaining a status of equality for Mary in the midst of a male world implies the need to disembody and desexualize the female Mary. Paradoxically, she is saved as a servant of God by being *assumed* (co-opted) by maleness. In this sense, this type of feminist reading functions in ways astonishingly similar to those of the heterodox readings of nineteen centuries ago. If this is the case, we need to acknowledge that some feminist readings have already internalized hetero-patriarchalism and have begun to operate in that matrix, reinforcing and reiterating its mandates.[68]

The Gospel of John seems to value Mary in a prominent way. The placing of Mary as the first witness of the risen Christ situates her as the main leader in the disciples' band after the departure of Jesus. This is also present in verses 1–2 where John tells us about Mary alone visiting the tomb. She is usually mentioned as a member of a group of women who went to the tomb of Jesus to anoint him on the first day of the week and found it empty. But, in the Gospel of John, only Mary of Magdala goes to the tomb and discovers it empty. This is a notorious difference with the Synoptic Gospels and anticipates the theological construction of the pericope of 11–18 related to the whole purpose of the Gospel: seeking and discovering a Christ who is raised.

John's is the only Gospel that conveys a personal Christophany to Mary, and tells us about it in a narrative that reconstructs Old Testament narratives. It is a literary and theological reconstruction especially of the Song of Songs 3:1–4. If this is true, the Christophany of Mary allows us to read it from a sexual perspective, a fact that most feminist readings set aside.[69] It is also evident that the way John tells us about the episodes has something to do with the way that early Christian communities have discovered the risen Christ.

From all the narratives about the Christophanies, the one related to Mary is the most important. Why is the witness of the risen Christ so important for the Christian tradition? Perhaps Saint Paul, who wrote his letters some time before the oral traditions of the Gospels were written down, gives us a clue: 'If Christ has not been raised, then our preaching is vain, and your faith also is vain.'[70] Therefore, Mary is responsible, in John's Gospel tradition, for the credibility of the whole of the Christian faith.

Nonetheless, in reading the Christophany to Mary from a sexual perspective, our analysis becomes difficult for Christianity, and this applies also to some feminist readings, because it implies the consideration of human erotic feelings present between Jesus and Mary. In some Gnostic Gospels, such as the Gospel of Mary, and the Gospel of Philip, this line of interpretation could be found.[71] The orthodox party in the Church of the second century condemned those interpretations openly, but it never disappeared in heterodox interpretations at different times throughout Christian history. Althaus-Reid is, perhaps, one of the first theologians to recognize this openly. Using her category of *indecent theology*, we might wonder, for example, if a queer person could save humanity, or even, if the person who saves humanity – Jesus – could be a queer person as well? This question is at the core or our analysis, because traditional theology is willing to recognize the full humanity of Jesus but not to sexualize that humanity. The topic becomes even more difficult if we go further with the argument and ask what would happen if Mary were a lesbian, or Jesus bisexual, or transgender or intersexual. Can Jesus, the Trinity, or Mary the Virgin, embrace those genders and sexual experiences? Furthermore, what if in fact Mary of Magdala was a prostitute? Is she then less of a witness of the risen Christ? Certainly, as we have seen earlier in this article, she was destined for normalization in order to subordinate her to the power of Peter, and later, to the orthodox party.

We can agree with feminist theologians that the main value of this Christophanic event resides in the fact that Mary is the first witness of that event, in other words, she can corroborate that the core of the Gospel is true. But we also need to acknowledge that if the pericope of John 20:11–18 functions as a *midrash* of Song of Songs 4:1–4, then sexuality unavoidably comes on board as one of the primary layers of the text. By denying or occluding this element, both classical Christian tradition and feminist readings function according to the same pattern, making Mary a decent woman. On the one hand, the classical Christian tradition erased the notion of Mary of Magdala as the first witness of the resurrection and transferred that privilege to Peter, who then became the first apostle among the apostles. For her the classical Christian tradition reserved the place of a repentant sinner woman who cries at the feet of Jesus for her salvation. In becoming decent, she was relegated to a subordinate position. On the other hand, by denying her attributed past or a sexual reading of the Christophany of John's Gospel, some feminist readings inscribed Mary in a patriarchal pattern of normality that is acceptable to traditional Christian morality. In other words, through these decent readings, she has been perfectly co-opted by hetero-patriarchalism and in return she has recovered the recognition of her leadership. But, still remaining subordinate, she thus continues to be an icon for hetero-patriarchal oppression.

On Saints and Prostitutes

What does all this information about Mary of Magdala mean in the context of Argentina? Her case is symptomatic of the daily life experience of millions of human beings in Argentina, as well as in Latin America and the rest of the world. She functions as an archetype for binary thinking which labels and classifies human beings. As already noted, language used to label human beings is tied to mechanisms of oppression. It reiterates the matrix of hetero-patriarchal oppression. Therefore, the binary *saint/prostitute* is still present overtly and covertly in different technologies of discourse. These technologies of discourse set up polities that condition the very existence of human beings, whether through legal systems or through cultural/societal traditions. Theology is part of this process. As we have seen in the case of Mary, the basic process was to deny her body and sexuality in order to co-opt her as an archetype for decency, an understanding that could be used as a model to keep women in *her place* – that is, subordinate to males. Nonetheless, the ideology behind those theological understandings has not been overcome, and it continues to affect the lives of human beings.

In/decency is a dangerous binary still reiterated in Argentina. It represents the way through which Argentinean *machos* see women. A decent woman is the one who is mother, sister or wife; an indecent woman is one who does not embrace these categories of decency. As we know, Argentina is a mainly Roman Catholic country. The presence of other Christian confessions (mainstream and evangelical Protestant, Anglican/Episcopal, and Orthodox) as well as other religions (Buddhism, Islam, Judaism and Hinduism, among others) is represented among the population, but the majority still remain in the hands of Roman Catholicism.

When it comes to sexuality, we find that prostitution has been a prominent issue in Argentina since the times of the foundation of the country.[72] Christianity and other religions in Argentina have been witnesses of this social situation, but they have never worried about the causes of it. There are no official pronouncements by churches, nor are there demonstrations or movements to collect signatures for a change in legislation which could help people who are involved in prostitution, not least those who against their will have been drawn into becoming slaves in this growing market. Rather, there has been a concentration on moral statements, condemning women and men to become outcasts subject to double oppression, socioeconomic and religious. In relation to women, this double condemnation has also been used to keep them under patriarchal control, forcing them to marry in order to be considered *respectable*, something that we have already seen in the case of Mary of Magdala.[73] Looking back to history in Argentina, it is clear that the binary of in/decency embraced the categories prostitute and wife, something that is still in place today. In this respect Donna J. Guy says:

> Argentina['s] laws ... focused upon prostitutes and wives. As women whose sexual practices and relationships represented each other's antithesis, these two groups jointly defined the parameters of female citizenship in modern Argentina. Prostitutes determined the limits of socially-acceptable female sexual behavior so that self-identified female prostitutes lost the right to move freely within cities, work without medical inspection, and live wherever they pleased. In contrast wives,

by law and religion sworn to remain sexually faithful, enjoyed all those privileges taken from prostitutes though they still suffered other civil restrictions.[74]

In other words, the lives of prostitutes vanished under moral codes, and this still happens today.

Some years ago I was appointed by an ecumenical organization to act as its representative on a commission run by the Government of the City of Buenos Aires for the World AIDS Day commemoration. The task of the commission was to plan activities, including the distribution of red ribbons to government and religious organizations, as well as NGOs (non-governmental organizations). Specifically, we were to create a triptych signed by the organizations working on the topic. We gathered several times for discussions regarding the activities, and we designated a special task force for the basic redaction of the triptych. We had a plenary session for the discussion of the draft. We got to the point regarding the use of condoms, when a woman raised her hand and told us that the police of the City of Buenos Aires were incarcerating women and accusing them of being prostitutes if they found condoms in their purses. That denunciation made me feel very concerned about the situation of these women, and I asked the plenary session to include a paragraph in the document that explicitly stated that the use and possession of condoms was not a *privilege* but a *tool* that a person has for the protection of their own health. The woman looked at me in surprise, and then she asked which organization I represented. I told her that it was an ecumenical/religious organization. I asked her who she was and which organization she was representing. To my surprise, she replied, 'I am the president of the National Union of Sex Workers of Argentina,[75] and I never thought that churches were interested in our well-being.' I think that this struck me more than my previous reply to her. It was surprising for her that a religious person like myself would be worried about sex workers and their health or safety. But I was surprised that she was shocked because she never thought that the churches would be interested in her as a *person* beyond what she did for a living.

Reflecting on the example above, we need to look at the categorization of these women. The National Union of Sex Workers of Argentina (AMMAR) was aided since its foundation by the pastoral work of an ordained female minister and a female lay-leader from a Protestant church who worked in solidarity with them, despite the critiques and retaliations from their denomination. AMMAR was also recognized as a member of the Argentine Workers Unions Confederation (CTA),[76] and they have an office at CTA headquarters. Churches did not recognize their pastoral work. Instead, they tried to ex-communicate those female leaders for responding with love and commitment to those who needed help in the midst of their struggles, the prostitutes.

The story about the use of condoms and these prostitutes provides evidence of the need for a theology that stands up when people feel like outcasts, not only from society but also from Christianity. We need a theology that is not afraid of *indecencies*. We are not talking about acknowledging prostitution when it makes human beings objects and colonizes their lives. Even members of AMMAR struggle to make the broader society understand this.[77] The striking aspect of this story is the unwillingness of the churches to recognize the image of the Trinitarian God in somebody who has been led into prostitution by social and economic realities or conditions. It is possible to advocate the case of poor people, even fight their cause within some churches, but when it comes to discussing these difficult issues, the silence in most churches in Argentina is suspiciously deafening. As in the case of Mary of Magdala, it is difficult for prostitutes in Argentina to find a place in the normalized discourse of traditional Christianity.

At the same time, despite the fact that two actively Christian women were working closely with AMMAR as a result of their gospel response to human beings, the story shows that Argentinian churches are far from *disrupting* and *distorting* of the order established by hetero-patriarchalism. This is not only present in the canonical and internal regulations of the Christian churches as *institutions*, but also shows how dependent those churches are on prejudices already present both in the broader secular culture and in the legal system.

The action of embracing different experiences of gender and performances of sexualities situates us in a liminal space, a space of marginalization as well as resistance. As with the term 'queer', originally used as a degrading word, now been recovered as a word of resistance, a counter-language is needed to resist and distort the order of traditional/decent theology/ies. The radical philosopher, bell hooks, relates language and spatiality to recover the margins as a place for resistance against colonization:

> Understanding marginality as a position and place of resistance is crucial for oppressed, exploited, colonized people. If we only view the margin as a sign marking despair, a deep nihilism penetrates in a destructive way the very ground of our being. It is there in that space of collective despair that one's creativity, one's imagination is at risk, there that one's mind is fully colonized, there that the freedom one longs for is lost. Truly the mind that resists colonization struggles for freedom of expression. The struggle may not even begin with the colonizer; it may begin within one's segregated, colonized community and family. So I want to note that I am not trying to romantically re-inscribe the notion of that space of marginality where the oppressed live apart from their oppressors as 'pure.' I want to say that these margins have been both sites of repression and sites of resistance. And since we are well able to name the nature of that repression, we know better the margin as a site of deprivation. We are more silent when it comes to speaking of the margin as a site of resistance. We are more often silenced when it comes to speaking of the margin as a site of resistance.[78]

This position of marginality as a space of resistance is determined by language. As I have previously said, language is a very important instrument for colonial hetero-patriarchalism in maintaining its hegemony, mainly through the process of labelling. Labels degrade differences in gender and performances of sexualities. Sometimes those experiences are lived not only through the psychological violence that the process of labelling encourages, but also through physical violence. These words set up boundaries as well as building binaries (as well as providing the foundation in society for oppressive laws and cultural and religious practices) that confine people's sexual experiences in strongly policed categories. The results are categories that function within the logic of the *either/or* binary thought such as *good/bad*, *right/wrong* and *correct/incorrect*. In mapping different sexual orientations as positive/negative binaries, there is no room for those elements that do not fit into the binaries. The result is either exclusion or *normalization*, as has been historically the case of Mary of Magdala. Real people in Argentina – prostitutes, single mothers, GLBTTIQ folks, non-*machista* males – face the same destiny every day.

As I have said before, the process of labelling acts in different guises, *silencing* being one of the most insidious ways, since it makes people *invisible*. For centuries, because of her *sinful past*, Mary of Magdala was silenced as the witness of the risen Christ. In the same way, today's Christianity seeks to silence people with experiences of gender and performances of sexualities that do not fit into the normalized understanding of the body and sexuality as regulated by Christian morality. The result is that there are people in many churches who are invisible and oppressed. They are told to keep silent about their rights and needs, in society as well as in the churches. But it is not only people with different gender or different performances of sexualities who have been made invisible, ordinary, decent women who speak out against the oppression they have experienced go unheard, especially when they are told by clergy to go back to their abusive husbands and maintain a marriage that enslaves them. And beyond this we have not even begun to comment on how many children are not baptized because the sin of their mothers is to be a single parent or a prostitute, as if the child should be condemned in the same way that her/his mother is condemned by hetero-patriarchal Christian morality. It is that morality that has co-opted a particular interpretation of Mary of Magdala and Mary the mother of the Lord in order to rule over people, especially women.

Therefore Mary has been historically used not only as an icon for pleading mercy at the feet of Jesus, but at the same time, as a model of subordination for everyone who defies the dictums of traditional Christian morality. They have to either accommodate themselves to an order created by Christianity and moral codes based on particular interpretations of the teachings of Jesus or leave the communities of faith to live as spiritual outcasts. Normalization, usually read as *conversion*, has created situations of oppression and occlusion by imposing on the shoulders of people whose sexuality differs from the dictums of classical theology a way of life that is exogenous to them.

Conclusion

By examining the case of Mary of Magdala, I have attempted to show how the body and sexuality have played an important part in the denial of her leadership as well as her historical function as an icon for decency and normalization of people. The search for the historical Mary is an enterprise hard to achieve due to centuries of occlusion towards her persona. What we can say about her, based on biblical or archaeological data, is minimal and skewed by the lenses through which that reading is made. Therefore the different understandings of Mary are based on academic speculation. By examining the three – but not exclusive – understandings of Mary, we saw how her body and sexuality have been denied over the centuries in order to replace them with a character that functions for different purposes. Paradoxically, those readings carry the assumption of Mary as a modelling instrument for normalization/oppression of people. As I have explored in the last section of this article, this affects the life of people today in Argentinian society.

Language has played an important role in this process, enhancing and reiterating the oppression of people at different levels. A counter-language that could transform those oppressions into real and concrete freedom is necessary in Latin American theology/ies. This would involve going back to the roots of Latin America Liberation Theology, according to which the task of theology is 'to transform the world'.[79] Perhaps this transformation should begin by embracing God in creational reality beyond our logics of normalization and oppression. Boff sees the core of this in the action of the Trinity as the 'inspiration for human society'.[80] Argentinean society is learning to embrace diversity, but churches are making the process harder, based on a fear of abandoning a morality that has oppressed people for centuries. Christian churches should re-explore their theology/ies and embrace new horizons in the same spirit that Jesus embraced the wholeness of human beings.

Gustavo Gutiérrez points to this when affirming that the *utopia* of building community as a just communion of sisters and brothers becomes the goal for the transformation of the world in doing justice through economic, social and political liberation.[81] In order to achieve part of this utopia, the recovery of the person of Mary of Magdala as a counter-icon could be a means by which Christianity could embrace people whose gender and performances of sexualities disrupt and distort the assumptions of normalization carried out through centuries by classical theology. In doing this, Latin American Liberation Theology/ies would move towards the recovery of a truly Incarnational theology. A dialogue with indecent/queer theology/ies is extremely necessary. The path that lies before us is to liberate Mary from the prison of oppressive hetero-patriarchal readings. In this way it would be possible for her witness to become guidance towards freedom for those in Argentinean society who are outcasts and excluded because of their gender or performances of sexuality. In doing this we will walk towards the encounter of the new life fully manifested in the risen Christ.

Notes

1   I am very grateful to Gary Smith for editing early drafts of this paper. Also the Rev. Dr Charles Buck, Dr Ibrahim Abdurrahman Farajaje, Cristina Conti, Dr Althaus-Reid, Dr Diana Rocco Tedesco and Thom Longino for their support.
2   Queer theorists denounce, 'the *either/or* thinking' or 'binary thinking' as the *inner logic* of the heterosexual system. (See Althaus-Reid (2000), 13.) Ibrahim Abdurrahman Farajaje goes beyond the gender binary – heterosexuality/ homosexuality – and explores the intersections of gender, class and ethnicity where binary thinking also plays an important role. Therefore, he points out: 'Now either-or thinking erases millions and millions of people. It sets up mixed-heritage or multiracial people to have to make the choice to identify with only one group as opposed to being able to define ourselves as we choose, acknowledging our place within the people-of-color communities. So now some mixed-heritage people begin to challenge a purely black-or-white way of seeing race' (Farajaje, 2000: 17). Sexuality is but one of the multiple layers where the *either/or* thinking expresses.
3   I will use the terms *humanity* and *human beings* not in the sense of women and men in the biological sense, but in the variety of experiences of sexuality and gender performances: heterosexuals, bisexuals, gays, lesbians, transgender, and intersex people. To make this list also presents us with a big problem: the *liberal list* or the process of naming the *differences* and making of those *differences* a list of categories. This carries the risk of marginalizing people that do not fit into those new categories. Being conscious of this risk, I believe that it is important to take into account this effort of queer theory to demystify the binary women/men as well as the *liberal list*. Therefore, this list, as well as the acronym GLBTTQI, is provisional.
4   In this regard, L. Davis points out that the notion of *deviancy* comes from Sir Francis Galton who made some revisions to the notion of *normalcy* as an statistical (Davis, 1997: 17). He also offers a history of this notion of body *normalcy*. He recognizes that Adolphe Quetelet (1796–1847), a French statistician, is considered the father of modern conception on *norm* or *average*. He developed this concept after his application of the astronomic 'law of error' to 'the distribution of human features such as height and weight'. From his studies, he developed the idea of the *average man* [*l'homme moyen*] as the abstract human through which the middle way of life of all humanity have to be measured by. Furthermore, it was desirable to become like this 'average man.' (See ibid., 11–12.)
5   The Eurocentric understanding of humanity, sexuality and gender performances that has colonized different cultures marks this. *Eurocentricism* is a process through which Europe labelled itself as *civilization*, and the rest of the world was labelled as *barbaric*. Ella Shohat and Robert Stam say, 'Eurocentrism sanitizes Western history while patronizing and even demonizing the non-West; it thinks of itself in terms of its noblest achievements – science, progress, humanism – but of

the non-West in terms of its deficiencies, real or imagined' (Shohat and Stam, 1995: 3). When we look at the past whether events or personages like Mary of Magdala, this constitutes part of the lenses through which our reading of that past is made. Queer theory seeks to *disrupt* those readings by using new tools in order to develop new readings.

6   For a detailed analysis of normalization as the stigmatization of deviancy, see the book of Goffman (1986).

7   *Silencing* is a way of not recognizing *the other/s* as individual/s and, therefore, to make them *invisible*. In his book *Outspeak*, S. O'Connell analyses this topic of language and violence taking into account the work of Paul Ricoeur, Judith Butler, Jacques Derrida and Emmanuel Levinas, among others. O'Connell chooses to read language as violence in order to resist its oppression (O'Connell, 2001: 148). The combination of language and power carries out the seeds of all sorts of violence when the interlocutor is disqualified as such. *Authoritarianism* is the most common form, but not the only one. Experiences of beating and rape are, in some cases, the continuation of verbal offences. But there are other kinds of violence like the privation of food or shelter, or even the lack of job or friendly/ familial relationships. In order to be treated as *equal*, one needs to *be recognized as equal*. This implies a grade of respect necessary to recognize *the other/s* as individual/s and not as object/s (which the process of labelling does), as mere abstractions.

8   Michel Foucault in *Discipline and Punish* analyses the idea of this *normalizing gaze* as follows: 'In short, the art of punishing, in the régime of disciplinary power, is aimed neither at expiation, nor even precisely repression. It brings five quite distinct operations into play: [1] it refers individual actions to a whole that is at once a field of comparison, a space of differentiation and the principle of a rule to be followed. [2] It differentiates individuals from one another, in terms of the following overall rule: that the rule be made to function as a minimal threshold, as an average to be respected or as an optimum towards which one must move. [3] It measures in quantitative terms and hierarchizes in terms of value the abilities, the level, the "nature" of individuals. [4] It introduces, through this "value-giving" measure, the constraint of a conformity that must be achieved. [5] Lastly, it traces the limit that will define difference in relation to all other differences, the external frontier of the abnormal (the "shameful" class of the Ecole Militaire). The perpetual penalty that traverses all points and supervises every instant in the disciplinary institutions compares, differentiates, hierarchizes, homogenizes, excludes. In short, it normalizes' (Foucault, 1977: 182–183).

9   The contribution of Gayle Rubin regarding this *good/bad* binary of sexuality is very important. She denounces a whole sexual value system determined by the supremacy of white middle-class heterosexuality (Rubin, 1993: 13–14).

10   Butler described this as follows: '[...] neither grammar nor style are politically neutral. Learning the rules that govern intelligible speech is an inculcation into normalized language, where the price of not conforming is the loss of intelligibility itself' (Butler, 1999: xviii).

11   Butler points out: 'If gender itself is naturalized through grammatical norms, as Monique Wittig has argued, then the alteration of gender at the most fundamental epistemic level will be conducted, in part, through contesting the grammar in which gender is given' (Butler, 1999: xix).

12   I take this idea from the work of Judith Butler, especially in her work *The Psychic Life of Power*. There she analyses the connection between language and its power to name and fixed identities that get *ad-eternum* connecting to whoever formerly pronounced the naming of that identity (Butler, 1997: 110–111).

13   Cf. Althaus-Reid (2000), p. 19.

14   I take this notion from Ibrahim Abdurrahman Farajaje when he speaks about class, gender and ethnicity: 'Queer-in-intersection is where we acknowledge that race and class and gender and sexuality and spirituality and embodiment are not monolithic, distinct categories, where we as queers can see notions of race that must include an understanding of the elements of class, gender, sexuality, geography, embodiment, spirituality, that go into the shaping of notions of race, how race and gender and sexuality and geography and embodiment and spirituality go into the shaping of notions of class, how race and sexuality and geography and embodiment and spirituality are factors and facets of the shaping of gender' (Farajaje, 2000: 20–21).

15   In this respect, Farajaje points out: 'One of the greatest acts of resistance and decolonization is to move beyond binary thinking, race and gender, invested with particular meanings, are categories created by human beings – men, to be specific- to support and reinforce economic and social power' (ibid., 17).

16   One of the most famous plays about Mary of Magdala is Digby's *Mary Magdalene*. Theresa Coletti offers an exhaustive analysis of this play in relation to its medieval context. See Coletti (2001), pp. 337–378.

17   See Norman Jewison's *Jesus Christ Superstar* (1973) or Martin Scorcese's *The Last Temptation of Christ* (1988).

18   The fact that Mary of Magdala is the first witness of the risen Christ cannot be ignored. Perhaps the Apostle Paul makes the most remarkable and earliest occlusion of her as the first witness of the risen Christ in the way he describes the events of the resurrection: '. . . he appeared to Cephas, then to the twelve. Then he appeared to more than five hundred brothers at one time, most of whom are still alive, though some have died. Then he appeared to James, then to all the apostles. Last of all . . . he appeared also to me' (1 Co. 15:5–8). There is neither mention of Mary of Magdala nor of any other woman among the company of Jesus in St. Paul's description. Schüssler Fiorenza affirms that the purpose behind this occlusion of women by St. Paul is necessary to justify not only the 'male chain of authority' but also his own apostolic tradition (Schüssler Fiorenza, 1999: 122–123). Nonetheless, Schüssler Fiorenza affirms that the basic problem regarding the resurrection is not related to traditions related to geography, but the classification of 'canonical and extra-canonical texts' should be done 'in terms to female and male witness traditions of the resurrection' (ibid., 124).

19   'The consequences of an analysis of sexual constructions carry important implications in any contextual theology. Basically they destabilise [*sic.*] the sexual foundations of economic and political theories and unveil the sexual ideology of systematic (even liberationist) theology' (Althaus-Reid, 2000: 7).

20   Jonathan Goldberg has noticed this in his work on *Queering the Renaissance* and in explaining this notion of risk, he points out: 'Indeed, to follow Foucault à la lettre, the Renaissance comes before the regimes of sexuality, and to speak of sexuality in the period is a misnomer. This is indeed the case if sexuality is taken as a marker of identity, definitional or a core of the person [. . .] can be found in the texts at hand. *Yet this does not mean that the anachronism of speaking of*

sexuality in the Renaissance is not to be risked, especially if the failure to invoke sexuality means acting as if texts of the period can always be explained in other terms, and in ways in which anything like sex disappears ...' (Goldberg, 1994: 5–6. italics mine).

21 Brown (2003).

22 Bernabe Ubieta (1994).

23 Sewicki (2000).

24 Horsley (1996).

25 See Mk 8:10.

26 See Mt. 15:39.

27 The Greek word *Tarixeiai* is used to describe factories for salting fish, or for pickling, salting, or otherwise preserving any food. Josephus calls the city by this name (see Sewicki, 192, note 23). This makes evident the interconnection between Magdala and the fishing economy of Galilee. On this see Hanson (1997), pp. 99–111.

28 For further geographical and archeological data on this topic, see 'Magdala'. Available at: http://www.ourfatherlutheran.net/biblehomelands/galilee/magdala.htm.

29 See Horsley (1996), p. 117.

30 See Sewicki (2000), pp. 183–184.

31 Horsley points out: 'The hypothesis of extensive international trade between Galilee and other areas of the Roman empire supports the claim that Galileans would not have been so isolated and backward economically and culturally as had previously been suggested by outsiders, from the early rabbis to romantic Western European writers such as Renan' (Horsley 1996: 67).

32 Ibid., pp. 44–45.

33 Ibid. The author also quotes two other works: Overman (1988), pp. 160–168; and Edwards (1998), pp. 169–182.

34 '*haitines diēkonoun autois ek tōn huparchontōn autais*' (Lk. 8:2–3).

35 Mary is mentioned only in the crucifixion, burial and resurrection narratives. Apart from those narratives and the list in Lk. 8:1–2, she is not mentioned in other passages. The fact she is mentioned previous to Joanna suggests 'Mary of Magdala was a person of greater importance in the early church than Joanna, wife of Herod's steward' (Thompson, 1995: 50).

36 Mk. 14:3–9; Mt. 26:6–13.

37 Lk. 8:2.

38 Thompson (1995), p. 14.

39 Saint Ephrain the Syrian. 'Homily on Our Lord' [#47] in Schaff and Wace (1983), pp. 326–327; quoted by Thompson (1995), p. 14.

40 Gregory the Great. 'Homilarum Evangelii' in Migne, *Patrologiae Latina* (Parisus, 1844) Vol. 76. 2.23.76; quoted by Thompson (1995), p. 15. (Translation by M. Thompson.)

41 Paul Veyne explains that under this new morality or new code, the status of married women changed. Based on Stoic tradition and Ovidian concept of *Amicitia* [friendship] women were invited through marriage to a relationship of friendship with their husbands. We need to notice that friendship played a very important role in Roman society. (See Veyne, 1992: 42–43.)

42 There were strict rules for enjoying the pleasure of sex and sexuality. Noble men in Greece and Rome had to fulfil expectations coming from their understanding

of body and sexuality rigorously controlled by the dictums of society. As a noble-man has to learn to exercise control over women, slaves, properties and lower classes, he also has to learn how to control his own body. (See Brown, 1988: 9, 11.)

43   While for Greco-Roman society this is mainly a description of an accepted and even welcomed custom, for patristic writers is a denunciation of a condemnable act. Saint Gregory of Nazianzus wrote a letter that in fact is an excursus where he apologizes for not attending the wedding banquet of Olympia. In that letter, St Gregory praises the marriage of Olympia but *criticizes* the contract of prostitutes to entertain at Christian weddings. (See Gregory of Nazianzus. *Ep. Ad Olimpiae*, in Teja, 1986: 147–151.) In *On Vainglory and the Education of Children*, Saint John Chrysostom advises Christians not to continue with such a custom, especially since children should not see nude women in those parties, a fact that implies how much the social custom was still part of Christianity. (See St John Chrysostom (1977) *De inani gloria et de educandis liberis*, 78, 88.)

44   Petronius Arbiter in his *Satyricon* quotes a paragraph from Tacitus that illustrates this: '*For Visitilia, born of a family of praetorian rank, had publicly notified before the aediles, a permit for fornication* [= prostitution], according to the usage that prevailed among our fathers, who supposed that sufficient punishment for unchaste women resided in the very nature of their calling.' (See Petronius Arbiter. *Satyricon*. Translated by W. C. Firebaugh. Available at: http://ancienthistory.about.com/library/bl/bl_prostitutionnotes.htm. Italics mine.)

45   In Greek history, the case of Aspasia is notorious. She was a prostitute and later became Pericles' companion and main counsellor. There were two types of prostitutes in Athens: (a) In the upper classes there were the *hetairai*, prostitutes with the social and intellectual skills necessary to entertain upper-class men at the symposiums, and (b) *pornai*, slave prostitutes who did not have these skills and entertained men from the lower classes. Aspasia was a *hetairai*. (See Jill Kleinman. 'The representation of prostitutes versus respectable women on ancient Greek vases', available at: http://ancienthistory.about.com/gi/dynamic/offsite.htm?site = http://www.perseus.tufts.edu/classes/JKp.html.) When Pericles died, she took his place in the political arena. Centuries later, in the midst of Christian Roman Empire, we find another example: Empress Theodora, wife of Justinian I. She was born in Constantinople in 497 CE and reigned from 527 to 548 CE. (See J. Irmscher. 'Teodora', in Di Berardino, 1998: 2069.) She was in her youth a striptease dancer who performed at the public theatre in Constantinople (Brown, 1989: 245). The case of Empress Theodora is rare because she also converted to Christianity and protected the monks of Syria. According to John of Ephesus, she was remembered among the monks as 'Theodora, she of the brothel' (John of Ephesus, *Lives of the Eastern Saints* 12: *Patrologia Orientalis* 17:189; quoted by Brown, 1988: 431). Both examples show how prostitutes were present in Greek and Roman societies, and how hard it was for Christianity to displace them from that social recognition.

46   They share common concepts, but we need to remember that stereotyping them is not helpful to understand their particularities. Veyne points out regarding matrimonial concepts: 'Clearly we must not argue in terms of stereotypes and imagine a conflict between pagan and Christian morality. The real cleavage lay elsewhere: between a morality of matrimonial duties and an internalized morality of the couple. The latter, which originated somewhere in the heart of pagan

culture, was commonplace by A.D. 100, shared by both pagan culture and Christians under the Stoic influence' (Veyne, 1992: 47). Brown goes further and explains: 'It is important to note at the outset the crucial difference between the widespread morality adopted by the Christians and the codes of behavior current among the civic elites. Much of what is claimed as distinctively "Christian" in the morality of the early churches was in reality the distinctive morality of a different segment of Roman society from those we know from the literature of the wellborn. It was a morality of the socially vulnerable' (Brown, 1992: 260–261).

47 We need to keep in mind that the Gnostic movement was a movement for elites and at the borders of main Christianity, that is, the arising orthodoxy in formation in the second century CE. Gnostics had to leave Rome and Alexandria, or remain underground to survive the increasing intolerance of orthodox Christianity. The Gnostic groups are never massive but small in number, usually women and men gathered around a leader or teacher who resembles the place of Jesus and his followers: '*The teacher relived among them the role of Christ and His disciples.* Here was "a guide, restful and leisurely." Like Christ, he unfolded an account of the origins of the world and of nature of the soul that brought intellectual certainty and moral purpose to all who heard it' (Brown, 1988: 106; italics mine).

48 See ibid., Chapter 4.

49 Ibid., Chapter 5.

50 *Gospel of Mary* 9:6b-9. [Available at: http://www.gnosis.org/library/mary-gosp.htm.]

51 The term *encratites* comes from the Greek *encrateia* which means *continence*. It is a form of radical asceticism that developed especially in Marcion's movement. According to scholars, it is doubtful to think that there existed a group with this name because it refers to behaviours and ideas that nurtured different movements. This kind of asceticism prohibited marriage and procreation as well as promoting abstinence from meat and wine. (See F. Bolgiana. 'Encratismo', in Di Berardino, 1998: 711–712.)

52 See Brown (1988), p. 84.

53 Ibid., p. 85.

54 *The Dialog of the Savior*, translated by Stephen Emmel. (Selection made from James M. Robinson (ed.), *The Nag Hammadi Library*, revised edition. San Francisco: HarperCollins, 1990. Available at: http://www.gnosis.org/naghamm/dialog.html.)

55 Clement of Alexandria. *Strom.* III.6:63. (J. E. L. Oulton and H. E. Chadwick. *Alexandrian Christianity*. (Philadelphia: Westminster Press, 1954); quoted by Brown, 1988: 85.)

56 Pagels (1979), pp. 66–67.

57 *Gospel of Thomas*, 114. ('The Gospel of Thomas', translated by Thomas O. Lambdin, in Robinson, 1977: 130; italics mine.)

58 According to the medical information of that time, women was a failure of nature, and thus, inferior to males. In the words of Aristotle, '[. . .] a woman is so to say a sterile man, [. . .] a woman, so to say, is a mutilated man; menstruations are sperm, but an impure sperm' (quoted by Rouselle, 1989: 45). What is astonishing is that heterodox writings, without denying the inferiority of women and the requirement to be assimilated to maleness, also allowed Mary of Magdala to be recognized as a prominent leader, especially since in most of the heterodox

writing, she is the one to close the discussions or to offer final responses. Even more, among certain Gnostic groups like Montanism, an active group of women embraced the leadership of the movement.

59   This is evident not only in the Gnostic groups but also in orthodox Christianity. The case of Saint Thecla is profound in this sense: 'Thecla begins as a "regular" engaged young woman from Iconium and end up being an anachoret transvested as a man with her hair cut in order to emphasize more, if possible, her vocation of overcoming her female condition' (Rocco Tedesco, 2002: 21). The case of Perpetua is more notorious since she became *mulier virilis* on her way to martyrdom; she had a vision before her combat where she saw herself transformed into a male gladiator. (See ibid., 26.)

60   Giovanni Filoramo explains: 'The symbolism of the androgyne, so widespread in the history of religions and found alive in ancient mythological thought also by virtue of the particular good fortune enjoyed by the Platonic androgyne, tends to express as its most general content the concept of *coniunctio oppositorum*, or joining the opposites, to embody the conquest of all duality in an image that for the most part is constructed on a sexual paradox, by denying sex itself or affirming the wealth and fruitfulness of a full sexual life' (Filoramo, 1991: 61).

61   The Valentinian divine *Pleroma* is formed of 30 aeons in partners (*sizigiai*). The first four partners are the most important and form the primal *ogdoada*, from which the rest of the aeons are formed. The unity of both elements of the *sizygia* is presented as the model of unity (C. Gianoto. 'Valentin Gnostico', in Di Berardino 1998: 2173–2174).

62   Rocco Tedesco (2002), p. 27.

63   Brown (1988), p. 113.

64   'The spiritual self-fertilization of the archetypical Androgyne is also represented, in a favourite theme of ancient thought, as contemplation of the male principle in the female "mirror" that constitutes its vital and emotional dimension' (Filoramo, 1991: 62).

65   Ibid., p. 177.

66   See Sewicki (2000), p. 193.

67   I disagree with Benedicta Ward in this regard. In her book *Harlots of the Desert*, she argues: 'Mary Magdalene, for the evangelists and for the Fathers, is not just a historical character or characters; she is the new Eve, the first sign of the reversal of the fall of Adam. She is also, because of her great love, the woman in the Song of Songs, and she is, for the same reason, the Church as well as the individual soul redeemed from sin' (Ward, 1987: 14). Furthermore, she concludes: 'I suggest that her identification as a prostitute lies deeper, in the imagery of sin throughout the whole of the scriptures. Mary Magdalene takes to herself the image of unfaithful Israel, so graphically described by the prophets as a prostitute in relation to God. This image transferred by the New Testament writers to the whole of humanity in the new covenant and therefore each soul in sin can be described as a prostitute, as unfaithful to the covenant of love between God and man. It is in this profoundly illuminating sense that Mary of Magdala assumes the character of a prostitute, not because lust is a specially *[sic.]* terrible sin but because she is all sinners insofar as all sin is unfaithfulness to the covenant of love. Just as the sin of Eve was described as lust because that image best describes the disobedience of the Fall. So the sins of Mary of Magdala were seen as prostitution; that is, unfaithfulness to the love which is the name of God' (ibid., 14–15).

Unfortunately, Mary of Magdala never was associated with Eve as an archetype. Since early writings in Christianity, especially in the letters of Saint Paul, who wrote before the writing of the Gospels, Mary the mother of Jesus has been associated with Eve. Despite the fact that Mary of Magdala in fact turned to be an icon for those who repent, she never occupied the place that was assigned to Mary, the Virgin.

68 This notion of internalization comes from the works of Hegel in relation to the dialectics of master and slave, taking by authors such as Fanon (1963), Freire (1981) and Butler, among many others. In this respect, Butler points out: 'Feminist critique ought to explore the totalizing claims of a masculinist signifying economy, but also remain self-critical with respect to the totalizing gestures of feminism. The effort to identify the enemy as singular in form is *a reverse-discourse that uncritically mimics the strategy of the oppressor* instead of offering a different set of terms' (Butler, 1999: 19; italics mine).

69 For example, although Sandra Schneiders identifies the connection between the Gospel of John and the Song of Songs, she suggests that at the time of the writing of the fourth Gospel, the Song of Songs was understood as a 'covenant' between Israel and Yahweh (Schneiders, 1996: 161).

70 1 Cor. 15:14.

71 For the texts of this passages of the Gnostic Gospels, see Ricci (1994), pp. 147–148.

72 An excellent historical survey on this topic can be found in the article of Guy (1992), pp. 201–17.

73 The role of wives was defined by Bialet-Massé in a study made at the beginning of the nineteenth century, where he expresses: 'Woman's mission, as far as each sex has a part in the perpetuation of the species, is maternity, and the raising and education of children; in women's wombs lie the strength and greatness of nations ... Among us there are marriages that have six or eight children; twelve or more are not rare, and up to twenty children born of one mother, and cases are known of twenty-five children in one home. Let us not snatch this crown of glory from the Argentine woman's brow' (Juan Bialet-Massé. *El Estado de las Clases Obreras Argentinas a Comienzos de Siglo*; (Córdoba: Universidad Nacional de Córdoba, 1968), p. 426; quoted by Salessi (1995), pp. 52–3; translation by Salessi).

74 Guy (1992), p. 204.

75 AMMAR stands for *Asociación Mujeres Meretrices de Argentina*. (Available at: http://www.ammar.org.ar/hisoria.htm)

76 CTA stands for *Central de los Trabajadores Argentinos*. The CTA is a union formed in 1992 based on three principles: direct affiliation, direct democracy and political autonomy. (Available at: http://www.cta.org.ar/institucional/institucional.shtml)

77 In this respect, AMMAR states: 'In the 10 years of our organization, little by little we have begun to demonstrate to a part of society that we exist. Our struggle is doubly hard: we have to achieve a change in the conscience of the people and the governments in office. Concerning the people, so that they do not see us as "the girls easy life" ["*las chicas de vida facil*"] and so that they can understand that our life is hard and that we are not promoting sexual work. We do not choose, but rather we opt for this form of earning life. Our bigger achievement would be that never a woman would have to be forced into this profession. Concerning our governments, our main struggle is that once and for all they stop using repressive

politics and criminalizing us, since the only thing they achieve is that many of us have to resort to pimps, who say they "protect us." In fact, this establishes a net of corruption that we are forced to obey in order to be able to work without being incarcerated and mistreated by the police.' (Available at: http://www.ammar. org.ar/futuro.html)

78 bell hooks (1990), pp. 150–51.
79 This is based on Marx's 'Eleventh Thesis on Feuerbach', 'The philosophers have only interpreted the world in various ways; the point is to change it' (Marx, 1976: 5).
80 'Trinitarian communion is a source of inspiration rather than of criticism of the social sphere. Christians committed to social change based on the needs of majorities; above all, see tri-unity as their permanent utopia' (Boff, 1988: 151).
81 'The historical project, the utopia of liberation as the creation of a new social consciousness and as a social appropriation not only of the means of production, but also of the political process, and, definitively, of freedom, is the proper arena for the cultural revolution. That is to say, it is the arena of the permanent creation of a new person in a different society characterized by solidarity. Therefore, that creation is the place of encounter between political liberation and the communion of all persons with God, a communion which passes through liberation from sin, the ultimate root of all injustice, all dispossession, all divisions among persons. Faith proclaims that the human fellowship which is sought through the abolition of exploitation of some by others is something possible, that efforts to bring it about are not in vain, that God calls us to it and assures us of its complete fulfillment, and that what is definitive reality is being constructed within what is provisional ... If utopia gives a human face to economic, social, and political liberation, this human face – in the light of the gospel – reveals God. If doing justice leads to the knowledge of God, finding God in turn requires a commitment to doing justice' (Nickoloff, 1996: 205).

References

Althaus-Reid, Marcella (2000) *Indecent Theology: Theological Perversions in Sex, Gender and Politics*. London: Routledge.
bell hooks (1990) *Yearning: Race, Gender, and Cultural Politics*. Boston: South End Press.
Bernabe Ubieta, Carmen (1994) *Maria Magdalena. Tradiciones en el Cristianismo Primitivo*. Estella: Verbo Divino.
Boff, Leonardo (1988) *Trinity and Society*. Maryknoll: Orbis Books.
Brown, Dan (2003) *The Da Vinci Code*. New York: Doubleday.
Brown, Peter (1988) *The Body and Society: Men, Women and Sexual Renunciation in Early Christianity*. New York: Columbia University Press.
Brown, Peter (1989) *The World of Late Antiquity AD 150–750*. New York: W. W. Norton & Co.
Brown, Peter (1992) 'Late Antiquity', in Paul Veyne (ed.) *A History of Private Life: From Pagan Rome to Byzantium*, translated by Arthur Goldhammer, pp. 235–312. Cambridge: The Belknap Press of Harvard University Press.

Butler, Judith (1997) *The Psychic Life of Power*. Stanford, California: Stanford University Press.

Butler, Judith (1999) *Gender Trouble: Feminism and the Subversion of Identity*. New York: Routledge.

Coletti, Theresa (2001) '*Paupertas est donum Dei*: Hagiography, Lay Religion, and the Economics of Salvation in the Digby *Mary Magdalene*', *Speculum* 76:2: 337–378.

Davis, Lennard J. (1997) 'Constructing Normalcy: The Bell Curve, the Nobel, and the Invention of the Disabled Body in the Nineteenth Century', in L. J. Davis (ed.) *The Disability Studies Reader*, pp. 9–28. New York: Routledge.

Di Berardino, Angelo (ed.) (1998) *Diccionario Patristico y de la Antigüedad Cristiana*, 2 vols. Salamanca: Sígueme.

Edwards, Douglas R. (1988) 'First-Century Urban/Rural Relations in Lower Galilee: Exploring the Archeological and Literary Evidence', in David J. Lull (ed.) *Society of Biblical Literature 1988 Seminar Papers*, pp. 169–182. Atlanta: Scholars Press.

Fanon, Frantz (1963) *The Wretched of Earth*. New York: Grove Press.

Farajaje, Ibrahim (2000) 'Queer: We Are All a Big Mix of Possibilities of Desire Just Waiting to Happen', *In the Family*: 15–21.

Filoramo, Giovanni (1991) *A History of Gnosticism*, translated by Anthony Alcock. Oxford: Basil Blackwell.

Foucault, Michel (1977) *Discipline and Punish: The Birth of the Prison*, translated by Alan Sheridan. New York: Pantheon Books.

Freire, Paulo (1981) *Pedagogy of the Oppressed*, translated by Myra Bergman Ramos. New York: Continuum.

Goffman, Erving (1986) *Stigma: Notes on the Management of Spoiled Identity*. New York: Simon & Schuster.

Goldberg, Jonathan (1994) *Queering the Renaissance*. Durham, NC: Duke University Press.

Guy, Donna J. (1992) ' "White Slavery," Citizenship and Nationality in Argentina', in Andrew Parker et al. (eds) *Nationalisms and Sexualities*, pp. 201–17. New York: Routledge.

Hanson, K. C. (1997) 'The Galilean Fishing Economy and the Jesus Tradition', *Biblical Theology Bulletin*, 27: 99–111.

Horsley, Richard A. (1996) *Archeology, History, and Society in Galilee: The Social Context of Jesus and the Rabbis*. Valley Forge: Trinity Press.

Marx, Karl (1976) 'Theses on Feuerbach', in Karl Marx and Frederick Engels, *Collective Works*, vol. 5 (1845–47). London: Lawrence & Wishart.

Nickoloff, James B. (ed.) (1996) *Gustavo Gutierrez: Essential Writings*. Maryknoll, New York: Orbis.

O'Connell, Sean P. (2001) *Outspeak: Narrating Identities that Matter*. Albany: State University of New York Press.

Overman, J. Andrew (1988) 'Who Were the First Urban Christians? Urbanization in Galilee in the First Century', in David J. Lull (ed.) *Society of Biblical Literature 1988 Seminar Papers*, pp. 160–168. Atlanta: Scholars Press.

Pagels, Elaine (1979) *The Gnostic Gospels*. New York: Random House.

Ricci, Carla (1994) *Mary Magdalene and Many Others: Women Who Followed Jesus*, translated by Paul Burns. Minneapolis: Fortress Press.

Robinson, James M. (ed.) (1990) *The Nag Hammadi Library*, revised edition. San Francisco: HarperCollins.

Rocco Tedesco, Diana (2002) 'La exclusión del discurso femenino en la Iglesia antigua', *RIBLA*, 42–43: 18–34.

Rouselle, Aline (1989) *Porneia*. Barcelona: Peninsula.

Rubin, Gayle (1993) 'Thinking Sex: Notes for a Radical Theory of the Politics of Sexuality', in Henry Abelove, Michele Aina Barale, and David M. Halperin (eds.) *The Gay and Lesbian Studies Reader*, pp. 3–44. New York: Routledge.

Salessi, Jorge (1995) 'The Argentine Dissemination of Homosexuality, 1890–1914', in Emilie L. Bergman et al. (eds) *¿Entiendes? Queer Readings, Hispanic Writings*, pp. 49–91. Durham: Duke University Press.

Schaff, Philip and Wace, Henry (eds) (1983) *Nicene and Post-Nicene Fathers of the Christian Church*, vol. XIII. Grand Rapids: Eerdmans.

Schneiders, Sandra (1996) 'John 20:11–18: The Encounter of the Easter Jesus with Mary Magdalene – A Transforming Feminist Reading', in Fernando F. Segovia (ed.) *'What is John?' Readers and Readings of the Fourth Gospel*, pp. 155–68. Atlanta: Scholars Press.

Schüssler Fiorenza, Elizabeth (1999) *Jesus: Miriam's Child, Sophia's Prophet. Critical Issues in Feminist Christology*. New York: Continuum.

Sewicki, Marianne (2000) 'Magdalenes and Tiberiennes: City Women in the Entourage of Jesus', in Ingrid Rosa Kiztberger (ed.) *Transformative Encounters: Jesus and Women Re-viewed*. Leiden: Brill.

Shohat, Ella and Stam, Robert (1995) *Unthinking Eurocentrism: Multiculturalism and the Media*. London: Routledge.

St John Chrysostom (1977) *La Educación de los Hijos y el Matrimonio*, Spanish translation by A. M. Malingrey. Madrid: Ciudad Nueva.

Teja, Ramon (1986) *Olimpiade. La Diaconessa*, Italian translation by Silvia Acerbi, pp. 147–151. Milan: Jaca Books.

Thompson, Mary (1995) *Mary of Magdala: Apostle and Leader. An Amazing Re-Discovery of a Woman in the Early Church*. New York: Paulist Press.

Veyne, Paul (1992) 'The Roman Empire', in Paul Veyne (ed.) *A History of Private Life: From Pagan Rome to Byzantium*, translated by Arthur Goldhammer, pp. 5–24. Cambridge: The Belknap Press of Harvard University Press.

Ward, Benedicta (1987) *Harlots in the Dessert: A Study of Repentance in Early Monastic Sources*. Kalamazoo: Cistercian Publications.

Chapter 7

Liberation Theology, Modernity and Sexual Difference

Frederico Pieper Pires

Introduction[1]

The English anthropologist Peter Fry, trying to understand Brazilian homosexual followers of *Candomblé*,[2] realized that the working concepts in use in Britain are not adequate for analysing the Brazilian situation. Here, in Brazil, things depend on the way people get together. The chief problem faced by Fry was that the active partner in this kind of relationship never considers himself to be a homosexual. On the other hand, the passive partner accepts as a matter of fact his homosexuality and, generally, considers the active partner to be a heterosexual person. He wishes to relate sexually with a man (a *macho*, in colloquial jargon) and never with one of his own kind. Fry comes to the conclusion that sexual relations in Brazil cannot be analysed in themselves, but depend on many factors, such as the roles represented by the involved actors. This example demands some consideration about the limits of European concepts when applied to the explication of Latin American reality, especially in the field of sexuality.[3] It is important to note that when the first Jesuit missionaries came to Brazil, their chief concern was with what they considered moral life or, explicitly, Christian morals. We can read in the *Atas do Concílio de Lima* (1582–1583) the affirmation of the Jesuit José de Acosta that America does not need theology but catechesis. We do not need reflection in America because there is nothing to be reflected down here. We need action. And such an action should be the urgent battle against matters including witchcraft, immorality, fornication, misbehaving.

Latin American Theology of Liberation represents also the appropriation of two European modes of thinking: Marxism (especially the version of the School of Frankfurt) and Christian faith. These two ways of thinking, obviously, were adapted to the Latin American situation. This was a slow process, always working from its origins in relation to the local context, methodologically critical and somehow creative. In this essay I want to concentrate my attention on the concept of inclusion as it has been used by Theology of Liberation theologians. I will try to demonstrate the existing articulations between inclusion and modernity in order to deconstruct the modern notion of inclusion in its relation to the question of difference.

At first sight the term 'inclusion' is fascinating. It seems to erase differences. However, the passion of inclusion for difference aims at overcoming it, even if assuming it in itself.[4] This concept is very similar to the Hegelian concept of Absolute Spirit when considered inside the metaphysical tradition, widely employed through modernity. In order to ground this thesis, I will explain the relation of this term with Hegelianism, here understood as the ultimate expression of metaphysics within modernity. In doing this, I hope to make clear its limits, visible in the inclusion/exclusion dichotomy. From this we shall see that the concept of inclusion presupposes the will to system in order to reduce existential and pluralistic ambiguities with the intention of overcoming (*Verwindung*) them.

Leftist ideological tendencies employ generously the concept of inclusion in their debates. Marxism, for instance, when criticizing the dominant ideology, points out its deficiencies, reclaiming the inclusion of the excluded by the capitalist system. In the historical process the marginalized are the excluded. Since 1990 it is common to hear from pastors and theologians of liberation claims such as, 'The church must be inclusive', 'The gospel is for everybody', 'The gospel is inclusive', 'Jesus' practice was inclusive'. For Theology of Liberation, at least in its first phase, the poor were the excluded. Pastors and theologians tried to raise their consciousness in order to emancipate them, transforming them into what they were always supposed to be, social subjects. Emancipation was understood as inclusion in the historical process. Recently, as the result of criticism and reflection, the scope has been extended. Indigenous people, workers in general, African-Brazilians, women, and more recently homosexuals, have been brought together under the same roof of exclusion. In short, all persons outside the pattern of the adult, white and European male were considered excluded. The concept of inclusion follows the same model. The question remains: to what extent does this proposition take seriously the complexity and multiplicity of social relations. Besides this, the question of sexual difference has not been tackled accordingly.

Let us go back to Hegel in order to understand the relationship between modernity and difference. Hegel represents the climax of the metaphysical tradition in the realm of modernity. This German thinker, at a time when metaphysics was severely criticized, worked hard to save that tradition, setting it against the background of modernity. His efforts were indeed compensated through his enormous influence in the work of many philosophers after him. Even in the thinking of his critics his influence can be felt. Karl Marx, for instance, in his early writings, tries to illuminate what seemed to him obscure in Hegels theory of the state. Starting from Hegelian categories, Marx develops his theory of the totality of reality, holding together the philosophical thinking and the social reality, taking into consideration both philosophy and the world because, after all, 'both are partial in their own right' (Oliveira 2001: 13). Nietzsche, on the other hand, tried to reveal what is more original in the system even if not always said, which is the will to system and the dialectical synthesis, understood by him as 'lack of honesty'. My criticism of Hegelianism, and consequently the use of the concept of inclusion, will follow this tendency.

Truth is the Whole

Hegel was the first philosopher to recognize the historical aspect of philosophy. Dealing with this problem criticizes especially the thinking of Kant. Hegel considered Kantian philosophy a/historical. Hegel starts from Kantian anthropocentrism, inserting it into the dialectical movement of history. From the Absolute Spirit, Hegel envisages the dialectical movement of history, pretending to put everything in its proper place inside of the system. In this regard, his *Phenomenology of the Spirit* occupies an important place in the effort to explain the development of consciousness towards Absolute Knowledge.

Hegel also inverted the Kantian methodology. Instead of beginning from the finite to arrive in the infinite, Hegel establishes the Absolute as the starting point for any philosophical thinking, avoiding the Cartesian problem of the relationship between God and human beings. Hegel establishes this axiom: being and thinking are identical. If, on the one hand, Kant affirmed the impossibility of any absolute thinking, Hegel, on the other, affirmed the contrary, the identity of being and thinking. But being is also becoming. For that reason there is no static affirmation once they are all identified with thought. With this premise Hegel departs from the dogmatism of classical metaphysics. However, it should be observed that the becoming happens inside the frame of an ontotheology of the Absolute Spirit, logically organized. Hegel tries to overcome not only the finite/infinite dichotomy, but also many others present in Descartes and Kant, such as noumenon/ phenomenon, truth/reality. In order to be absolute identity, the Absolute Knowledge has to overcome also the subject/object and the universal/ particular dichotomies.

But if being and thinking are the same thing, how is it possible to know what is true and what is false? It is possible, starting from the absolute, to take historical truth as relative, and to locate absolute truth in the totality. For Hegel all things are essential. He surpasses classical metaphysics because it contrasted essential to inessential. The system, in his conception, accords to each thing its own place in relation to the development of the consciousness of the self. Philosophy becomes philosophy of history, ordaining locally the entire production of human beings. There is no truth or falsehood as such. The things we consider true or false have to be adjusted to the different stages of the development of consciousness. Things considered false in earlier stages can become true in the next stage. Hegel thought that classical metaphysics wanted to establish truth and falsehood without any consideration of the dialectical self-movement of the Spirit. This was for him a mistake. Consequently, everything belongs to being, even nothingness. Châtelet comments on this position in relation to the *Phenomenology of the Spirit*: 'Plato's philosophy stated the truth which it was able to state in its own context, that is, the Greek city with its intellectual, political and affective context. In a way, Aristotle also surpassed Platonism, but also expressed the truth' (Châtelet 1994: 117).

What is the relation between this aspect of the metaphysical philosophy of Hegel and the concept of inclusion? Both appeal to difference with the intention of homogenizing. Both accept the different, but always with the purpose of including him/her in a certain system, all-encompassing and comprehensive. This system is enclosed and becomes unique. There is nothing outside it – nothing inessential – because it includes everything within it. Apparently nothing and nobody is rejected or discriminated against. The question is not to know who deserves be included in the system but where to be included in order to overcome all differences, for the establishment of identity, erasing all differences. Following this it is easy to proclaim the ideal of accepting differences in unity. At this point, truth is no longer the difference but, as Hegel would insist, the whole. Difference is never considered in itself, but always in relation to its placement in the system. Alas! Is this not the same logic of globalization?

In Christian liturgy the moment of absolution is an outstanding occasion. Sinners kneel repenting of their sins before God and the priest proclaims God's forgiveness with the absolution of their faults. The word 'absolution' comes from the Latin, *absolutus*, meaning unattached, loose, fulfilled and released. *Absolutus* also originated the term 'absolute'. To be absolved means to be fulfilled and participative in the absolute. The inclusion of sexual differences looks much more like the process of absolution[5] than respect for and acceptance of differences. The absolved persons are those who have transgressed the established rules of behaviour; they are the transgressors, the queers. The different is absolved and, after that, disappears in the absolute.

The Will to System

In the background of inclusion, hidden, there remains the will to system. In order to be included in the system, someone or something has to be previously excluded from it. It is presupposed that there is an organizing centre determining whom or what is included. The system is the pattern, the measure, for establishing inclusion and exclusion. But from where comes the power to fix such a system as the regulative centre and measure? Who has the power to build its foundations? Here we are facing the complex relationship between power and the will to system. All systems create criteria to distinguish truth from untruth. The truth of the system is not at stake here. On the contrary, every system produces its own truth and policies of truth in order to control existing differences and indicate the transgressors (Foucault 1980).

The first step for deconstructing the concept of inclusion, understood as system, is the criticism of the static foundation,[6] or ground, taken as the organizing centre of the entire system. Summing up all this, metaphysics can be seen and the belief in an objective world order be apprehended by reason and expressed by language. Human discourse could, then, be constructed from the stable foundation, certain and normative. Derrida has offered a very precise definition of foundation. According to him, the play of metaphysics reveals itself as play, 'grounded and constructed from a founding immobility with a peaceful certainty, arising from the same play. From such a certainty, anxiety can be conquered' (Derrida 1995: 231). If this is true, we have to bring this stable point inside of the play in order to destabilize it.

The concept of foundation or ground brings us to Nietzsche. From his notion of the death of God and of the surpassing of values, he questions the very idea of foundation. As Vattimo affirms: 'In sum, for Nietzsche "God is Dead" means nothing else than the fact that there is no ultimate foundation' (Vattimo 2002: 3). The death of God means the loss of any fixed or stable point. Everything becomes fluid and unstable. According to Wrathall, 'God served as a land and horizon, giving the sensible world a fixed point of reference' (Wrathall 2003: 71). When this God dies, there is no candidate to substitute for him. Indeed, what appears is that the subject also dies with him. For Heidegger, after the death of God everything loses its value and gravity (Heidegger 1977: 53).

Consequently, there is nothing original to be looked for, nor ultimate ground to be found. 'There are no facts, only interpretation, and this is already an interpretation', Nietzsche says. It is not possible to make safe affirmations about the first mover imagined by Aristotle, named afterwards by theologies as God. If we cannot affirm God nor any ground, we are left with a feeling of absence and emptiness. Derrida reminds us of the process developed in the Western metaphysical tradition of replacing the foundations for something else. According to him, the history of metaphysics is realized through:

> ... a series of substitutions from one center to the other, a chain of determinations arising from the center. The center receives, one after the other, regularly, forms and different names. The history of metaphysics as the history of the Western world is the history of these metaphors and metonymies. Its matrix would be ... the determination of being as presence according to all meanings of this word. It would be possible to show that all names used for foundation, in the beginning and in the center, always pointed to the invariant of a presence (*eidos, arché, telos, energeia, ousia, aletheia*, transcendence, conscience, God, man [sic] etc.).
>
> (Derrida 1995: 231)

But in Hegelianism (and as we are trying to show, in the concept of inclusion), what determines the centre? The metaphysical system of Hegel and the concept of inclusion presuppose ontotheology. Ontotheology thinks the beginning and the end with certainty. When we face the abyss, where we have been thrown, we are tempted to appeal to God (or to the Absolute Spirit,[7] in the case of Hegel), transforming it into a foundation. That which is not determined is transformed into something determinate. This became possible in the Western metaphysics because Being was transformed in a being (*entis*). Such foundation reified has been always explained as absolute identity and presence. According to Aristotle, he (always considered in masculine terms by tradition) is equal to himself and thinks himself: being, therefore, thinking of thinking, in the words of Aristotle. In his *Science of Logic*, Hegel also affirms self-identity as the characteristic of being. Hegel, at the end of his *Phenomenology of the Spirit*, makes this clear:

> *Wenn in der Phänomenologie des Geistes jedes Moment der Unterschied des Wissens und der Wahrheit und die Bewegung ist, in welcher er sich aufhebt, so enthält dagegen die Wissenschaft diesen Unterschied und dessen Aufheben nicht . . .*[8]
>
> (Hegel 1952: §805)

Besides that, it is important to remember that for metaphysics, since its beginnings in Greece, reality was organized in the *logos* (logically) and was believed to be apprehended by the *logos* (reason). Hegel radicalizes this metaphysical presupposition. Reality and history are organized according to his dialectical method. History moves dialectically from the beginning, through the medium, towards the end. Consequently, the individual consciousness and the different are conceived in relation to the dialectical march of history towards its *telos*, the Absolute Knowledge. This implies that the different can only be understood inside of the system. Thus, any possibility of *aporia*, or chaos, is eliminated. All differences can be fitted inside of the system. Differences can be in an hegemonic way organized in relation to the historical objective or, in other words, according to the objective of the system (Hegel 1989). So, if the ground of the system is the identity with itself, then, its beginning and its end is absolute identity.

Starting from that, it is necessary to establish the basic principle of every system: the principle of non-contradiction. This is also the principle of any metaphysics depending on logic. Because in our metaphysical tradition our human experience is contradictory and ambiguous, the *logos* (or thinking) has the task of organizing experience from the principle of non-contradiction. This means that the system overcomes all ambiguities and determines all relationships in a unilateral fashion. In the system individuals are mirrors of the macho monotheistic God. Each individual is identical to himself and clear to himself. The affirmation of the unity of God (God is one) means that God is centred in himself and is the centre of all things. God's unity is intimately linked to his immutability and eternity. Plurality is always submitted to change. Immutability cannot bear 'many' and must be 'one'. This is why God's transcendence always points to his identity (Taylor 1992: 32). Inclusion, then, presupposes an absolute identity as the organizing centre of all differences. Everything moves towards an absolute identity. If this macho God, identical to himself, is the mirror of man, of the white adult man, and inclusion, finally, aims at absolute identity, the phalocentric mythology has a chance to remain untouched. Ingenuously, the reaffirmation of absolute identity triumphs through differences.

Criticism of Foundation

I am trying to show that the criticism of the notion of inclusion is linked to the criticism of foundation, for 'to establish a centre is, on the one hand, to organize, orient, balance a movement, release its forces, allow its progress and liberate the "play of elements inside the total form", but, on the other (and at the same time), is to fix it in an oppressive and irremediable prison' (Pecoraro 2002: 49). In the process of overcoming foundations, Derrida suggests the word 'vestige' instead of *arché*. Vestige, then, is the most original element possible to be reached by analysis. Something without origin constitutes the dimension of the original. Consequently, the beginning and the end of the system, taken without doubt until recently, are now contested. We do not know any more from whence we came, neither where we shall arrive (in the case of arriving somewhere). Erring (Taylor 1992) is the most likely possibility when we do not have certainties any longer. The logically constructed system is shaken and falls down when it loses its foundation. The metaphor of foundation, or ground (*Grund*), becomes an abyss. Instead of walking on secure ground, we are now over the abyss. At this point the concept created by Gianni Vattimo of 'weak thinking' or 'debilitated thinking' seems to be a good workable concept (Vattimo and Rovatti 1983).

Starting from the premise that there is no ultimate foundation ('this is an interpretation'), Vattimo conceives truth only as hermeneutical truth. Accordingly, truth is always interpretation and never a description of reality. It abandons what could be called 'strong ontology', recognizing its debility, being nothing else than a perspective. On this, Vattimo observes: 'the weak thinking signifies not so much or not essentially an idea of thinking aware of its own limits, avoiding the pretension of great and global metaphysical visions etc., but, above all, a theory of weakness considered a constitutive trace of being in the time of the end of metaphysics' (Vatimo 1998: 25). The relation between being and language established by Heidegger from the 1930s is basic for Vattimo. The being given through language is far away from the metaphysical tradition. Being loses its *ousia* and opens new possibilities for thinking. Vattimo, then, radicalizes the Heideggerian notion of 'ontological difference'. Being annuls itself in such a way that any effort towards establishing foundations contradicts its dynamic. Consequently, being can only be apprehended as remembrance, memory and vestige. It cannot any longer be understood in absolute terms or identity. According to the weak thinking, all strong categories of the metaphysical tradition are denied. The weak thinking recognizes and accepts instability, precariousness, the absurd and the contradiction without the need or intention of imposing closed schemas of interpretation or, in other words, without the will to system.

Broadly speaking, we can say that the weak thinking is composed of two steps. The first was expounded above and can be synthesized in this way: 'If I profess my system of values – religious, ethical, politics, ethnic – in our world of plural cultures, I have to have also a clear consciousness of the historicity, contingency and limitation of all these systems, beginning with my own' (Vattimo 1992: 43). Vattimo shows how limited, precarious, contingent and determinate are all philosophical projects. At this point, we can ask: what remains? What remains is the multiple character of the play of interpretations, resulting in hermeneutical nihilism. However, it should be stressed, such a nihilism is not the same as atheism, according to Vattimo. 'Wherever there is an absolute, even if it is the sheer affirmation of the nonexistence of god, metaphysics is always present in the form of the supreme principle' (Vattimo 2002: 3).

The difference between the thinking of Vattimo and other postmodern philosophers is his hermeneutical emphasis. For example, he affirms that 'probably there is no aspect of the so-called postmodern world not marked by the spread of interpretation' (Vattimo 2001: 26). He thinks that hermeneutics has a certain nihilist vocation, resulting in the frustration of establishing any ultimate foundation. His criticism of the foundation arises from his hermeneutics and ends up in no foundation at all. His nihilism is a play of interpretations, that is, a hermeneutical nihilism. Our task consists in stressing the difference, that is, the plural character of all narratives. Criticism does not come from the unmasking of ideologies. If that were so, we would be building new ideologies and foundations. Criticism starts from the explication of pluralism. Let us turn to an example.

Ideology, according to Marx, is the necessary representation that each social class produces about itself. The resulting image does not always coincide with reality. From that premise ideology would function in the masking of social relations, building a distorted and inverted vision of reality. Even Marx, in the second phase of his writings, could consider ideology to be pure illusion and fantasy, as opposed to his early criticism that limited it to the inversion of reality. This inversion (or false impression of reality) created by the ideology, resulting in the alienated knowledge of reality, happens in two stages: (1) the domination of one social class over others, and (2) class struggle.

In Marxism, the form of overcoming ideology creates in the end another ideological form considered to be the true description of reality. This is evident when Marx refused the term 'Marxism' because it would mean the transformation of his ideas into another ideology. But this is precisely what would happen later on when Lenin described Marxism as 'the ideology of the proletariat'. Theology of Liberation tried to follow these steps. In many cases, especially in relation to sexuality, it became oppressive. In the first decades, theologians of liberation did not consider the theme. Their concept of the poorman as an integral person was confined to his sociopolitical situation. The sexuality of the poor was subtlety sublimated. Very few liberation thinkers in Latin America paid any attention to the relationship between sexuality and Theology of Liberation.[9] What is to be done in face of the many difficulties for unmasking the gaps left by ideology? In his book *The Transparent Society*, Vattimo risks some possible trails:

> If we cannot anymore deceive ourselves about the possibility of revealing the lies of the ideologies and reach an ultimate and firm foundation, we can, however, show the plural character of all 'narratives' in order to make them function as a liberative element in face of the monologist narratives.
>
> (Vattimo 1992: 33)

The term 'inclusiveness' finds here its major problem: it presupposes monologist narratives. To include and to exclude presuppose, as we have already seen, a centre engaged in determining who or what is included or excluded. Differences have to be overcome and taken into a phallic-centred identity. Multiplicity is, then, reduced (again) to the One, which is the Christian mirror of God. Is this God, the beginning and end of history, the only macho for whom there is no place in multiple narratives? Every narrative of difference must necessarily converge towards the only narrative of the One.[10]

Similar, in a way, to Vattimo's thinking is the contribution of Deleuze. This French philosopher defines the contemporary thinking as *Rhizom*. This is a kind of root in which the old parts are replaced by new ones in such a way that the whole plant is changed and renewed. According to Manfredo de Oliveira:

> Rhizom is always a net in which each point is bound to the other: it is a non-centralized system, or multiplicity, non-hierarchical and non-significant, without organized memory, defined only and exclusively through the articulation of different situations. Against the traditional concept of system, all differences keep their autonomy; they are not overcame through a common ground nor eliminated through an homogenous configuration, though there are still many parallel developments, remaining all the time deeply different among them.
>
> (Oliveira 2003: 51)

These differences, however, maintain relationships and links without any unifying purpose. On the contrary, these links promote a much higher level of complex relations. This ontology is against the homogenizing principle of Hegel. It does not seek the unification of differences around an organizing centre. Relationships result in encounters without previous orientations. *Arché* and *telos* are only traces, vestiges, footprints. The affirmation of absolute plurality is therefore impossible, for the only things given to thinking are differences and links. Thinking is a passage and the difference appears through crossings and crossroads.

(In)conclusion

If origin comes to us as vestige (trace or footprint), the will to system becomes impaired. Relations happen through encounters and passages without any organizing centre. Besides that, relations are complex and plural against the limits of inclusion and exclusion. Each one of us is included in some particular context or group and equally excluded from others. This results from the plurality of relations and interests alongside existence. We are never identical with ourselves as it was believed by the system based on absolute identity. We are, as in the gospel passage, possessed by a thousand demons, with many diverse faces and 'identities' which do not need to be synthesized. These identities are determinate by encounters and situations and do not need to remain the same forever. This critique is specially important for sexual difference when we remember that the centre of inclusion is always a God identical to Himself, One and phallocentric. Before this God the transgressor has to be absolved from his/her 'sin' and become one with him, losing his/her difference. In the case of Latin America, where sexual differences are suppressed in the name of a hierarchic and a phallocentric society, the mirror of a Christian God, the affirmation of difference as difference, is especially important. In this respect, Theology of Liberation has an important task and must be critical of words which come from the metaphysical tradition that always has absolute identity as its basis. According to Lévinas, love 'is a relation with that which always escapes from us' (Levinas 1969: 67). Love, therefore, preserves the other in his/her singularity, always avoiding any attempt to include him/her in a system. Love means to let the other be the other, commemorating together the revelation of differences. However, as Heidegger reminds us, revelation implies concealment. The being never reveals itself entirely. So, commemorating the revelation of the other (different) is also to respect what is not accessible and remains hidden, as a fascinating mystery.

Notes

1 Chapter 7.
2 African-Brazilian religion brought by slaves in the sixteenth century. It is characterized by a syncretistic religiosity mixing Catholic and African elements.

3   I am not defending the idea that in order to be Latin American we should be free from any external influence. For Schwarz the problem with Brazilian intellectuals consists in trying to found their national identity on the elimination of everything not native. For him, what remains from this subtracting operation would be the authentic substance of the country. According to some authors (especially at the beginning of the twentieth century) the major Brazilian problem was the copy. It was impossible to create anything new in Brazil. I am not defending this thesis. I only want to show some existing limits for understanding our Latin American reality. Cf. Schwarz, Roberto, 'Nacional por subtração', in Roberto Schwarz, *Que horas são? Ensaios*, São Paulo: Cia. das Letras, pp. 29–48.

4   The German term employed by Hegel is *aufeheben*. In German it has the meaning of preserving and also of destroying. The best translation seems to be 'overcoming', though some authors use the concept of suppressing. The original meaning indicates that the initial stages of a natural developing process are taken up in the higher stages. So, for instance, the ancient philosophies are both overcome and at the same time preserved in the new philosophy of Hegel. According to the *Hegel Dictionary*, 'this is a movement from below to above and never, for instance, from an animal to a corpse; Hegel perceives a deep connection between the development of concepts and the development of things: this is essential for his Idealism' (Michael Inwood, *Hegel Dictionary*. Oxford, Blackwell, 1992).

5   In Portuguese it is possible to play with this word and to write the two meanings of *absolutus* in one word: 'Absol(r)ver'.

6   The term 'foundation' is a translation of *Grund* used by Heidegger and other philosophers. In English it can also be 'ground'. This term appears, for instance, in Paul Tillich when he calls God 'the ground of being'.

7   Frequently in Hegel's thought Absolute Spirit and God seem to be the same. In *Lectures on Philosophy of Religion,* Hegel analyses the concept of religion and affirms, 'Our starting point (namely, that which we generally call "God", or God in an indeterminate sense, as the truth of all things) is the result of the whole of philosophy'; '... God is substance is part of the presupposition we have made that God is Spirit, absolute spirit, eternally simple spirit, being essentially present to itself'. (Hegel, G.W.F. *Lectures on Philosophy of Religion.* pp. 367, 370).

8   'If in the *Phenomenology of the Spirit* each moment is the difference between knowledge and truth, and (is) the movement in which that difference is taken up'; Hegel still affirms: 'on the other side, science does not contain this difference and this overcoming; but as far as the moment has the form of a concept, it unites in its immediate unity the objective form of truth and (the form) of the self who knows.'

9   There is no doubt that Jaci Maraschin is one of the pioneers and important contributors to Theology of Liberation in this respect, establishing a close relationship between the body and liberation. In the 1980s, at a time when theologians of liberation paid no attention to this subject, Maraschin made key contributions in this area.

10 After the crisis in Marxist theory, many theologians of liberation have been trying to find another way of reflection that does not depend so much on Marxist philosophy of history. In Marxism, due to its derivation from Hegelianism, there is an idea of a unique sense to history. Recently some theologians in Latin America have been using Michel de Certeau on daily life theory and how people create multiple ways of resisting. This approach is only possible after the end of

metanarratives (announced by Lyotard). The history of daily life fights against dominant ideologies and normative discourses from the past and tries to open new ways of approaching to experiences lived in a short time. In this context there have developed many research topics seeking to articulate body, sexuality and Pentecostal movement in Latin America, especially concerned with the situation of women. As yet queer theory has not made a significant impact on the production of theology in Latin America.

References

Chatêlet, F. (1994) *Uma história da Razão*, translated by Lucy Magalhães. Rio de Janeiro, Jorge Zahar.

Derrida, J. (1995) *A Escritura e a Diferença*, translated by Maria Beatriz Nizza da Silva, 2nd edn. São Paulo: Perspectiva.

Foucault, M. (1980) *Power-Knowledge: Selected Interviews and other Writings, 1972– 1977*. New York: Knopf Publishing Group.

Hegel, G. W. F. (1952) *Phänomenologie des Geistes*, 4th edn. Hamburg: Verlag.

Hegel, G. W. F. (1981) *Reason in History: A General Introduction to the Philosophy of History*. New York: Liberal Arts Press.

Hegel, G. W. F. (1995) *Hegel Lectures on the Philosophy of Religion*, Vol. I, edited by Peter Hodgson. Berkeley: University of California Press.

Heidegger, M. (1977) 'The Word of Nietzsche: God is Dead', in *The Question Concerning Technology and Other Essays*. New York: Harper Trade.

Lévinas, E. (1969) *Totality and Infinity*, translated by A. Lingis. Pittsburgh: Duquesne University Press.

Oliveira, M. Araújo (2003) 'Pós-Modernidade: Abordagem Filosófica', in José e Gonçalves Transferetti, and Paulo Sérgio, *Teologia na Pós-Modernidade*. São Paulo: Paulinas.

Oliveira, M. Araújo (2001) *A Filosofia na Crise da Modernidade*. São Paulo: Loyola.

Pecoraro, Rosário Rossano (2002) 'Niilismo, Metafísica, dDsconstrução', in Paulo César Duque-Estrada (ed.) *Às Margens – A propósito de Jacques Derrida*. Rio de Janeiro: Editora PUC, pp. 49–72.

Schwarz, Roberto (1999) 'Nacional por Subtração', in Roberto Schwarz, *Que horas são? Ensaios*. São Paulo: Cia. das Letras, pp. 29–48.

Taylor, Mark (1992) *Erring. A Postmodern A/Theology*. Chicago: The University of Chicago Press.

Vattimo, G. (1992) *A Sociedade Transparente*, translated by Hossein Shooja e Isabel Santos. Lisbon: Relógio D'água.

Vattimo, G. (1998) *Acreditar em Acreditar*, translated by Elsa Castro Neves. Lisbon: Relógio D'água.

Vattimo, G. (2001) *A Tentação do Realismo*, translated by Reginaldo di Piero. São Paulo: Instituto Italiano di Cultura.

Vattimo, G. (2002) *After Christianity*, translated by Luca D'Isanto. New York: Columbia University Press.

Vattimo, G. and Rovatti, P. (eds) (1983) *Il Pensiero Debole*. Milan: Feltrinelli.

Wrathall, Mark (ed.) (2003) *Religion after Metaphysics*. Cambridge: Cambridge University Press.

Chapter 8

Liberating Mary, Liberating the Poor

Mario Ribas

The intention of this chapter is to explore how Christian iconography reflects a heterosexual paradigm of dogma, thereby becoming a source of control upon the Latin American masses that make use of iconography in popular religiosity. Popular religiosity in Latin America is, to a large extent, expressed through *Mariología* (Mariology). This *Mariología*, paradoxically, is either expressed in ways that are sanctioned by the Church, or in ways that bring together elements that are alien to the Christian tradition. Icons and portraits of Mary are fundamental for Marian devotion, but the main question we should address is how they relate to the struggle of women, sex workers or single mothers, to name a few of the categories of marginalization amongst women, and how a sexual Liberation Theology should consider these Mariological representations in its reflections.

Iconographic art has for a very long time been part of Christian tradition and central in popular religious expressions mainly in Roman Catholicism, the Orthodox Church and also in Anglicanism. The famous paintings in the Sistine Chapel by Michelangelo, the icons of *Christo Pantocrator*, or the Madonna and the Child are good examples to be mentioned, but there are several others that were inspired by artists throughout the ages. There are also statues which are not viewed simply from an artistic or aesthetic perspective, but fundamentally as objects of veneration by massive crowds of devotees who gather around those representations to express their spirituality and beliefs. On the other hand, the way popular religiosity is expressed is not always sanctioned by the clergy in terms of imagery. Models can be established and imposed by them as a way to exercise social and religious control upon the masses.

In popular religiosity Mary's representations are the most venerated. Mary's central role in popular expression is affirmed by the large crowds of pilgrims that visit her sanctuaries every year in Fatima, Lourdes, Walsingham, Aparecida and other locations around the world. The sanctuary in the City of Aparecida in Brazil, for example, is taken over by hundreds of thousands of pilgrims that gather especially on the festival day, the 12 October, to venerate the virgin or beg her for a blessing. *Nossa Senhora de Aparecida* (Our Lady of Apparition) is one of the black versions of Mary in Latin America. This statue was originally discovered by fishermen in a river, and became the patron saint of Brazil. Many pilgrims travel more than one thousand miles by bus or car. And each goes either to thank the virgin for a blessing already received, or to ask her for a healing, a job, or the solution to any problem the devotee may have. It is common to find in the sanctuaries in Latin America photos, wheelchairs, or anything that relates to an illness that has been healed, placed there by those who attribute the miracles to the Virgin.[1] In a context of poverty and oppression, the Virgin represents the last hope for many people.

Religious portraits and icons are to be found on the hands of ordinary people who find in them inspiration and a source of hope to cope with the hardship of life, and cope also with the fear of death. They are intended to symbolize faith, but as religious objects they can be sacralized in every sense and used as amulets for protection against all sorts of evil. But what icons and portraits of Mary and Jesus can address us in relation to our bodies and sexuality? What could they say to us in terms of the social and ecclesiastical interests controlling our bodies and sexuality? If icons and portraits are representations of a system of belief, they could have implications regarding bodies, sexuality and society. The Church as well as society can profit from them as instruments that can exercise control on the poor through their own popular expression of religiosity.

Liberation Theology, generally speaking, did not pay much attention to popular religion in terms of its more mystical aspects. Rather, it tried only to rationalize the struggle and liberation of the poor, as though liberation would happen through a sometimes rhetorical process. This would be in the fashion of European academia, rather than in the way many Latin Americans have their system of beliefs constructed and expressed, that is the veneration of the Virgin and other saints. Therefore popular religion that articulates itself through veneration of the Virgin and other saints would be forgotten, especially the visual representations that maintain a system of beliefs and institutions unchanged, unless these representations are also the focus of liberation.

Icons and portraits of saints are for most of the population a source of inspiration and hope. Religious dogmatics can be a field dominated, if not monopolized, by theologians and professionals of religion. Ordinary people would mostly express their faith through symbolisms, such as veneration of saints through imagery and pilgrimages to their sanctuaries. However the standard applied to each image embodies the results of that belief system, established by the Church and society and in the end consumed by ordinary men and woman who need objects to give meaning to their spiritual journey. And their purpose is to be an instrument of control, which maintains the power structure unaffected. Gerd Lüdemann argues that the representations of the Virgin, which were brought by the European conquerors and applied as an instrument for the maintenance of the power structure, were not transformed by Liberation Theologians, since in 'its roots this theology has not revises its theological claim for power' (Lüdemann 1998: 143). Mary, therefore, has been used for the same purpose as in the time of conquistadors, that is, to oppress and later to maintain the status quo. Many Christians and theologians, as well as social movements, in Latin America might enthusiastically 'defend and apply Liberation Theology' (Mott 1999: 37) in their projects of liberation, but they would still treat those who do not conform to the hetero-patriarchal structures of Christianity as if we still lived under the whips and fires of the holy inquisition. In this way, liberationists may have made a great contribution to academic reflection, but in terms of concrete liberation for the poor they have failed. Basically, they forgot that the poor are illiterate, and as such they would be more likely to find the use of popular religious symbols more attractive and meaningful to represent their struggle for liberation than words. On the other hand, the same icons that symbolize the faith of the poor can be perceived as instruments of alienation. This should be a good starting point at which to mount a Liberation Theological challenge at all its levels.

There is the need to re-evaluate this structure of power in terms of seeking the liberation of those who prefer the way of non-assimilating themselves into the 'hetero-normality'. The way to do this is to take seriously theological questions previously suppressed concerning who are *indecent* people and how authentic are they and how relevant are they when we seek ways to liberate them from economic and social exclusion. And in this way it should also be possible to take into account the ways in which they express their religiosity and how this religiosity is still controlled through portraits that support a system of belief that is still responsible for their exclusion and oppression.

A Liberation Theology for all the people should not ignore their faith and devotion as expressed in daily life. Brazilian spirituality is rich in symbolism that gives meaning to the religiosity of ordinary people. A Liberation Theology, in this case as a theology from the margins, should start from popular religion and its expressions rather than from the rhetorical arguments that apply mostly to academia and the clergy rather than to the illiterate masses. But apart from these expressions, it should also attend to its economic and social implication, especially regarding the place of the body and sexuality. The questions that arise from the current iconography and portraits of Mary are those related to the repression and stigmatization faced by sex workers, single mothers, gays and lesbians, transsexuals, the sexually impotent, or anyone else who does not fit into the heterosexual model and paradigm.

We should explore how the model offered by the current iconography of Mary and Jesus – and we could add the names of other saints – helps to maintain the present structure of power. We can talk about queer reality, taking into account how Christian iconography can also be a source of oppression, or used to maintain hetero-patriarchal control over those who do not fit into this category.

Body and sexuality are also elements that cannot be denied in Latin American reality, since we live in a culture famous for its 'sensual approach' to life, where male and female bodies are, without shame, visible on the beaches, and dance in sensual ways, most of them half-naked, during the carnival processions. These elements cannot be denied, especially in view of the great numbers of European tourists that pour into Brazil every year in search of a Latino sexual experience with one of the *mulatas* (girls of mixed race) in Rio de Janeiro or Salvador. Sexuality and economy, in this case, are intrinsically linked, but often this is at the same time a source and result of social and economic exclusion for those who are the subjects of the pleasure-seekers. This is also intrinsically linked to our cultural formation, the way we see ourselves, where our embodied state is a case of great concern and denial through the religious representation of the Virgin.

On the other hand, in Latin America the iconography of saints is not confined to churches or religious environments. Such icons are often found in public places, schools, government offices, courts of justice and homes. They can also be found in bars, cabarets and brothels as well as in garages, displayed alongside pictures of naked women. The icons, therefore, in popular religion are part of daily life, mixed with the profanity of every aspect of human life. There is also the syncretism of Latin American popular religiosity as the icons of the saints are often placed alongside Afro-Brazilian representations of spiritual entities. Sacred and profane are mixed up in popular expressions: the statue of the Virgin Mary or a crucifix can be placed on the wall above the same bed where sexual activities take place. But the statue of the Virgin can also be there as a reminder of the pure example of ideal womanhood.

Placing icons of Mary in brothels is the way in which prostitutes tend to symbolize their re-claiming of their faith in God and in Mary. It is at the same time a way to undermine the current theological assumption that procreation is the only purpose of sex, rather than pleasure, or the result of economic exclusion. In this way, placing an icon of the Virgin in a brothel illustrates to some extent a theological contrast, as was pointed out by Ruth Adams, in her essay 'Idol Curiosity – Andy Warhol and the Art of Secular Iconography' (Adams 2004: 92). She presents Marilyn Monroe as an antithesis of Mary. Mary in this case represents the one who reproduces without sex, while Monroe is the one who has sex without reproducing. The same antithesis applies to prostitutes, who find in their job a way to survive. In their case, they cannot procreate, although some of them do, accidentally. So it is that the situation of the children of a prostitute can be even worse, as shown in the popular expression *filho da puta* (son of a whore). Such an expression, often used in moments of anger, is applied to anyone who has been a source of annoyance: it symbolizes one of the lowest categories of people within society. On the other hand, Jesus himself might have been called *filho da puta*, either by his contemporaries, or even perhaps unconsciously by the current theological tradition that denies to Joseph the biological fatherhood of Jesus and by the current iconography that routinely portrays Mary alone with a child in her arms.

In my five years as a parish priest in Brazil, many women looked to our church to baptize their children, as they could not have them baptized in the Roman Catholic Church due to the fact that they were born out of the wedlock. Ninety per cent of baptisms I performed were for single mothers who were made pregnant by their boyfriends. More than half of these women had to bring up the children on their own since the boyfriends would not take co-responsibility for their actions. If we consider Mary's pregnancy to be not as the result of a sexual encounter between herself and Joseph, then in this case her story forms a parallel to the reality of other single mothers: she faced rejection in the town of Bethlehem, since accommodation had been denied to her and consequently she had to give birth in a manger, amongst the animals. In this way we can argue that if the rejection was a result of prejudices towards single mothers, they have no place in the church; they need to go to the manger. However, in the end her image is used in a different direction, to point out the mistakes single mothers have made and reinforce condemnation upon them. The way she is portrayed is as if she had never had sexual intercourse, or faced the hardship of having a child outside of wedlock. In her portraits, single mothers find further reason for their alienation, rather than identification with their own reality and healing for the traumas caused in bearing a child without being married. This can all be found in the veneration of Mary and in the machismo way of exploring the veneration of the Virgin. In her representation is found the symbolism for the ideal woman that unites both aspects of virginity and maternity (Urán 1983: 55). This symbolism divides women into those who are confined to the home, silent and submissive, and those who must live on the streets. The latter do not fit into the social and economic framework imposed by a patriarchal culture and legitimized by the religious representations of Mary.

There is another example that could be mentioned, the case of a young man whom we can call Andre. Andre started his pastoral counselling with me to try to fix his own sexual orientation, which was unacceptable to him. His own priest, not knowing how to deal with the situation, would encourage him to go and pray to the Virgin. He said that every time he had a sexual encounter with another man, he would then go and pray to the Virgin and ask her forgiveness. I asked him why he would pray to the Virgin. His reply was that it was because she actually represents one of the highest virtues he did not have, that is, being able to control his desires for sexual intercourse. He expressed also his feelings of unworthiness to approach God directly in his prayers; therefore the Virgin would be the one who was able to understand him and approach God on his behalf. This case not only illustrates the way the Virgin is held up as an example over and against those who want to express their sexual desires, but also the way the Latino male's relation to Mary is culturally constructed by his inability to cut the umbilical cord that keeps him united to his mother. In the case of Latino women, whose piety focuses on their veneration of the Virgin, it might be thought that this represented a matriarchal rather than a patriarchal culture. However, the matriarchal aspect in this context functions only to legitimize and strengthen the patriarchal foundations on which our society is built.

Mary has been the most venerated saint in popular religiosity, and in the Christian tradition she has been seen as a possible intermediary of masculine sovereignty (Ruether 1993: 119), but she is still the one who helps to maintain male control, which in this case is represented in a religious discourse. In order to perform this function, it has been necessary to deny her body and her sexuality. This is true also of very religious women in Latin America. They are the ones who see themselves as the guardians of the hetero-patriarchal structure, adopting the Church's moral standards and reinforcing them through the piety of discourse and actions. In this, they create a sort of matriarchal culture, which does not exists as an end in itself, but as only as intermediation to preserve the hetero-patriarchal structure. The consequence of this system is that women who do not conform to this pattern are subjects of stigmatization by other women as well as by men. Ivone Gebara point out that:

> Prostitutes, single mothers, black and indigenous women, and lesbians, were not and are not considered as examples to be followed. This discrimination was not practiced by men alone, but also by women. Through the education received, mothers of families reproduced behaviour that reinforced their superiority before the others. In the end it is not enough to be a mother to be socially accepted, it is necessary to be a mother according to the rules established by those who retain the power.
>
> (Gebara 2000: 150)

The role played by many of the Latino women, by their acceptance of current patriarchal structures, may constitute the key element in the endurance of patriarchalism in Latin America. On other hand, they were not responsible for the creation of this structure: as noted earlier their role has been as intermediaries rather than principal actors in this scenario. As intermediaries they have acted in such a way as to maintain the binary structure of powerful and powerless, oppressor and oppressed, decent and indecent, straight and queer. Women can act as intermediaries in this process, but they themselves are victims too, since in the end while assimilating themselves into this structure they have to asexualize themselves to conform to the established parameters. The image of Mary is fundamental to this process of asexualization, as her icons are imposed as mirrors to reflect the imagery of the perfect and decent woman. The icons and portraits of Mary always represent her as a young woman, overdressed and for the most part entirely naïve. The outcome is the image of an asexualized woman whose body is hidden by layers of theological concepts which impose virginity upon her and deny her as sexual being. This in turn governs the approach of the male Latino to Mary and the way they see their mothers and wives. Mothers are not seen as sexual beings, but nor are the women who become their wives and the mothers of their children. Women, after they are married, unconsciously cease to exist as women, but are asexualized in order to fulfil the roles of wife and mother. The terms 'woman' and 'wife' are then not so much synonyms as antonyms, expressing different realities within the subconscious in our culture. In this popular mentality it is not surprising to see how the male is proud of being sexually involved with another woman, other than his wife, while society at large praises him for such behaviour. By comparison, the woman who becomes involved in a sexual relationship with another man who is not her husband must hide herself away. She knows that she will be condemned: to this popular mentality the sin of the wife who betrays her husband is much more serious than the adultery of the man. After a woman becomes a wife she must desexualize herself. By the same token the husband will not see his wife as a woman who can fulfil his sexual fantasies. That would be indecent: the mother of his children is viewed and judged according to the idealized type of woman. Once again, we see the role played by Virgin in this process of imposing religious and social models upon women. In this respect, Lüdemann says:

> Mary, as a humble virgin chosen by God, serves to prompt women to desexualise their bodies and to be humble. At all events the plaster figure in the grotto of Lourdes virtually invites this interpretation. There one sees a Mary with downcast eyes and a body veiled to the point of being unrecognisable. However, for reasons of depth psychology men too find pleasure in such a de-sexualized pure saint. But male fantasies, which style Mary a pure virgin in order to master sexual problems, are unable to sublimate sexual drives in the long run. These drives discharge themselves by refunctionalizing, if not Mary herself, at least other women, as whores. Women are women and not whores or madonnas.

Virginity becomes not only an ideal to be followed by other women, it becomes an intrinsic part of male fantasies: the fantasy for a woman who has never been to bed with another man, the desire to be the first one to have her. This is connected to the mentality of wife-property which is prevalent in many parts of the country. The result is that women who have been abandoned by their boyfriends or husbands, with children to bring up, are for the most part condemned to live on their own. Most men would not want to be involved with someone who already 'belonged' to somebody else and bears the result of that relationship. The parameters set here are still on the binary scale of the decent and indecent woman; on the one side, those who conform to the institutional norms of control, on the other side the whores. Whores in this case are not only the ones who make their living out of prostitution, but also the ones who either choose or are forced to abandon the model established through the representations of the Virgin.

Mary's representations in religious art and in popular consciousness simply reproduce the model of repression and alienation that is intrinsically found in the current established paradigms of dogmatic theology. A theological construction that brings justice to the reality of the poor and indecent people can therefore begin through liberating Mary: the starting point can be Mary's vagina and breasts, or the lack of these elements in cultural and religious images. Yes, those are private aspects of Mary's life, aspects normally ignored since she has not been considered sufficiently human to be associated with our desires, passions and our fears of loneliness. Undressing Mary can be a way to overcome the shame of our bodies, which the narratives of Adam and Eve in Genesis express so well. In the narrative of Genesis the awareness of nakedness came through knowledge of good and evil. This narrative functions also as an analogy for the reality of indigenous people in Latin America. When the conquerors arrived, indigenous people would be unaware of their state of nakedness, but all that would change as soon as the gospel was preached to them and they were made to relate their bodies to shame and hide them with clothes. The worship of the overdressed Virgin was established as a reminder of the way of decency and a symbol of a theology of shamefulness. The irony is that later Brazilian people would adopt the indigenous way of life insofar as they appeared half-naked in public on beaches and at carnivals. The mixture of races in Latin America has resulted in a very sensual culture where people are deeply aware of their bodies and are not ashamed of baring their chests and legs during the summer, especially on the beaches. The Brazilian beaches could be very good sites at which to re-create a theology of the body, a theology that liberates the body from all the denial of sensuality that has been imposed through the veneration of the Virgin.

No doubt such a theological development would be met with resistance from the Church. Since popular religiosity is in constant conflict with the institutional forms, there are attempts to control the veneration of the Virgin in its public manifestations. At the carnival, for example, which is a time when crowds become ecstatic as they make their way through the streets, measures have been taken to exclude expressions of popular spirituality. During the carnival the crowd, of mostly half-naked bodies, dance in sensual ways, to songs and themes describing myths that are part of the popular consciousness, myths that reproduce historical facts in their allegories. It is a time of sensuality and the body is an integral part of the procession. It has thus become a source of conflict with the Church, especially when attempts are made to include representations of the Virgin in the allegories. The archdiocese of Rio has, on several occasions, taken the samba schools to court, to prevent them taking religious icons into the streets. It forgets that spirituality and sensuality cannot be entirely separated in Brazilian culture. But in any case, the Virgin is denied to the *carnavalescos* (carnival people) since there is a contradiction between what is represented by the icon and what is represented in the carnival feasts. The processions of carnival are like parades of liberation from all oppressions for the body. It is a time when gender dualism is overcome by straight men, who dress up either as women, or at least in a very feminine way with lots of make-up and feathers. It is a time when it is permissible, especially for men, to ignore the structure of power and all the requirements expected for the maintenance of this structure, to dress up and express themselves without being called *viados* (fags). Women, on the other hand, may not dress up as men for carnival, but they are allowed to be topless and half-naked. To be topless in such an event is liberating, since on the beaches women are not allowed to show their breasts, while men are always bare chested. As the Virgin is denied to the *carnavalescos*, they would in the end recover Iemanja or other African entities to replace Mary in the carnival. The African slaves were forced to replace their representations of entities by the Christian saints. Ieamanja was replaced by the worship of the Virgin. But with the religious freedom we are envisaging, Iemanja might now go back to the streets and be the mother of *carnavalescos*.

Icons of Mary always show a woman looking down as a sign of humbleness, holding the baby Jesus in her arms and, as we mentioned before, this icon can be found in such places as garages, displayed alongside the mechanics' pictures of naked women. This juxtapositioning of images constitutes a dynamic contradiction from a theological point of view, but it can be understood through the way heterosexual paradigms structure our society. The picture of the naked woman is the icon of indecency, what Ivone Gebara describes as the icon of woman ' "of the public world" that for diverse reasons and ways entered the world of men' (Gebara 2000: 151), but which is still subjected to them as pleasure giver, and fulfils male sexual fantasies. On the other hand, the Virgin represents the ideal type of women, those who reproduce according to the established rules, asexualizing themselves in order to fulfil the economic and social interests of men. The current theological tradition denies womanhood to Mary and consequently to other women. In the end, indecent and decent ones are still alienated, either as objects of desire or as subject to the *machista* control, the first being alienated socially and economically and the second sexually. Undressing Mary in this case does not necessarily mean producing her as an object of sexual desires, but rather bringing back awareness of the body and sexuality as a way to liberate those who have found themselves alienated and oppressed by the current social and economic structures which are legitimized by the religious discourse and symbols. Showing Mary's vagina can be a way to make us aware that the salvation came into the world through female intimate parts, unless we want to believe it happened through a Caesarean.

Mary's vagina has been dislocated by the current theological establishment from between her legs up to between her ears, as we believe that the pregnancy was the result of the words of the Holy Spirit. So a simple thought of Mary's menstruation, or even the dilation of her vagina by the introduction of a penis or during labour, is entirely dismissed by current theology. Mary is forced into the closet, where her sexuality is entirely hidden. She becomes a co-adjutant only, in the process of bringing Christ into the world, since her sexuality plays no role in the incarnation. In this, instead of becoming a source of liberation, she becomes a source of repression, where all must repress their sexual orientation and/or condition and submit to the current hierarchical establishment. The result of this system of beliefs is intrinsically represented through the icons and portraits of a desexualized Mother of God, castrated from her sexuality and consequently from her humanity. Her icons are imposed in this format in order to maintain the dichotomy of life, where sexuality and body are always in contradiction to the spiritual life.

In parallel to Mary, in images of Jesus his penis is always hidden by a white cloth. Although the current iconography allows male saints, including Jesus, to be portrayed with bared chests and legs, the same is not permissible for female saints. But in spite of their bared chests and legs, there is always a white cloth placed over their genitals. In the Gospel of John, we find the narrative of the Word becoming flesh and dwelling amongst us. The Word became flesh, but how could this happen if Mary's vagina was left untouched? What kind of flesh could be conceived by words penetrating a woman's ears? Why did it not happen through a sexual encounter between Mary and Joseph? Would a sexual encounter have affected in some way God's purpose through Jesus Christ? Those are the kinds of questions that I have often heard from those who found themselves alienated due to either their sexual orientation or condition. The fear of sex and body amongst early Christian theologians stripped the *logos* of its flesh, penis, ejaculation and any feeling towards somebody else. The current theology denies the corporeity of Jesus, and in doing so denies the reality of the incarnation of the *logos* of God. He comes to us as one who is for all practical purposes asexualized (Musskopf 2002: 60).

One day, during a visit to London, I found a beautiful stone carving in the main porch of the Church of Saint Martin in the Fields, in the centre of the city. This carving was a representation of Jesus in the manger, but two details caught my attention: unlike most carvings of the baby Jesus I have seen, in this one his penis was uncovered: there was also the umbilical cord. That carved image led me to reflect again on the Gospel of Saint John, chapter 1, '. . . the Word became flesh and dwelt among us'. The Word overcame the dichotomy that fragments our lives and make us ashamed of our corporeal state. That carving represented God acquiring the fragility and beauty of a human body, including the fragility of all the desires and frustrations we face as sexual beings. However, throughout the centuries theologians have been responsible for stripping the Word of its corporeity, giving Jesus an androgynous or asexual appearance. Mary was also stripped of all female beauty and sensuality and given heavy clothing to wear at all times. In this way, she would serve as a role model for the hetero-patriarchal interests of domination.

But if we liberate Mary and Jesus and strip them of their clothing, perhaps we would be able to construct a theology that relates to the reality of poor and indecent people. To liberate Mary and Jesus, perhaps would be the way to create a theology that heals the trauma faced by those who experience rape, or those who are infertile, or those who suffer from any venereal disease or even those who are diagnosed with HIV/AIDS, but are ashamed to talk about their reality and suffering. To create a theology that is able to out Jesus and Mary could be the way to break the silence of the voiceless. To give a voice to those who have none would open up a path to take away the shame and fear of the parents who always face a huge barrier to talk openly to their children about sex, pregnancy and sexually transmitted diseases. Outing Mary would be make a major impact on Latin American people, who see in her a mother for all, one to whom people mostly pray and the one who is venerated in every sphere of life, especially by poor people and any one of those in the margins of society.

How about adding wrinkles to the face of Mary, in a new iconography that would relate her to the reality of poor or old women? Such an icon could portray her as overweight, or as a strong woman. Poor women in Latin America do not have plastic surgery or use cosmetic products to eliminate the signs of ageing or to satisfy the parameters of beauty set up by the television soap operas and advertising. Most women do not follow the fashion trends and feel therefore frustrated at not being able to conform to the imposed ideal of womanhood. We need a Mary reflecting real Latin American women, even physically, in terms of ageing processes and the ravages of time amongst the poor.

The body and sexuality are in this context intrinsically attached to economic exclusion. They suffer the consequences of a system that determines beauty and fashion standards and employs media icons to protect and advertise economic interests. For cosmetic products and fashions the icons are ideal types of women to best promote the brand, typically tall, young and white. Women who are short, fat or old are therefore excluded. The icons of the Virgin are, in this case, in accordance with the ideal woman projected in the media. Mary is always represented as a lady with a perfect complexion, young, slim and, normally, white. A theological construction can begin from aesthetic concepts of the body, but first we need to recover the appreciation of the body and sexuality in theology, to be able to address oppression from that perspective. A good way to begin this theological construction could be by painting a new picture of Mary that relates to the reality of poor as well as old women, instead of one that always has smooth skin and with lots of make-up, which does not incarnate the reality of those who cannot afford beauty treatments.

However, people might want to maintain Mary in the same way she is represented, as a denial of their own reality. They might not want a woman who is exactly like their own image, which expresses hardship of life and exclusion. But liberation, in the end, never happens if reality is denied. Liberation happens when we acknowledge our own state of oppression, even if it first comes with the recognition of our feelings of inadequacy. Then we go on to find what represents best our own reality, giving symbolic meaning to our struggles and hopes. Such hopes are not of accommodating ourselves to the parameters imposed through the image of Mary, but rather to be accepted and recognized inside our own reality.

In addition to the carving of the baby Jesus in the Church of St Martin in the Fields, I should also mention another statue I found in Rio de Janeiro. In a gay bar in Copacabana beach there is a statue of Marlene Dietrich dressed up as *Nossa Senhora de Aparecida*. For many, Marlene Dietrich is a symbol of liberation and subversion, for others she is a model of perfection, beauty and sensuality. The statue was not dressed in the style of Marlene Dietrich but in the overdressed style, with cope and crown, of the statue of the black Virgin Mary. The use of Marlene Dietrich in this icon also represents the desire for overcoming dualism. Dietrich herself is recognized as bisexual, one who would not conform herself to the imposed limits on gender expression. This statue is of a sensual and sexualized woman, not a naïve one; one who would dare to challenge the structures, since she would not live according to imposed requirements regarding sexual expression. This could be seen as an act of sanctifying Marlene Dietrich, but more importantly it is a way of liberating Mary so that she could be a free woman, aware of her body and desires.

A sexual Liberation Theology must take into account popular religiosity that is reproduced and controlled by the use of imageries. These are set in place to desexualize the body and at the same time function as tools for the maintenance of hetero-patriarchal economic and social interests. Iconographies and portraits that are established to represent a spiritual reality in fact promote male dominance. They are consumed in a large part unconsciously by the masses. As we saw previously, icons can still find a place in houses used by prostitutes. They can assist prostitutes in reclaiming their faith, but at the same time they express the contradictions between the popular and institutional religiosity. But the private expression of faith inside a house of prostitution cannot be controlled by the Church, in the way that it can be controlled in its public manifestation, for example in carnivals. In the end, popular religiosity plays an important part in Latin American culture and it can be manifested in different ways. A Theology of Liberation which takes into account the body and sexuality, along with other aspects of life, must pay attention to the expressions of Mariology and how it symbolizes not only faith, but also the heterosexual paradigm. A Liberation Theology that began with the struggle of the poor and oppressed – those who prefer the way of non-assimilation by the institution and its paradigms – should pay attention to popular religiosity and its symbolisms and begin the liberation process from there. And instead of adopting the iconoclast route, rationalizing the struggle of the poor and the liberation process, it could find ways to re-create icons and portraits that meet the reality of the oppressed. Such icons would give meaning to their struggle for liberation through the way of non-conformity, through awareness of the similar situation in which they find themselves. Icons can be effectively used to maintain the oppressed in silence and alienation: they could also be effective in focusing on liberation, symbolizing and bringing together faith and the struggle for liberation. It is important to take into account the questions which are disallowed, the questions of those who are 'indecent'[2] or do not assimilate themselves into hetero-normality. How do such indecent people relate to the symbolism set up to represent and maintain those paradigms unchanged and unchallenged? Liberating Mary could be a good starting point in the process of liberating the poor and indecent, and for this we should look unashamedly upon the breasts and vagina of the Virgin. It was by this passage that God chose to communicate Godself to the world and by these breasts that God's Word was nourished in his development. These features can also be objects of desire, but why should we deny the association of Mary with our desires, fantasies, sexuality and fear of loneliness? Consequently those considered to be indecent (or theologically transgressive) can find ways that symbolize their own reality and produce concrete tools for action towards their liberation.

Notes

1 Usually, these small tokens are made of tin and represent the body part which has been healed, for instance a hand, a leg or a heart. It is also common to find these tokens fixed to crosses.
2 The concept of 'indecency' comes from Marcella Althaus-Reid. See Althaus-Reid *Indecent Theology* (London: Routledge, 2001).

References

Adams, R. (2004) 'Idol Curiosity: Andy Warhol and the Art of Secular Iconography', *Theology and Sexuality*, Vol. 10.2, March 2004. London: Continuum.
Gebara, I. (2000) *Rompendo o Silencio – Uma Fenomenologia Feminista do Mal*. Petrópolis: Editora Vozes.
Lüdemann, G. (1998) *Virgin Birth? The Real Story of Mary and Her Son Jesus*. London: SCM Press.
Mott, L. (1999) 'A Igreja e a Questão Homossexual no Brasil' in NETMAL, *Religião e Homossexualidade*, Revista Mandrágora Ano 5, nr. 5. São Bernando do Campo: Universidade Metodista de São Paulo.
Musskopf, A. (2002) *Uma Brecha no Armário – Propostas para uma Teologia Gay*. São Leopoldo: Editora Sinodal.
Radford Ruether, R. (1993) *Sexismo e Religião*. São Leopoldo: Editora Sinodal.
Úran, A. M. Bidegain de (1983) 'Sexualidade, Vida Religiosa e Situação da Mulher na América Latina in CEHILA', *A Mulher Pobre na História da Igreja Latino Americana*. São Paulo: Edições Paulinas.

Chapter 9

Seriously Harmful For Your Health? Religion, Feminism and Sexuality in Latin America[1]

Elina Vuola

Let me start by sharing the story of a nine-year-old Nicaraguan girl, named 'Rosa' by the media, whose little body became a public battleground in Central America in 2002.[2] She was raped at the end of October 2002 in the countryside of the neighbouring Costa Rica, where her parents had arrived as illegal migrant workers a few years earlier. Rosa, eight years old when raped, not only contracted a venereal disease from her rapist but also became pregnant, apparently during the month that would have brought her first ever period. To make a long and appalling story short: when her parents found out about her pregnancy, they took her back to Nicaragua, where an abortion was performed on 20 February 2003. The Nicaraguan law still allows a 'therapeutic abortion' if the mother's life is in danger – a law that has been under much fire from opponents of abortion. Thus, the abortion was considered legal, and the doctors and parents are not facing criminal charges. However, the Catholic leadership of both Costa Rica and Nicaragua has publicly denounced the abortion as an 'elimination of an innocent and defenseless human being'.[3] This was considered by the Archbishop of Nicaragua, Monseñor Miguel Obando y Bravo, a homicide, which is why he excommunicated the girl's parents and the medical doctors involved. He saw himself, as does the entire institution he represents, as defending the rights of an unborn child, apparently never noting that the whole issue was about an already born child's right to life and integrity.

I myself am a mother of a girl of Rosa's age, but this is not why I start with this story. Nor do I make direct references to Rosa's case in this chapter. However, I will keep her in mind, because in all its repugnancy the case is a perfect example of what is at stake when we speak of the problematic role of religion, especially Catholicism, in relation to women, sexuality, reproduction and public policy in Latin America. Her story also was the springboard for some of my thoughts on the Virgin Mary and virginity.

The statistics concerning the reality of women in Latin America demonstrate the interconnection between poverty, the lack of reproductive choices and mortality. According to the World Health Organization, globally some 529,000 women died from pregnancy-related causes in 2000, 99 per cent of them in the so-called developing countries. Some 22,000 of these maternal deaths[4] occurred in Latin America and the Caribbean, with enormous disparities within the region and higher rates for indigenous groups.[5] Women in their prime reproductive period (20 to 35 years of age) number among these deaths. These women are more likely to have young dependent children, whose own survival and wellbeing is usually seriously compromised by the death of their mother, often the only or primary career.[6] This obviously reflects the fact that protecting the reproductive choices and the wellbeing of adult women is the best guarantee for defending children, unborn and born. According to the Pan-American Health Organization, relatively little progress has been made in recent years in the reduction of maternal mortality in Latin America, in comparison with reductions in mortality from other causes.[7]

About 78,000 women die globally every year from unsafe abortions.[8] According to the reports by the Alan Guttmacher Institute, each year, more than four million women in Latin America undergo an induced abortion. Because most abortions are illegal, these procedures are performed under clandestine and often dangerous conditions.[9] Abortion is one of the leading causes of death for Latin American women between 15 and 39 years of age.[10] Because of the illegality of abortion, the statistics are not reliable, the reality being probably much harsher than the statistical estimates. In spite of its illegality, abortion is available all over Latin America for women who live in cities and have the financial means to obtain a safe abortion. Abortions amongst poor rural women often happen under dangerously unsanitary conditions.

Nicaragua, the second poorest country in the Western hemisphere, because of its very poverty, has one of the highest rates of maternal mortality, and this has been ascending in the last ten years. Also (having little Rosa in mind) most of the incidences of sexual violence against women and girls in Nicaragua take place in the family: 65 per cent of the victims of this violence, including rapes, are girls – adolescents and younger; 30 per cent of all maternal mortality in the country is of adolescent girls; 26 per cent of abortions are practised on girls younger than 19 years.[11]

Much of my research work over the years has taken place in Nicaragua, but since my research interests – the interplay of religion and feminism, especially for women from the poorest sectors of society – are relevant all over Latin America, I will by and large be speaking on this more general level, problematic as it is. However, the predominant role of the Catholic Church is one of the reasons why we can make some generalizations about the region, the Church being the only important institution that has survived since the times of the Conquest, five hundred years ago. Also, in spite of losing its colonial power, the Catholic Church is far from being a marginal institution in Latin America. The power of the Catholic Church is related to traditional ways of interaction of Latin American elites.[12] In some countries, conservative Catholics and politically powerful elites are forming new alliances between the Church and the state in spite of the legal separation between the two.

In issues of sexuality, reproduction and the family, the Catholic hierarchy, and groups close to it, are launching campaigns against any political, social or legal changes that might question its teaching. Having lost much of its legitimacy and power in issues of sexual ethics in European Catholic countries (for example, Italy, the Vatican's front yard, has the lowest birth rate in the world), the Vatican has turned to Latin America as a region not yet lost to secularism. Similarly, in all Catholic countries, including those in Latin America, ordinary people do not necessarily follow the official teaching. One of the ways in which the Vatican has tried to compensate for this loss of influence over individuals is its ever-growing activity in secular circles – be it United Nations conferences, international finance institutions or national governments.

The Catholic Church in Latin America is the main social and political institution shaping population policies and values around family, sexuality and women: by and large its teaching is patriarchal and sexist. This in itself is hardly news. I will argue that a critical analysis of important changes in Latin American Catholicism, such as Liberation Theology, would help us to understand why issues of sexuality, sexual ethics, and reproduction have been so difficult to talk about in the context of organized religion. I also will argue that most 'secular' feminist movements and feminist scholarship have not been able to adequately tackle the sexism of the Catholic Church and especially its important role in creating a climate in which it is practically impossible to speak of women's reproductive realities in honest and open ways. This creates an often awkward situation in which a good part – if not the great majority – of Latin American women consider themselves Catholic (and if not Catholic, Christian) but cannot live according to the Church's teachings. They also have an understanding of feminism as something secular and anti-Church. I will take the devotion of the Virgin Mary as an example of this tension between 'secular' feminist critique and women's religious experiences. In feminist writings from inside and outside the region, *marianismo* is understood both as the explanation of women's subordinate status and as the legitimization of their sufferings. However, I claim that this is an inadequate way of understanding both women and religion.

Liberation Theology, the Catholic Church and Feminism

It is fairly common that a fundamentalist interpretation of women's rights is justified by cultural differences – a discussion that is too large and complicated to take up here. Briefly, human rights, especially women's rights, are in this so-called cultural relativist position seen as a form of Western imperialism, which pretends to legitimize the cultural superiority of the West. This discourse is especially true in some Muslim countries, but more and more one can hear these sorts of arguments being expressed in Latin American Catholic countries as well. Thus, it is not any longer about Christianity as the religion of the 'West' and Islam as the religion of the 'East', but also about the growing gap between the 'North' and the 'South'. The Church of the 'West', the Catholic Church, wants to be seen as defending and representing the 'South' in Latin America, emphasizing its cultural differences from the Church in Europe. The secularized North, with its moral decline and lack of values, is seen as controlling the South, where values concerning the family and the patriarchal social order are considered so central that without them the entire culture is in danger of collapse. This explains, at least partly, why feminism – both the one born in the industrialized countries and a more indigenous feminism – is experienced as such a threat, and even the principal sign of social degradation.[13]

This is also the context in which the activity and collaboration of certain Muslim governments and the Vatican becomes more understandable. Especially during the reign of the late Pope, John Paul II, the Vatican became a strange mixture of one of the most imperialist (Eurocentric, or rather 'Vati(can)centric') institutions in strictly Church-related issues in which, on the one hand, all the orders come from above, from Europe (for example, the nomination of conservative bishops against the preference of the local churches in Latin America; the silencing and expulsion of Liberation Theologians; a direct open political pressure on national governments, especially on issues of sexual ethics) and, on the other hand, of an institution which pretends to represent the weak, the poor, the South, in the larger society, both nationally and internationally. Obviously, the lacking bridge between these two faces of contemporary Catholicism would be seeing the poor also as reproductive, gendered and sexual beings. It is poverty and lack of power that makes sexual relations, reproduction and mothering deadly for so many women.

The phenomenon of an active US-style 'pro-life' coalition, with the Catholic Church in the lead, is a quite new phenomenon in Latin America, born – or rather imported – as a reaction to the growth of feminism in the region and worldwide. In Latin America, the situation is historically without antecedent. The popular church type of Catholicism, influenced by Liberation Theology and the ecclesial base communities of the 1960s to late 1980s, and today's very different kind of political and public role of the Catholic Church, are both new phenomena in the history of Catholicism in Latin America.

Liberation Theologians have until now been more or less unable to analyse critically the complex and often contradictory role of the Catholic Church, which partly explains why there is no alternative sexual ethics being developed in Latin America, even though it is the most Catholic region of the world and one where new, sometimes radical, reinterpretations of Christianity are being developed in other areas of ethics and theology.[14] If Liberation Theology would seriously tackle this double role of the Church, it would become clear how difficult it is to speak in an undifferentiated (and unsexualized) way of 'the poor'. The Latin American Catholic Church is, even formally as an institution, a critic of the effects of neoliberal economic policies on the poor and thus sides with Liberation Theology, but it is also one of the powerful institutions which stubbornly refuses to look at the statistics on maternal and infant mortality or to revise its teaching on sexuality, gender roles and reproduction. It would help Liberation Theologians to give the option for the poor new depth and meaning, if they would take seriously the feminist claim that there is no one 'essential' way of being a 'woman' or 'poor' or even 'Latin American'. It is not women *per se*, but poor women and often very young women, who die for reasons directly related to sexuality, reproduction and maternity, and women's lack of power to decide over these. If Liberation Theology takes this challenge, including a serious dialogue both with feminism and the Church hierarchy, it is not only being faithful to and deepening the epistemological and practical meaning of the option for the poor, but possibly will also offer an interesting example of a positive synergy between Liberation Theology and feminism in a Third World setting.

Taking up this challenge would also make it necessary for Liberation Theologians to look at their use of concepts such as life, defence of life, or Liberation Theology as a theology of life (*teología de la vida*). To defend the life of poor women means defending their right for reproductive choice derived from a sexual ethics rooted in the practical and concrete life conditions of these women. What we see, instead, is a discourse of life which excludes women, and even makes allusions to an absolutist Vatican type of sexual ethics.[15] As long as women are not seen as fully moral agents, who by and large are also in a privileged but silenced position to define what we mean when we speak of life, the defence of life, and the right to life, Liberation Theology will not be able to have a say in today's struggles to combat poverty and needless death in poor countries.

Liberation Theology has always been an ecumenical endeavour, even when the base communities were principally a Catholic phenomenon. Some of the so-called historical Protestant churches (mainly Lutheran, Baptist and Methodist, in Nicaragua also the Moravian), which arrived in Latin America mainly in the nineteenth and early twentieth centuries, played an important role in the development of Latin American Liberation Theology and actively participated in the political struggles against military dictatorships. Since the 1980s, the number of Protestant groups, especially Pentecostalism, has grown rapidly in the region: the estimates varying from 10 to 15 per cent of Latin Americans considering themselves *evangélicos*.[16] These newer churches often distance themselves not only from the Catholic Church but also from the more mainline historical Protestant churches, which is not without significance in issues of gender relationships and sexual ethics.[17]

With the birth of Liberation Theology and the popular church, and the visibility of such Latin American Catholic bishops as Monseñor Oscar

Romero of El Salvador and Dom Helder Camara of Brazil, it became impossible to speak of the Catholic Church as one monolithic hierarchical system. The changes and the inner divisions in the Latin American Catholic Church have been widely documented and need not be repeated here. However, in issues related to women, feminism, sexuality and reproduction, the Catholic Church was always much more unanimous and less divided.[18]

Liberation Theology has represented a new way of thinking, not only from the South as the geographical location of the so-called Third World, but from the South also as a space of resistance and suffering, of widespread poverty and huge class and income differences, and as a space colonized and marginalized first by Europe, then by the United States. Central in this Liberation Theological understanding of the impoverished South, and the poor as its *locus*, was an understanding of people as subjects, individually and collectively. Nevertheless, this great insight of Liberation Theology has fallen short or stayed mute when it comes to issues of racism and sexism. The voices of women, as well as those of indigenous and Afro-Latin American people, have too often been merely added to the endless list of the oppressed in need of liberation, without clearly analysing the roots of their specifically experienced oppression. In order for Liberation Theology to do this, it needs to break theologically with the model of the Church, which is patriarchal, Eurocentric, authoritarian and anti-sexual.

By and large, Liberation Theology has not been able to create alliances with new social movements, such as the feminist movement, the gay and lesbian movements the indigenous people's movements, the black movement and the ecological movement. At the level of the contemporary array of social movements in Latin America, issues considered 'feminist' are being addressed and reinterpreted in not only the narrowly understood feminist movement, but in any other movements in which an adequate analysis of the political sphere cannot afford excluding an analysis of gender dynamics, issues of sexuality and sexual identities, and the relationship of these to issues of power, authority, repression, and political change. The lack of interaction between Liberation Theology (including feminist Liberation Theology) and feminist movements in Latin America has led to an absence of concrete (political) demands in a theology which twenty years ago was seen as the vanguard of political struggle.

Feminism and Religion

Much of social scientific research on religion and women is guided by two opposite stereotypes. On the one hand, there is a kind of feminist 'blindness' of, or resistance to, the importance of religion for women, especially in its possible positive or liberatory aspects, even when women from different religious traditions claim this to be true for them. On the other hand, there is something that could be called a 'religious paradigm' type of feminist study in which women are seen mainly or only through the lens of religion, especially in research done by Western scholars on Muslim and Third World countries, or at least on a culture and tradition not one's own. For example, Islam may be seen as the almost sole signifier of women's lives in certain countries.[19] I do not think Catholicism is any less 'other' to most feminist research than Islam.

This way of seeing religion probably has several origins. One of the most important is a supposition that secularization is both a universal and unavoidable path of development, whereas in reality, the kind of secularization announced by much of social science has happened only in Western Europe.[20] Another reason is the recognition of the historical fact that different religious traditions and communities have been some of the main obstacles for women's liberation, and continue to be so in many ways. However, it is also true that many early feminists, for example, were motivated by their faith in a God who grants an absolute equality and freedom for human beings. Thus, we are dealing with the Janus-like face of religion, which makes it difficult to speak of religion in too oppositional terms: the one and the same religious tradition often offers tools, interpretations and motivation for radically different views and practices. Women's position in most religions is a clear example of this dynamic. It is not in the interests of either women or feminist research, if a too stereotypical image of a religion is being drawn, be it Islam or Latin American Catholicism.

The above-mentioned polarity of stereotypes has some interesting and important consequences for women, feminism and feminist studies. I will only mention three. All of these have relevance also in the Latin American context. First, the historical, social, political and ethical importance of a given religious tradition is negated, because secularization is considered to have won over religion in modern societies. Second, many people in different cultures are deprived of their agency if their religious traditions are considered immutable and unchangeable. If contemporary forms of, for example, Islam or Catholicism, are seen as powerful, immutable power systems over people's decision-making and possibilities for change, both the dialogue and critique inside these religious traditions are ignored, as well as their historical changes over centuries – some of them major, like the Reformation in Europe, or like Liberation Theology in Latin America. An important distinction to be made is also that between the official teaching and popular religiosity.

Third, we are witnessing a rise of fundamentalism in all major religious traditions. This often state-legitimized 'social fundamentalism'[21] is creating new political alliances between, for example, the Vatican and some Muslim governments, especially in issues that have to do with women's rights. I have elsewhere called these alliances of old enemies 'fundamentalist or patriarchal ecumenism'.[22] If at the same time feminists are unable to analyse this phenomenon adequately, including taking seriously women's positive identities as Muslim or Catholic, it becomes difficult to understand the complex and often tense relationship between women and their religious traditions, identities and beliefs.

If the Catholic Church in Latin America is portrayed by the secular feminist movement as the 'arch-enemy' – even if for understandable reasons – many Latin American women will feel alienated not from the Church but from a feminist discourse and practice that is so anti-Church. Women may find themselves on a battleground between two clashing ideologies in which it is hard to discuss issues such as sexuality, reproduction and violence in a way that reflects their lived experiences. The chilling statistics mentioned earlier are some testament to this. However, these experiences also entail deeply internalized views of right and wrong, sin and guilt, but also of forgiveness and grace, as well as women's everyday resistance to their oppression.

Given the importance of religion in Latin American culture, I believe that a large part of the region's female population would like to remain Christian but also to have a greater say in their Church's teaching on women. There is practically no public space for discussion about realities, which include women not living according to the teachings of the Church, committing acts considered by the Church as major sins, such as abortion, but understanding themselves as Catholics or Christians, nevertheless. The spheres of private and popular religiosity, which may include an image of a forgiving and understanding God (in the Catholic tradition, often in the figure of the Virgin Mary), and the public role of the Catholic hierarchy, do not meet each other in any meaningful way in a society and in a Church where women's ways of perceiving religion, god, sin and justice have no legitimacy or importance. Most Latin American women who decide to have an abortion (mostly illegal, as we remember) also believe in God. To justify their decision, they need either to create an alternative understanding of a God who also forgives or to live with a constant sense of guilt and shame. Probably all these are part of many women's life experiences. This lived experience of moral and religious contradiction, and women's ways of resolving it, do not form any part of the public discourse on abortion, reproduction and sexuality.[23]

Many ordinary women probably feel the need for both a non-sexist interpretation of their religious traditions and for a feminism which would be less hostile and ignorant about religion and which would stop seeing women, for whom religion is important, as the most alienated and in need of a feminist saviour. Polarized explanations omit the practices of agency and the experiences of conflicting images of selfhood in women, both individually and collectively, which again may lead to researchers seeing women as a homogeneous group of 'poor Third World women', passive victims of colonialism, patriarchal religions, and sexism.[24]

In order for us to understand and analyse the complex and often contradictory relationship between women and their religious traditions, identities and beliefs, it is important to recognize that women have different ways of opposing cultural stereotypes concerning them, including some of those represented by feminists. The stereotypical image of poor women as the passive victims of religious indoctrination is one of the most common. However, one of the most powerful means of women's resistance has always been the reinterpretation and reappropriation of religious practices and theories for their own ends. Scholars would do well to recognize that for many women in different societies, their religious identities are intimately tied to their identities as women, even as resistant or rebellious women.

Harmful For Your Health? *Marianismo*, the Virgin Mary and Feminism

In the title of my article, by 'seriously harmful for your health' I refer, on the one hand, to the Catholic Church as an institution of power, especially in relation to the lived realities of women and their health in particular. The poorer the women, the more harmful the institution. On the other hand, I also refer to such feminist discourses and practices that see all established religion, including the popular type of Catholicism in Latin America (*religiosidad popular*), as harmful and alienating for women. The favourite woman of the Catholic Church, the Virgin Mary, is a case in point. Women's love of her and devotion to her can be seen as the worst sort of alienation. Hardly any differentiation in much feminist research is made between institutional, official religion, on the one hand, and the lived religious practices, on the other hand.

I definitely agree with the first, the dangerous and even life-threatening impact of the Catholic hierarchy on people's – especially women's – health and wellbeing. As has become clear, I do not easily agree with the second, the feminist conviction of the harmfulness of religion for women, almost without qualification. Both 'secular' feminism and 'progressive' Catholicism (Liberation Theology) have been, by and large, unable to simultaneously question the official religious tradition and teaching and take seriously women's sexual and reproductive realities, leaving one more time an open (public) space to be dominated only by the aggressive and authoritarian policies of the Church hierarchy. I wish to look at the lacking but crucial space between official Catholic teaching, sexist no doubt, the more progressive and critical interpretations such as Liberation Theology, which has no explicitly feminist agenda, and the secular feminist discourses and practices which lump all things religious in one and the same basket of powerful and blatant sexism. What do we see in that ignored space? Women, of course, and their own reinterpretations of sexist religious practices and theories, sometimes in open contradiction with all groups mentioned above. I will take some examples of this tension in the image of Virgin Mary.

Why Mary? For the following reasons, at least. First, she is the central, if not the sole, female figure in the Catholic imagery and cult. Second, she is of central existential importance for ordinary Catholics, especially women. Third, she is the main figure in Latin American grass-roots popular religiosity, often in syncretized forms and in tension or even in contradiction with the official teaching on her. Fourth, there is an international, ecumenical, feminist theological interest in her, aiming at both a substantial critique of traditional Mariology as well as possible liberatory aspects of her. And fifth, Mary is a central object of the feminist critique of both sexist Catholicism and women's overall subordinate status in Latin America.

The term *marianismo*, widely used in contemporary (social scientific) research on Latin American women, originally comes from an early article by Evelyn Stevens called 'Machismo and Marianismo' (1973).[25] Stevens' article is by now dated, reflecting maybe an early stage of feminist critique, carrying presuppositions that later feminist theories have, by and large, questioned and put aside. However, we should not look at Stevens' texts not as some historical remnant of feminist theorizing, because, curiously enough, in contemporary feminist research on Latin American women, both inside and outside the continent, her bipolar *machismo* vs. *marianismo* model is being reproduced over and over again, to such an extent that the terms have gained some sort of a foundational status among feminist Latin American scholars. This happens even in spite of well-founded critiques of the model. Interestingly, the feminist theological interest in the figure of Mary has, as far as I know, nowhere entered into dialogue with this mainly social scientific feminist critique of her.

In her early texts, Emily Stevens delineates two different moralities and sources of identity for Latin American men and women: *machismo* for the first, *marianismo* for the latter. As I said, this configuration appears in one form or the other in several subsequent social scientific studies done on Latin American women, sometimes evaluated critically.[26]

According to Stevens, *marianismo* is a 'secular cult of femininity drawn from the adoration of the Virgin Mary'.[27] Marianismo 'pictures its subjects as semi-divine, morally superior and spiritually stronger than men. This constellation of attributes enables women to bear the indignities inflicted on them by men, and to forgive those who bring them pain. (...) Men's wickedness is therefore the necessary precondition of women's superior status'.[28] *Machismo* is the 'other face of *marianismo*'; together they create two opposite moralities for Latin American men and women, 'a stable symbiosis in Latin American culture'.[29] Women are deliberate perpetrators of the *marianismo* myth,[30] which is characterized by the female ideals of semi-divinity, moral superiority, spiritual strength, abnegation, an infinite capacity for humility and sacrifice, self-denial and patience.[31] All this 'a considerable number' of Latin American women freely choose and support.[32] Both *machismo* and *marianismo* are syndromes, fully developed only in Latin America.[33] Even though Stevens says that *marianismo* is not a religious practice,[34] she nevertheless uses the term almost interchangeably with Mariology and marianism.[35] For her, *marianismo* is, however, a secular edifice of beliefs and practices related to the position of women in society.[36]

To analyse Stevens' depiction of Latin American women's lot and its relationship to the figure of Virgin Mary (including the pathologization of an entire culture, the image of men in the *machismo* myth, and women's compliance with it all) would demand more space than is possible in this chapter.[37] I will shortly refer to some critiques expressed by other scholars, but my own interest – not taken up by the few other critics of *marianismo* – is the confusing interplay between *marianismo* (as defined by Stevens), the Virgin Mary, Latin American women, and their oppression. I hope to offer examples of a very different image of Mary, alive among ordinary Catholic women, and often in open contradiction with the official teaching on her. The religiously or theologically unanalytical lumping together of *marianismo* and the devotion of Mary by Stevens and others is based on the formal, official, and undoubtedly sexist, teaching on her of the Church. What it omits are the discourses and practices of women themselves, which do not reinforce the traditional impossible model of womanhood presented through Mary.

The *marianismo* model and its frequent use in even contemporary feminist scholarship have been criticized, for example, for oversimplification of the reality of Latin American women and for investigators' failure to consider the material bases of manifest behaviour,[38] for blaming the victim, not taking the force of patriarchal social relations seriously enough (neither *machismo* nor *marianismo* exist in a cultural vacuum or are inherent characteristics of one gender or the other) and reflecting only a middle-class ideal or reality.[39] Further, the concept has been practically warned against by Marysa Navarro in a recent article called simply 'Against Marianismo', in which she criticizes the term for being seriously flawed, essentialist, anachronistic, sexist and ahistorical.[40]

The importance of the Virgin Mary as symbol and the Church's teaching about her – but not necessarily in the *marianismo* type of configuration – is evident also in several other forms in feminist research on Latin American women, for example in relationship to motherhood and maternalism (as the use of motherhood to justify political activism[41]);[42] the symbol of the Virgin (good woman) as opposed to the symbol of the whore (bad woman);[43] and more specifically, the Virgin of Guadalupe as opposed to Malinche (in the Mexican context);[44] or the Mary symbol as opposed to *las locas*, the *Madres de Plaza de Mayo* (in Argentina),[45] the *loca* here referring also to a prostitute;[46] or (good) Mary as opposed to (bad) Eve.[47] For different scholars and in different contexts, the Virgin Mary symbol can serve both as a corollary of the female submission, 'the ultimate female icon',[48] and as the 'mother as political actor who subverts marianist notions of motherhood'.[49] Sometimes *marianismo* is not used as Stevens meant it (as the cult of female spiritual and moral superiority), but simply or mainly as the cult of the Virgin Mary.[50] The Suffering Mother (*la madre sufrida*, *Mater Dolorosa*) is another theme that appears constantly in relationship to Latin American women and the Virgin Mary symbol,[51] as is the interpretation of women's public identification with the Virgin Mary and their conscious use of the Mary symbol for their own political ends (for example, Evita Perón and Violeta Chamorro), even when people do not always identify them as imitating the Virgin Mary.[52] One can ask if combining the cult of Virgin Mary with all these issues is a correct thing to do, and if yes, on what basis; that is, why do scholars make the Virgin Mary the reference point for both motherhood and maternalist politics in Latin America. It is possible that this is a correct thing to do, but it is also possible that it is more a scholarly construction than a reality. And, even if so, women still might have far more varied interpretations of Virgin Mary than scholars usually see.

Women's Mary?

In my ongoing research, I hope to offer the rich and controversial Marian tradition – both 'the official' and 'the popular' versions – as a critical corrective to the often ahistorical *marianismo* type of reducing the Virgin, and women's devotion to her, to a mere concept, which does not really illustrate or explain or even do justice to the richness of the tradition or to the women themselves who think she is worthy of their devotion.

Also, in feminist theological research, there is a renewed interest in the Virgin Mary, ecumenically and cross-culturally, which may imply the importance of the Mary symbol for women beyond traditional confessional limits of Marian piety.[53] In my own research, I am asking how and why women in different cultural settings, and in different times, approach Mary in their everyday experiences of being women in patriarchal societies and religious traditions, and give her their 'own' meanings, sometimes independently of the formal teaching on her. I claim that there is a living tradition of devotion to Mary with a very human (feminine) face, coming close to women in their most intimate and real experiences.[54] In the following, I will briefly delineate some of the most important themes in that 'women's tradition'.

An understanding of Mary as somebody who affirms and shares but also transcends and is beyond human womanhood is sometimes in open contradiction with the 'official' Mary of the churches and with theological doctrines, especially when it comes to her bodiliness, sexuality and motherhood.[55] Interestingly, these same Marian doctrines have perhaps best maintained something that could be called a feminine principle in Christianity, from its beginnings up to our own time, distorted as it may appear from contemporary women's perspective. According to Jaroslav Pelikan, the Marian doctrines are good examples of how doctrinal development has followed popular beliefs and lived spirituality, and not the other way round. Classical Mariology is not as much 'from-top-down' as one might first think.[56] He makes the point that we should not automatically assume that what the councils of the Church legislated as dogma was what the common people actually believed, or conversely, that what the common people actually believe is always different from dogma and creed. According to him, the veneration of the Virgin Mary is one of the clearest examples of how ideas and practices have moved from the faith of common people into liturgy, creed, and dogma, rather than the other way around.[57] This is a related argument to mine: women's popular beliefs about the Virgin Mary may be, and in fact often are, in tension with the creed and dogma of the official Church, but not necessarily, because over the centuries, many so-called popular beliefs have in fact been integrated into the dogma. It is about a two-way influence.

Since Mary is in heaven (the dogma *Assumptio* of 1950), she can act as the Mediatrix between humanity and God. This is also her most important role in the popular piety. She is simultaneously a divine (or divine-like) being and a human being. The term Mediatrix refers to her twofold mediatory function: she is the one through whom humans have access to her son, on the one hand, and through her the son was incarnated, given to humans.[58] Pelikan combines Mary's role as Mediatrix with her portrayal as the *Mater Dolorosa* (Mother of Sorrows).[59]

If this is true, it is important to note that this is exactly how women in different cultures and religious traditions approach her: the one who understands women's sufferings, as mothers but also as women in other respects, because she has gone through it all herself, unlike the masculine divine figures who seem to be so much more disassociated from the complexities of human life. This means that there is a clear continuation between women's sometimes unorthodox veneration of her as a heavenly sister or mother and the Western Catholic understanding of her, even when the same tradition also carries most of the sexist weight of traditional Mariology. Women themselves, over the centuries, have given her meanings in which her femininity and closeness to human females does not centre in her impossible combination of motherhood and physiological virginity or her chastity. Women see her as a suffering sister or mother, who knows the pains of childbirth, raising the child, and then losing the child to death, and this is why they prefer talking and praying to her, not because she is the model of chastity and impossible motherhood. It is easy to see how this sort of understanding of her is very different also from the *marianismo* type of 'syndrome'.

As becomes clear from my examples from Latin America and Finnish-Russian Karelia,[60] the main element in women's popular Marian piety centres in their understanding of her as both 'like myself', another woman, and as somebody who transcends women's experiences by being a divine figure, a goddess. Unlike Christ and God (understood as the male monotheist God the Father), Mary combines humanity and divinity, immanency and transcendence, in her person, at least in women's religious experiences.

It is this combined role of Mary that I claim to be of central importance in both the official tradition (to some extent), in (women's) popular Marian piety and in a possible feminist re-appropriation of her. This 'both-and' character of Mary can have many faces and names: the Mediatrix, the *Mater Dolorosa*, the gateway to heaven (unlike Eve, the *porta diaboli*), 'someone like me' but also divine for ordinary women, the exemplary (deified) human. In less direct terms, she exemplifies and is an incarnation of the traditional female role of bridge-builder and someone who keeps an impossible whole together.

Jaroslav Pelikan notes this role of hers in the context of other cultures and religions:

> One of the most profound and most persistent roles of the Virgin Mary in history has been her function as a bridge builder to other traditions, other cultures, and other religions. From the Latin word for 'bridge builder' came the term *pontifex*, a priestly title in Roman paganism. (...) Ultimately it applied to all those concepts and personalities whose fundamental message and significance could be expressed better by saying both/and than by saying either/or.[61]

This is exactly how women venerate Mary in different cultures: someone who is both-and and not either-or. And, of course, this is close to women's traditional roles as providers and sustainers of the family, community and culture. No wonder, then, if women want to see that important role reflected in divinity. For them, it is in Mary that they can see their often down-played important roles divinized and exalted.

This both-and role of Mary seems to have something to do also with crossing (different) boundaries, and her body, as any female body, metaphorically also embodying the fusion/disappearance/crossing/mixing of boundaries. Of the many visual presentations of Mary, this aspect of her becomes most clear in those paintings and sculptures in which her body literally contains all humanity, at times even divinity. She opens up her gown or her body, and inside are not only her child Jesus, but all the apostles and saints as well. She as a person, she in her body, is the primordial sacred space.

Ordinary Christian women identify themselves with Mary and fate with intensity and 'blur' the boundary between her and themselves, between 'the religious' and 'the ordinary', between the immanent and the transcendent. Mary is a perfect channel of and object for this sort of (female) experience. This *imitatio Mariaea* has much more to offer for women than the classical *imitatio Christi* type of Christian life, and conversely, women have much to offer in the realm of religion in the context of a Mariology, which presents Mary as the all-encompassing maternal force and as the personification of the liminal character of human life.

Mater et Femina Dolorosa

Suffering seems to be one important factor in trying to understand Mary's meaning for women. It is also a theme that runs through all the material I have used here. Some feminist researchers use the term *culture of suffering*, especially in reference to women's roles in lamentation, death and burial rites.[62] It is not only about maternal suffering. Through lamentation, women are seen to convey to themselves and others that it is a role and burden of women to be both sufferers and social actors who take upon themselves the responsibility of coping with everyday life. A woman's selfhood shows up as clearly intersubjective.[63] The language of lament is based to a large extent on the mother-child relationship and in which the father is presented in 'matrilineal' terms. The intersubjectivity of lamentation comes to the fore in the ways in which lamenters construct a perspective of time, which unites the past and the future, mother and daughter, death and life.[64]

Ritual lamentation, but also the almost ritualized speaking of suffering, seem to be women's way in different cultures to speak of something that would otherwise be difficult or impossible to express. Here it is obvious how the Virgin Mary as *Mater Dolorosa*, the premium female sufferer, plays an important role. As we have seen, she is both an object of identification and a channel of emotions and social expectations, and still, something beyond ordinary female womanhood. This does not only or necessarily mean the impossibility of being like her for any other woman, so often taken up by feminists, but it may also refer to how she transcends ordinary womanhood. If women's own social and ritual role is to be 'on the boundary', mark the boundary or to be the boundary itself, Mary again is a perfect example of that role, even in traditional teaching.

Thus, the emphasis on suffering in much feminist analysis on Mary, both theological and non-theological, has this concrete base. However, the meaning and language of suffering need not necessarily be simplistic, as if there were a one-to-one relationship between women's lives and suffering. It is 'real', especially in contexts of poverty and death, but it is also a common social role of women in different cultures. Laments are, in the end, also about communication with the dead. And finally, the language of laments and suffering could be women's own 'meta-explanation' of their lives, at least in certain contexts, and especially for women of a certain age and life situation. As such, it may reflect women's feelings of powerlessness: suffering is offered as a meta-explanation of women's lives (*ay, yo que sufrí tanto*, something one hears from, especially older, Latin American women constantly). The language of suffering is an acceptable language in the context of religion and women's role within it. According to Terhi Utriainen:

> The message of the laments has perhaps at certain times and in certain places appeared as a form of metacommunication (Gregory Bateson), as tidings and language, resounding in the drum formed by the bodies of lamenting women, a situation in which the women are able to see through and above a given (cultural situation). Using the meta-message of lament, women have perhaps been able to communicate meanings on a number of different levels as well as various messages concerning the existence of motherhood, womanhood and relations among women in a situation in which such communication would not have been possible in any other form.[65]

The Virgin Mary is thus both one of the lamenting women and the Mediatrix of not only grace but of suffering, negotiating the boundaries of immanence and transcendence, the mundane and the sacred.

The Virgin Mary, Sexuality and Virginity

Based on the above, I would claim that issues of sexuality and reproduction should not be treated only in a legal or socio-political framework, as issues of rights, important as this is. In the context of religion it is important to be able to distinguish between different levels. When speaking of women's religious and sexual experiences together, it is of special importance to look at women's (possible) own interpretations and meanings and ways of creating ethical discourses, because women are *de facto* excluded from positions of power and authority in the Catholic Church.[66] This is a huge task, and here I am only hinting at some possibilities of doing so in recreating values, norms, and beliefs about sexuality, based on people's real everyday experiences of suffering and exclusion, but also of joy, sensuality and belonging.

To conclude, I would like to briefly present some thoughts on virginity. It is widely accepted that the name Mother of God refers to pre-Christian deities. In the pre-Christian Mediterranean and Near Eastern religions, 'the Mother Goddess' played an important role. Long before Mary, there existed the myth of the virginal Mother Goddess who created all life from herself. She was considered to be the origin and foundation of all being, the original feminine condition, the cosmic womb. Virginity could symbolize her eternally renewing youth, autonomy, integrity and self-fulfilment. This original motherhood, 'the beginning of all', was virginal motherhood. In this sense, Mary is but one link in a long chain of symbols that offer an image of an independent, creative feminine consciousness.[67] These myths are often enthusiastically and uncritically (ahistorically) revived by modern feminists, whereas Mary is not seen on the same continuum.

Without doubt the mythical and art historical connections between ancient goddesses and Mary do exist.[68] Nevertheless, according to some interpretations, one central characteristic makes 'the official' Mary very different in the chain of great goddesses: she alone is completely disassociated from sexuality.[69] Her fertility is not seen as opulent and optimistic. Her maternity is taken away from her: the birth of her child was unlike all other births. In her, fertility and maternity are not affirmations of natural life as in the pre-Christian goddesses. Even her virginity – her most precious gift, according to the tradition – is defined only in the narrowest physiological sense. Jesus was 'conceived by the Holy Spirit' (without a sexual act) and 'born of the Virgin Mary' (the hymen did not rupture even at delivery – a violent, even sadistic, image). In the (other) goddesses, virginal motherhood was understood as the mystical and powerful ability of women to create life from within themselves; in the case of Mary, this is reduced to a unilateral act, from above, by the

Holy Spirit, for whom Mary is no more than a vessel, a recipient, instead of an active subject. All these are seen as reasons for the rejection of Mary as a usable goddess for contemporary feminists.

The early understanding of Mary as *Theotokos* contains a contradiction between the affirmation of Jesus' humanity through his natural human birth, on the one hand, and the exceptional nature of his birth in relation to all other human births, on the other hand. If it is true that in Mariology there is an influence of (and battle with) the pre-Christian goddesses, then how should we interpret the dogma? If we interpret the miraculous virgin birth only as oppressive to women, because it makes the birth of the god-child different from all other human births, should we not make this same observation of the pre-Christian goddesses and their supposed virgin births? On what grounds are they considered as somehow more woman-friendly and supportive of natural biological processes, but not so in Mary's case? And conversely, if there is a feminist interest in restoring the ancient goddess myths, including the possibly positive symbolic meaning of their eternal virginity and virgin births, why not to apply that to the Virgin Mary as well?

In this context, it is important to see Mary in a historical continuum, including the pre-Christian and (in Latin America) the pre-Colombian goddesses, and not only as an anti-female and ahistorical product of patriarchal Christianity. If virginity and virgin birth really can be metaphors or symbols for women's autonomy, creativity and self-sufficiency (according to Jung, as the cultural archetype of the *Magna Mater*[70]), it certainly can be applied to Mary, too. Not even in the case of the goddess cults, did the veneration of women's miraculous capacity to create life from themselves mean an elevated social or religious status for them.[71] Nor did it in the case of the teaching on the Virgin Mary. In both cases we need to be cautious not to draw too easy causalities between a symbol and reality.

If the traditional presentation of Mary's 'yes' stresses her passivity and supposed consent ('I am the slave of the Lord'), her impregnation could be interpreted as the divine rape of the virgin and as a religious legitimization of sexualized violence against women and girls. This sort of conceptualization has also served as the model for the patriarchal Christian marriage: the man as 'the head', the rational, the active; the woman as 'the body', the emotional, the passive. But if the virgin birth is not taken literally, referring to physiology, but rather as a metaphor of something beyond its sexual connotations, there might be other ways to interpret even the traditional Marian dogmas. If we can attach meanings such as integrity and autonomy to virginity and, at the same time, denounce the violence against women and girls, we might be able to offer the image of the Virgin Mary as a healing image to women and girls such as Rosa. This may be very wishful thinking, but it is unfortunate if feminists revive pre-Christian and pre-Columbian goddesses without paying attention to some of their qualities preserved in the contemporary devotion to the Virgin Mary. I have been claiming that many women do in fact see her as a source for autonomy, integrity and strength. She helps them in areas of life of which she supposedly did not know anything: sexuality, abortion, violence, ordinary motherhood. We can only see and value this, if we ask ordinary women themselves. In different parts of the world women do not speak of a *marianismo* that oppresses them, but of a divine female figure, which sustains them, listens to them, is like them, but which also is able to transcend human experiences.

How are we to relate that to the cold statistics on women's mortality presented at the beginning of this discussion? How can we talk about reproductive rights, the reality of abortion, and women's interpretations of their lives, in a way that would respect their self-understanding as sexual, moral and religious beings, and which also would translate into concrete political action? Maybe a rights-based language, which opposes 'choice' and 'life', a woman and her foetus or child, does not take us any further than it has done up to now. Both Liberation Theology and feminism have wanted to represent the voices of the silenced in society, but since these voices speak of women's sexual lives, they have not been well heard by Liberation Theologians, and since they are often religious, they have not always been understood by feminists.

Notes

1   This article is partly based on a public lecture given at the Harvard Divinity School on 3 April 2003, while I was a visiting scholar at the Women's Studies in Religion Program of the HDS.

2   The case received publicity also outside Latin America. For example, 'Rosa's' mother was interviewed in a BBC documentary by Steve Bradshaw (2003).

3   *La Nación*, 24 February 2003.

4   According to the International Classification of Diseases, a maternal death is defined as a death of a woman while pregnant or within 42 days of termination of pregnancy, irrespective of the duration of the pregnancy, from any cause related to or aggravated by the pregnancy or its management. Thus, abortions, illegal or legal, are counted among these causes.

5   http://www.who.int/reproductive-health/publications/maternal_mortality_2000/mme.pdf

6   World Health Organization 1996, 3: 10–15.

7   http://www.paho.org

8   *The Bush Global Gag Rule: Endangering Women's Health, Free Speech and Democracy*. A report by the Center for Reproductive Rights at http://www.crlp.org

9   Alan Guttmacher Institute: *An Overview of Clandestine Abortion in Latin America*. At http://www.agi-usa.org/pubs/ib12.html

10 *Latin America and the Caribbean*. A report by the Center for Reproductive Rights at http://www.crlp.org

11 Pizarro (2003), 8, 11.

12 Hynds (1993), 1. Guillermo Nugent speaks of a 'tutelary system' (*orden tutelar*) as a way of understanding the conflict between issues of sexuality and public policy

in Latin America, based on a belief in the necessity of representation: groups seen as unable to represent themselves need the tutelage of others. In Latin America, the most influential institutions in supposedly representing the interests of large social groups have been the army and the Catholic Church. (Nugent 2002 and 2004).

13 See Vuola (2002b).

14 In Vuola (2002a) I develop and analyse this discussion in detail, especially in Chapter 4.

15 I have written more extensively on this in Vuola (2000).

16 In some countries, such as Guatemala, the number of Protestants has risen close to 40 per cent of the population.

17 According to Graciela Di Marco, the declaration of the Latin American Council of Churches (*Consejo Latinoamericano de Iglesias*, CLAI, the regional equivalent of the World Council of Churches, of which most mainline Protestant churches are members) on 'Population and Reproductive Health', together with the activities of local Protestant pastors, male and female, played an important role in the appropriation of the law. Di Marco also pays attention to how several Protestant churches and ecumenical organizations besides CLAI have in fact publicly taken another route than the Catholic Church in issues of population and reproduction. In countries where there is a strong presence of Protestant churches, some of them working with poor women and having gender programmes with a feminist framework, they could possibly play a similar role to that in Argentina. See Di Marco (2001), 11–13. Also Juan Michel: 'Iglesias apoyan ley de salud reproductiva'. Agencia Latinoamericana y Caribeña de Comunicación (ALC), 21 June 2000; and Juan Michel: 'Aprobaron ley de salud reproductiva', ALC, 23 June 2000. According to this information, five Protestant churches and eleven ecumenical organizations supported the law, whereas the Catholic Church strongly opposed it.

It is important to remember that by and large the Protestant churches have not as unified and absolutist a teaching in issues of sexuality as the Catholic Church. Of course, this does not mean that they are free of sexism and authoritarianism. Some of them are extremely conservative, reinforcing the patriarchal model of family and the church, but it is also women who mostly join these churches, leaving the Catholic Church behind in both its traditional and liberation theological form. It is impossible to analyse this here in more detail; I am rather pointing to a possible alliance between feminist organizations – especially the ones who work with poor women as many of them do – and at least some sectors of the Protestant churches.

18 I have documented and discussed the *de facto* inability of Liberation Theology to take up issues related to sexuality and sexual ethics in any new way in Vuola (2002a).

19 For more on this dilemma, see Sakaranaho (1998) on the Middle East and Turkey. She shows how 'the religious paradigm' is related to Orientalism in which Islam is seen as an immutable and stagnant belief system, and how most academic feminist studies take place within this paradigm.

20 Casanova (1994), 19–29.

21 According to John Stratton Hawley, 'until recently, it has been insufficiently appreciated (. . .) that issues of gender play a crucial role in the language of fundamentalism. While some thinkers continue to emphasize the appeal to inerrant scripture as a principal defining feature of fundamentalist groups, others

– myself included – have focused on the centrality of an appeal not to scriptural fundamentalism but to a certain "social fundamentalism". We have noted that shared fears about enlarged domains of relative autonomy for women are a major focus of attention (. . .). What is being championed is a divinely sanctioned vision of natural differences between the sexes (. . .)' (Hawley 1999, 4).

22 Vuola (2002b).

23 According to an article in *La Boletina*, the magazine of *Puntos de Encuentro*, a feminist organization, 'En Nicaragua la gran mayoría de mujeres que recurren al aborto creen en Dios. Ninguna de ellas considera que debe dejar de considerarse cristiana después de haberse practicado un aborto. Muchas dicen: "Yo hablo con mi Dios y sé que El me comprende." Según una encuesta que hizo el Colectivo de Mujeres de Matagalpa, 8 de cada 10 mujeres que alguna vez se han practicado un aborto creen en Dios. Tomaron su decisión de abortar porque sentían que, por una u otra razón, estaban "en la sin remedio".' http://www.puntos.org.ni/boletina/bole43/suplemento.html in an article with the title *Hablemos del aborto . . . Una decisión personal difícil*.

24 Mohanty (1991).

25 Stevens (1973a). A slightly different version of the same text appeared the same year. See Stevens (1973b).

26 See, for example, Brusco (1995), 79, 96; Chaney (1979), 49; Craske (1999), 11–15, 194; Eckstein (2001), 26; Fisher (1993), 3; González and Kampwirth (2001), 24; Melhuus and Stolen (1996), 11–12; Ready (2001), 174.

27 Stevens (1973a), 62.

28 Ibid.

29 Ibid., 63.

30 Ibid.

31 Stevens (1973b), 94.

32 Ibid., 99.

33 Ibid., 91.

34 Ibid.

35 Ibid. She uses Marianism and Mariology as synonyms to describe a religious movement around Mary, which is inaccurate, since the first term is something not used at all, the second refers to a distinctive set of theological teachings and dogmas on the Virgin Mary, since the first Christian centuries as well as to research related to her person.

36 Ibid., 91–92.

37 This is one theme in my ongoing research.

38 Browner and Lewin (1982), p. 63. They say, among other things, that self-sacrifice and patience are not ends in themselves but rather means or strategies for gaining economic and social rewards.

39 Bachrach Ehlers (1991), pp. 1, 4–5, 14.

40 Navarro (2002), pp. 257, 270.

41 González and Kampwirth (2001), 25.

42 For example Craske (1999), 13–18; Schirmer (1989 and 1993). They use terms such as militant motherhood and political motherhood. Also González (2001), 43–44; González and Kampwirth (2001), 23–25; Kampwirth (2001), 96.

43 For example Stephen (1997), 35, 283.

44 For example Melhuus (1996), 231, 236–239; Melhuus and Stolen (1996), 25; Rostas (1996), 217–220.

45 See, for example, Althaus-Reid (2001), 51, 176; Feijoó (1994), 121.
46 Althaus-Reid (2001), 51.
47 Melhuus (1996), 253.
48 Craske (1999), 127.
49 Ibid., 17.
50 Stephen (1997), 273; Drogus (1997), 60. In fact, Drogus uses the term in both meanings: '(...) *marianismo*, a complex web of beliefs about the Virgin Mary and devotional practices centered on her' and 'Catholic images associated with Mary – suffering motherhood, purity, and moral superiority, for example – become part of the cultural norm of the ideal woman' (ibid., 60–61).
51 For example, Bayard de Volo (2001), 99–100; Jelin (1997), 76; Melhuus (1990).
52 Bayard de Volo (2001), 157–159, 177; Kampwirth (1996).
53 Nevertheless, I have paid attention to the different ways Catholic and Protestant women approach 'a new Mary'. A hypothesis in need of being verified: Catholic women tend to be searching for the historical and even biblical Mary in order to humanize her, whereas Protestant women approach her divine aspect in order to replace the exclusive masculine image of divinity.
54 See my earlier work on Mary in Vuola (1993). On Liberation Theologians' Mariological interpretations, see Vuola (2002a), Chapter 3.4. When writing this article, I came across the doctoral dissertation in anthropology by Lena Gemzöe from the University of Stockholm, Sweden, and was pleased to find out that she came very much to the same conclusions as myself, when doing her anthropological fieldwork in northern Portugal. (See Gemzöe (2000).) Overall, ethnographical methods seem to make researchers more sensitive to both women's religious authority and interpretations as well as to the tensions between 'official' and 'popular' religion, thus providing examples of the kind of feminist research which is not insensitive to issues of women and religion. My critique is aimed at the sort of feminist research, which makes huge unfounded generalizations about religion, without really looking at women's experiences and listening to them, in the end, asking how women themselves perceive their religion.
55 This, too, was found by Lena Gemzöe in Portugal. See, for example, Gemzöe (2000), pp. 25, 28, 55–56. According to her, women in the village where she did her research seldom talked of Mary as a virgin. What they emphasized was her motherhood, the mother–daughter relationship, and the direct relationship between Mary and humans, for which the intermediary role of the Church and priests is not needed. According to Gemzöe, the most characteristic trait in women's approach to Mary is its intimate, personal and emotive character. Her similarity, rather than differences, with ordinary women is stressed (Ibid., pp. 64–65, 82, 194–195). See also Rodríguez (1994) for a similar interpretation of the Virgin of Guadalupe among Mexican-American women.
56 '(...) a basic aversion to the phenomenon of lay piety, out of which (...) so much of the history of the development of Mariology, including the assumption, had emerged' (Pelikan (1996), 210).
57 Ibid., 216.
58 Ibid., 131.
59 Ibid., 125–127. According to Atkinson, 'The appeal of the Pietà and of the Mater Dolorosa arose from Mary's symbolization of the pain and sorrow believed to be characteristic of all maternity. (...) Maternal anguish became the emotional center of Marian piety' (Atkinson (1991), 162).

60   See Vuola (1993) and Vuola (2006).
61   Pelikan (1996), 67. He then goes on explaining at length the important position Mary (Maryam) has in the Qur'an and Islam.
62   Utriainen (1998), 193, referring to Aili Nenola (Ingrian laments) and Anna Caravelli-Chaves (Greek laments). Nenola's research has since the publication of Utriainen's article been published as Nenola (2002).
63   Ibid., again referring to Nenola's research on Ingrian laments.
64   Ibid., 194–195.
65   Ibid., 194.
66   Again, see Gemzöe (2000) for several examples from her fieldwork in Portugal, of how and why women's religious practices and interpretations are in tension, and sometimes in open conflict, with the institutional, official Church.
67   For example, Atkinson: 'The figure of Mary acquired characteristics of the old goddesses, whose ancient shrines were revived in some of Mary's holy places. (...) devotion to Mary increasingly resembled devotion to the goddess' (Atkinson (1991), 107). See also Pelikan (1996), 56–58, 78. He warns of 'facile' modern theories about the mother goddesses and their supposed significance for the development of Christian Mariology, even if he also affirms that there are 'significant parallels' between the two phenomena. See also Christ (1997), 68–69.
    There is no necessary linkage between Goddess symbolism and women's social roles. The one does not predict the other, as is often claimed – at least implicitly – by such feminist researchers and activists who belong to feminist spirituality or Goddess spirituality movements. In them, the academic feminist research is often tied to religious convictions. Even among (feminist) theorists, there is no consensus of the historical, mythical, existential and religious meaning of the Goddess symbolism. See, for example Christ (1997); Gimbutas (1982); Gadon (1989); Diamond and Orenstein (eds) (1990). For a critical view, see for example Biehl (1991); Eller (2000). Biehl warns of ahistorical interpretations which can lead to further mystification of women and 'femininity'.
68   The same has been affirmed by several scholars in the case of pre-Colombian goddesses and Virgin Mary, most notably the hybrid image of Tonantzin and *Virgen de Guadalupe* from today's Mexico. See also Sigal (2000) for the hybrid Mayan image of the Virgin Mary Moon Goddess.
69   Carroll (1986), 5.
70   Jung (1989), 109–110, 132–134. Based on his conviction of the importance of the Mother symbol, he also ends up embracing the Catholic doctrine of the Assumption of Mary (ibid., 137–140).
71   Biehl (1991); Eller (2000).

References

Althaus-Reid, M. (2001) *Indecent Theology. Theological Perversions in Sex, Gender and Politics*. London and New York: Routledge.
Atkinson, C. (1991) *The Oldest Vocation. Christian Motherhood in the Middle Ages*. Ithaca and London: Cornell University Press.
Bachrach Ehlers, T. (1991) 'Debunking Marianismo: Economic Vulnerability and Survival Strategies Among Guatemalan Wives', *Ethnology*, 1: 1–16.

Bayard de Volo, L. (2001) *Mothers of Heroes and Martyrs. Gender Identity Politics in Nicaragua, 1979–1999*. Baltimore and London: The Johns Hopkins University Press.

Biehl, J. (1991) *Rethinking Ecofeminist Politics*. Boston: South End Press.

Browner, C. and E. Lewin (1982) 'Female Altruism Reconsidered: The Virgin Mary as Economic Woman', *American Ethnologist*, 1: 61–75.

Brusco, E. (1995) *The Reformation of Machismo: Evangelical Conversion and Gender in Colombia*. Austin: University of Texas Press.

Carroll, M. P. (1986) *The Cult of Virgin Mary: Psychological Origins*. Princeton: Princeton University Press.

Casanova, J. (1994) *Public Religions in the Modern World*. Chicago and London: The University of Chicago Press.

Chaney, E. M. (1979) *Supermadre: Women in Politics in Latin America*. Austin and London: University of Texas Press.

Christ, C. P. (1997) *Rebirth of the Goddess: Finding Meaning in Feminist Spirituality*. Reading, MA: Addison-Wesley Publishing Company.

Craske, N. (1999) *Women and Politics in Latin America*. New Brunswick: Rutgers University Press.

Di Marco, G. (2001) 'La constitución de nuevas identidades en los procesos de formación de las políticas públicas', unpublished paper presented at the XXIII International Congress of the Latin American Studies Association, 6–8 of September, Washington DC.

Diamond, I. and Orenstein, G. F. (eds) (1990) *Reweaving the World: The Emergence of Ecofeminism*. San Francisco: Sierra Club Books.

Drogus, C. A. (1997) *Women, Religion, and Social Change in Brazil's Popular Church*. Notre Dame: University of Notre Dame Press.

Eckstein, S. (2001) 'Power and Popular Protest in Latin America', in S. Eckstein (ed.), *Power and Popular Protest. Latin American Social Movements*. Berkeley, Los Angeles and London: University of California Press, pp. 1–60.

Eller, C. (2000) *The Myth of Matriarchal Prehistory: Why an Invented Past Won't Give Women a Future*. Boston: Beacon Press.

Feijoó, M. del C. with M. M. A. Nari (1994) 'Women and Democracy in Argentina', in J. S. Jaquette (ed.), *The Women's Movement in Latin America: Participation and Democracy*. Boulder, San Francisco and Oxford: Westview Press, pp. 109–129.

Fisher, J. (1993) *Out of the Shadows: Women, Resistance, and Politics in South America*. London: Latin America Bureau.

Gadon, E. W. (1989) *The Once and Future Goddess: A Symbol for Our Time*. San Francisco: Harper.

Gemzöe, L. (2000) *Feminine Matters: Women's Religious Practices in a Portuguese Town*, Department of Social Anthropology, Stockholm University, Stockholm.

Gimbutas, M. (1982) *The Goddesses and Gods of Old Europe: Myths and Cult Images*. Berkeley and Los Angeles: University of California Press.

González, V. (2001) 'Somocista Women, Right-Wing Politics, and Feminism in Nicaragua, 1936–1979', in V. González and K. Kampwirth (eds), *Radical Women in Latin America. Left and Right*. University Park: The Pennsylvania State University Press, pp. 41–78.

González, V. and K. Kampwirth (2001) 'Introduction', in V. González and K. Kampwirth (eds.), *Radical Women in Latin America. Left and Right*. University Park: The Pennsylvania State University Press, pp. 1–28.

Hawley, J. S. (1999) 'Fundamentalism', in C. W. Howland (ed.), *Religious Fundamentalisms and the Human Rights of Women*. New York: St Martin's Press, pp. 3–8.

Hynds, P. (1993) 'Poder y gloria: la iglesia católica en América Latina', *Noticias Aliadas*, 30 (38): 1.

Jelin, E. (1997) 'Engendering Human Rights', in E. Dore (ed.), *Gender Politics in Latin America. Debates in Theory and Practice*. New York: Monthly Review Press, pp. 65–83.

Jung, C. G. (1989) *Aspects of the Masculine. Aspects of the Feminine*. New York: MJF Books.

Kampwirth, K. (1996) 'The Mother of the Nicaraguans: Doña Violeta and UNO's Gender Agenda', *Latin American Perspectives*, 23:1: 67–86.

Kampwirth, K. (2001) 'Women in the Armed Struggles in Nicaragua. Sandinistas and Contras Compared', in V. González and K. Kampwirth (eds), *Radical Women in Latin America. Left and Right*. University Park: The Pennsylvania State University Press, pp. 79–109.

Melhuus, M. (1990) 'Una vergüenza para el honor, una vergüenza para el sufrimiento', in M. Palma (ed.), *Simbólica de la feminidad. La mujer en el imaginario mítico-religioso de las sociedades indias y mestizas*. MLAL and Ediciones Abya-Yala, pp. 39–71.

Melhuus, M. (1996) 'Power, Value, and the Ambiguous Meanings of Gender', in M. Melhuus and K. A. Stolen (eds), *Machos, Mistresses, and Madonnas: Contesting the Power of Latin American Gender Imagery*. London and New York: Verso, pp. 230–259.

Melhuus, M. and K. A. Stolen (1996) 'Introduction', in M. Melhuus and K. A. Stolen (eds), *Machos, Mistresses, and Madonnas: Contesting the Power of Latin American Gender Imagery*. London and New York: Verso, pp. 1–33.

Mohanty, C. T. (1991) 'Under Western Eyes. Feminist Scholarship and Colonial Discourses', in C. T. Mohanty, A. Russo and L. Torres (eds), *Third World Women and the Politics of Feminism*. Bloomington and Indianapolis: Indiana University Press, pp. 51–80.

Navarro, M. (2002) 'Against Marianismo', in R. Montoya, L. J. Frazier and J. Hurtig (eds), *Gender's Place. Feminist Anthropologies of Latin America*. New York: Palgrave Macmillan, pp. 257–272.

Nenola, A. (2002) *Inkerin itkuvirret. Ingrian Laments*. Helsinki: Finnish Literature Society.

Nugent, G. (2002) 'El orden tutelar. Para entender el conflicto entre sexualidad y políticas públicas en América Latina', unpublished manuscript, Lima.

Nugent, G. (2004) 'De la sociedad doméstica a la sociedad civil. Una narración de la situación de los derechos reproductivos y sexuales en el Perú', in C. Dides (comp.) *Diálogos sur-sur sobre Religión, Derechos y' salud, sexual y Reproductiva. Los casos de Argentina, Columbia, Chile y Perú*. Santiago: Editorial Universidad Academia de Humanismo cristiano, Programa de Estudios de Género y Sociedad, pp. 105–124.

Pelikan, J. (1996) *Mary Through the Centuries: Her Place in the History of Culture*. New Haven and London: Yale University Press.

Pizarro, A. M. (2003) *Nicaragua en el 2003: Derechos, salud, educación y desarrollo*, mimeograph, Managua.

Ready, K. (2001) 'A Feminist Reconstruction of Parenthood within Neoliberal Constraints: La Asociación de Madres Demandantes in El Salvador', in V. González and K. Kampwirth (eds), *Radical Women in Latin America: Left and Right*, University Park: The Pennsylvania State University Press, pp. 165–187.

Rodríguez, J. (1994) *Our Lady of Guadalupe: Faith and Empowerment among Mexican-American Women*. Austin: University of Texas Press.

Rostas, S. (1996) 'The Production of Gendered Imagery: The Concheros of Mexico', in M. Melhuus and K. A. Stolen (eds), *Machos, Mistresses, and Madonnas: Contesting the Power of Latin American Gender Imagery*. London and New York: Verso, pp. 207–229.

Sakaranaho, T. (1998) *The Complex Other: A Rhetorical Approach to Women, Islam, and Ideologies in Turkey*. Department of Comparative Religion, University of Helsinki.

Schirmer, J. (1989) 'Those Who Die for Life Cannot be Called Dead: Women and Human Rights Protest in Latin America', *Feminist Review* 32: 3–29.

Schirmer, J. (1993) 'The Seeking of Truth and the Gendering of Consciousness: The CoMadres of El Salvador and the CONAVIGUA Widows of Guatemala', in S. A. Radcliffe and S. Westwood (eds) *'ViVa'. Women and Popular Protest in Latin America*. London and New York: Routledge, pp. 30–64.

Sigal, P. (2000) *From Moon Goddesses to Virgins: The Colonization of Yucatecan Maya Sexual Desire*. Austin: University of Texas Press.

Stephen, L. (1997) *Women and Social Movements in Latin America: Power from Below*. Austin: University of Texas Press.

Stevens, E. (1973a) 'Machismo and Marianismo', *Society*, 10, 6: 57–63.

Stevens, E. (1973b) 'Marianismo: The Other Face of Machismo in Latin America', in A. Pescatello (ed.), *Female and Male in Latin America: Essays*, Pittsburgh: University of Pittsburgh Press, pp. 89–101.

Utriainen, T. (1998) 'Feminine and Masculine in the Study of Balto-Finnic Laments', in S. Apo, A. Nenola and L. Stark-Arola (eds), *Gender and Folklore: Perspectives on Finnish and Karelian Culture*. Finnish Literature Society, Helsinki: Studia Fennica Folkloristica 4, pp. 175–200.

Vuola, E. (1993) 'La Virgen María como ideal femenino, su crítica feminista y nuevas interpretaciones', *Pasos*, 45: 11–20.

Vuola, E. (2000) 'El derecho a la vida y el sujeto femenino', *Pasos*, 88: 1–12.

Vuola, E. (2002a) *Limits of Liberation: Feminist Theology and the Ethics of Poverty and Reproduction*. Sheffield and New York: Sheffield Academic Press and Continuum. Spanish translation (2001) *La ética sexual y los límites de la praxis. Conversaciones críticas entre la teología feminista y la teología de la liberación*. Quito: Abya-Yala.

Vuola, E. (2002b) 'Remaking Universals? Transnational Feminism(s) Challenging Fundamentalist Ecumenism', *Theory, Culture and Society*, 19, 1–2: 175–195.

Vuola, E. (2003) 'Option for the Poor and the Exclusion of Women: The Challenges of Postmodernism and Feminism to Liberation Theology', in J. Rieger (ed.), *Opting for the Margins: Postmodernity and Liberation in Christian Theology*. Oxford and New York: Oxford University Press, pp. 105–126.

Vuola, E. (2006, forthcoming) 'La Morenita on Skis. Women's Popular Marian Piety and Feminist Research on Religion', in S. Briggs and M. McClintock Fulkerson (eds), Oxford: Oxford Dictionary of Feminist Theology, Oxford University Press.

World Health Organization (1996) *Revised 1990 Estimates of Maternal Mortality: A New Approach by WHO and UNICEF.*

Chapter 10

Worship and the Excluded

Jaci Maraschin

Introduction

The theme of this reflection is a tricky one. It seems at the outset that we take for granted what the word 'worship' means as well as its relation to the persons engaged in it to the exclusion of outsiders whom we would call the excluded. Traditionally speaking, we have in our churches what we call worship and the worshippers. They belong together and this belonging is symbolized by the temple. The worshippers are inside the temple; the others, outside it. But there is another sense in which worship, temple, worshippers, outsiders and excluded can be interpreted. As worship happens in a social, political, economical and cultural context, it is possible to look at people from the perspective of the boundaries: the ones belonging to the context and the others excluded from it. The excluded would be those outside the boundaries, living on the other side of the walls, refused to be part of the congregation and, finally, despised and rejected. I will try, in the first place, to discuss the meaning and the practice of worship among Christians from the perspective of postmodern thinking and experience. Then I will proceed to analyse four types of exclusion in order to relate this to our common practices of worship in our Christian congregations. I am aware that it is possible to develop different approaches to this theme. This is my choice and it depends, naturally, on my own experience in Brazil and in my participation in the life and work of the Anglican Communion. As I do not live only in Brazil but, in a way, in our contemporary and postmodern world, and I do not limit myself to the denominational experience of my own church; some of my concerns may be also the concerns of other people around the world as well as of other people belonging to other diverse religious bodies. I will conclude this chapter not only with some critical, theoretical propositions but also with a few practical suggestions towards the overcoming of the polarity inclusion/ exclusion in the community of worshippers today not only in Latin America but also in some other places where they might fit.

What is Worship?

I do not want to risk a definition here, therefore I will start from the other end, that is, from our existential experience as persons in our contexts and outside them. The worship of the church is also known as liturgy. It is that which Christians do when they get together in their meeting place. What Christians do when they meet together? The obvious answer is this: they worship God. But when we say that we worship God we are taking for granted an image which we call God. When we do this, we transform God into an idol and our liturgy becomes idolatrous. This is what my friend Gabriel Vahanian says in his book, *The Anonymous God* (Vahanian 1989: 332–3). However, I propose to follow another way. Instead of naming the mystery, I prefer to experiment with it in different forms and contexts.

The first one involves the overcoming of our rational and dogmatic ways of thinking and feeling, turning to the experience of play. Religions, in general, start from myth and became alive in rituals and other liturgical performances. Worship, then, is like a play, like a game, a children's activity. It has no aim beside itself and it gives pleasure. Gadamer, for instance, understands that all play has no intention or aim and demands no effort (Gadamer 75: 91–99). In other words, people involved in play like to play. They do not pretend to perform utilitarian tasks towards the attainment of practical results. Play serves nothing. There is a sense in which play is the pure experience of *Dasein*, of being there, as Heidegger would call our human existence.

In the second place, worship has to do with aesthetic and mystery. It points to the experience of the sacred. It points to art instead of to technology. Langdon Gilkey says that our technological culture is voracious and devours: it consumes all non-technical cultural aspects and transforms everything in skill, in ways of how-to-do, in media. For him, only art is able to resist this tendency, though sometimes it is also used for utilitarian purposes (Gilkey 1996: 188).

Movement and speed, signs of the modernist movement, created the cinema, TV and computers. Many church liturgies surrendered to this wave of velocity and came out from their sober and contemplative spaces to the lights of cameras and stages. They ended in the electronic church. In this desire for speed nothing is better than show-masses, gospel music and thousands of slogans. Futurism was the most natural fruit of modernity. Pushed by speed the world became smaller and our society, global. In spite of this, mystics and poets are sleepwalkers like the Jesus of the gospels who had no place to rest his head (Matthew 8.20). They cannot find a place in society. It is most likely that they have to live on the borders of society or outside it in the desert. Artists and mystics are not interested in speed. We need time and leisure to listen to good music, reading poetry, contemplating painting and sculptures and dancing.

Thirdly, liturgy and worship are related to body and surface. This is why it is also related to art. There is nothing more bodily and physical than art. It has to do with our human sensibility: vision, touch, smell, taste and hearing. Jesus starts his ministry healing bodies: 'So his fame spread throughout all Syria, and they brought to him all sick ... and he cured them' (Mt. 4.24). He emphasized vision: 'The eye is the lamp of the body' (Mt. 6.22). Then, he enhances the body: 'Is not life more than food and the body more than clothing?' (Mt. 6.25). He enjoys eating and drinking even with sinners and publicans (Mt. 9. 10 and 11). He multiplies bread and fish in order to feed his listeners (Mt. 14.13–21), transforms water and wine at a wedding for the joy of the guests (John 2.1–10) and, finally, in the last meal with his friends, eating bread and drinking wine tells them that these were his body and blood. But this Jesus made of bones and flesh was mythologized by his followers and instead of the man whom he was, he became the second person of the Holy Trinity after a very complex and subtle process of theologizing, while also his mother was transformed into a non-sexual and immaculate virgin. The author of the Fourth Gospel, however, perceived that the *logos* (the word or reason) had become flesh. The fathers of the Church, paradoxically, under the influence of Platonism and neo-Platonism, tried to make him divine. If mythologically God had become flesh, ecclesial theology very early inverted the divine action, transforming the flesh of Jesus in the spiritual Christ. So, his flesh was erased and he became pure spirit. This affected the liturgy of the Church. The worship became memory and *propaganda fidei*, manipulation of the sacred, moralist and rationalist. Consequently, all forms of art at the service of the Church assumed the same functions of any other kind of engaged art. The liturgy, however, does not need to be engaged art. When we relate liturgy with body issues, we assume that we are bodies. Taking this corporeality seriously the liturgy becomes art of the body. Maurice Béjart, great master of dance, says, 'human beings are alone in face of the incomprehensible: and feel anxiety, fear, attraction and mystery. Words are, then, good for nothing. Why should we call this thing, God, absolute, nature, chance? ... dance – he goes on – springs from the necessity of saying the unsaid, of knowing the unknown and of relating to the *other*' (Garaudy 1973: 8). Dance is also contemplation in movement. This is the reason why biblical religion refers many times to it. Hans Urs von Balthasar tried to bring to the theological context the contribution of aesthetics, and he compares the Christian faith with aesthetic contemplation and its pleasure (von Balthasar 1975). For him, the Christian message does not fit in any rational system nor in existential or political projects. It is, rather, a fascinating aesthetical experience. So, in a liturgy of the body, it is that which pertains to the body that is important: and the most important element of the body is the skin. This surface can be vested with veils and colours, but in this revestment the body remains always capable of being undressed and, therefore, revealed.

The fourth element is called 'non-sense'. We read in Isaiah 29.14: 'I will again do amazing things with this people, shocking and amazing. The wisdom of their wise shall perish, and the discernment of the discerning shall be hidden.' This is liturgy, a non-sense activity, like art and children's play. The concept of a non-sense liturgy can be understood in two ways, a negative one and a positive one. In the first moment, as the expression suggests, it represents the postmodern 'non' in face of the imposition of the utilitarian and technological rationalism inherited chiefly from Greek philosophy and the Enlightenment. This 'non' applies to what can be called the uses of the liturgy (liturgy as memorial, manipulation of absence, marketing and moral teaching). The use of the liturgy in this way transforms it into works against grace. Christian communities used the liturgy for their own institutional profit. In this, they followed the way of logic. In the second moment, non-sense means the postmodern yes, beyond the liturgical uses of modernity. The abolition of sense (rational meaning) represented by the 'non' opens up the liturgy for the play and the game. It leans much more towards aesthetics rather than ethics in face of the mystery, emphasizing the human body, its expressions and senses, and, consequently, the skin. It does not mean that liturgical celebrations have to be irrational (an activity of the beasts). We still gather as rational beings and it is with our intelligence that we can make this option. In other words, I am proposing the abandonment of the modern technological reason of modernity for another kind of reason. It is much more like becoming aware of the limits of logical reason allowing us to go beyond it. Pascal in the sixteenth century had already perceived this possibility.

The ancient Greek philosophers thought that being and *logos* were the same. When, in the twentieth century, Heidegger criticizes that premise, he makes a completely different assertion: being and time are the same. This vision of reality opens up new possibilities for human existence. Time is precisely that which can never be fixed. It is a play without foundation. In his treatise on the foundation, he writes: 'Being and foundation: the same thing. Being as foundation has no foundation but, as the abyss, plays the same game as its mission, plays with our being and foundation' (Heiddegger 1965: 88). In the same essay, he affirms also that the mission of being is this play. Spoiled by our Greek inheritance we keep asking: what is the reason for playing? Why playing? But, obviously play has no finality outside itself. It has no why. It is like the work of art, always exhausted in it. The play for the players is an occasion of pleasure. It is always joyful. Myth is transformed in play through ritual, though this is not the only possibility left by the myth. But it is the supreme liturgical possibility.

Types of Exclusion

Marxists tend to say that all kinds of exclusion depend on economic factors and result from the existence of different classes in society. However, it is possible to face the phenomenon of exclusion from different angles. When we are dealing with the worship of the Church, trying to analyse the life of the Church in relation to contemporary society, it is impossible to limit the scope of exclusion to a single factor. The concept of exclusion can be applied both to Church and society in the same way, because the Church exists in society and cannot be abstracted from it. I have selected four types of exclusion present in our contemporary society and, consequently, in the Church. I will try to apply this to the liturgy as, so to say, a case among many other possible cases. The four types are the following: cultural exclusion; economic exclusion; religious exclusion and sexual exclusion. As is the case in almost all typologies, they are not pure types frequently exhibiting many problematic overlaps and intermingling amongst them. Typology works as a kind of scaffold to help us to construct the building as well as to deconstruct it.

Cultural Exclusion

Modern culture is logocentric. It depends on the metaphysics of presence and is based on the correspondence between concepts and things or persons. It is a logical culture, a culture of the *logos*. It is a literary culture. Truth is, then, the *adequatio* of the concept (or word) to the thing in such a way that being and word becomes the same thing. In this logocentric culture priority is given to words, spoken words and written words. A person of culture reads daily newspapers but also journals, books and magazines. McLuhan, some decades ago, announced the end of the book and the advent of the electronic media culture. Students in the 1960s and 1970s were waiting for the death of what was then called the Guttenberg galaxy. But this did not happen. In many cultural centres throughout the world, book fairs increase in size annually. The market in books is constantly growing and generating enormous profits for those investing in it.

The Church in many places throughout the world lives within the same logocentric culture. It is for the most part a religion of the book. In some instances, it is the religion of many books: the missal, the Bible, the hymnal, the catechism, together with manuals of theology, dogma, doctrine, canon law, constitutions as well as church journals and bulletins. In order to be a member of the Church one has to read all the time. To be a good member of the Church (an inclusive member) one has not only to be able to read but to read well. And here we have the first type of exclusion. Especially in Latin America, not everybody knows how to read: illiteracy rates are very high. When we come to the liturgies the result is tragic. Congregations are required to read responses, prayers, biblical lections and hymns, but illiterate people cannot do this. They are, then, excluded from that kind of worship.

Cultural exclusion also happens in the wording of the liturgy, through sermons and homilies, and in the space of the celebration. People are asked to understand the liturgy. The reformers were literate people and they wanted everyone to be part of the learned assembly. This is why they translated the Bible and the many parts of the Mass into the vernacular. The reformers resembled in some way the ancient Gnostics. A certain number of nice ideas developed by the Greek philosophers entered in the vocabulary of the

Church, always in a binary form. Among them, the opposite concepts of truth and error became prominent. This was part of the theological effort of establishing orthodoxy against heresy. Salvation became identical to knowledge. And knowledge had to be tested by the canons of right doctrine. This created also a new form of exclusion. Heretics had to be expelled from the congregations of the orthodox Christians. We all know how the history of the exclusion of heretics developed. It generated anger, persecution and, finally, torture and death. Some theologians of liberation in Latin America tried, unintentionally, to recreate the same climate of righteousness, changing the concept of orthodoxy to the equally modern and moralistic concept of orthopraxis. In order to have ortho/praxis we have to have also a rule, a pattern, a matrix idea and foundation. And this was found in reason.

The emphasis on reason is not new in the history of the Church: it is already present in the New Testament. In the First Epistle to the Corinthians, chapter 14, we read: 'In church I would rather speak five words with my mind, in order to instruct others also, than ten thousand words in a tongue' (v. 19). There are many more examples but, for the time being, it is sufficient to recall the counsel given to Timothy: 'give attention to the public reading of scripture, to exhorting, to teaching ... pay close attention to yourself and to your teaching, continue in these things, for in doing this you will save both yourself and your hearers' (First Epistle to Timothy, chapter 4, 13 and 16). Salvation would, then, come from rational knowledge. Throughout the history of the Church, this kind of rational religion was constantly in tension with the mysterious and mystic character of liturgical celebrations.

Another consequence of this emphasis on reason and understanding appears in the moral teaching of the Church. Preaching became central in many Protestant traditions, especially among Puritans and fundamentalists. The gospel of grace and absolution became the threat of condemnation and exclusion. The Puritan evangelical culture established commandments, moral canons and a very precise code with rules of behaviour. But, in order to be fair to the reformers, we have to recognize that this tendency was already present in some passages of the New Testament and the Church Fathers. We could even trace this to some Old Testament roots. The Lutheran doctrine of justification by faith through grace was much more accepted as doctrine than way of life. If for Luther it represented a spiritual experience of liberation, for his followers it became a doctrine. And doctrines are seldom liberative factors in the struggle for justice.

A rationalist religion is a religion of the book. Any religion of the book tends to exclude those who cannot take the book as revelatory. In order to transcend the literalism of rational religion we have to go from hermeneutics to deconstruction. And beyond reason (technical and scientific reason) the worship of the Church opens new possibilities which give priority to the body, to the senses and, consequently to aesthetics. Brazilian culture is a bodily culture. It leans toward Dionysian expressions of life much more than to Apollonian neatness and order. Carnival and soccer are, somehow, symbols of our way of living. Ours is also a culture of the open air. We love our beaches, the sea, the streets, the parks and our forests. People like music and dance. And our popular music is a mixture of African beats, native rhythms, Portuguese melancholic melodies and international influences brought through TV and cinema. All these elements constitute a very strong erotic and sensual dimension, visible in the way people dress, not only on the seashore but also in our sidewalks, in the way we move our bodies and through the style of our exchange of affections through hugs, kisses and different kinds of touch. I should add that our hot climate predisposes people for all these things. It follows, obviously, that we are not a people of the book. People prefer images to letters. They prefer art to philosophy and experience instead of theories.

The liturgy, however, may also be another hindrance to liberation when it is taken as given by God to be performed according to rules given by Church authorities, given once forever, unchangeable and sacred. Instead of being the expression of the people, it risks to be the expression of Church authorities. And this embraces not only the words of the liturgy, but also its space, its time and its performance. In a recent symposium held in Brazil, one of the lecturers proposed that our churches should stop reading the Bible for a certain time, giving place for other kinds of readings or expressions. I have, myself, proposed many times that the Church to which I belong (the Anglican) should allow a liturgical experiment beyond the Book of Common Prayer, leaving it aside for a while, liberating the people from the rigid forms that we have inherited from the English Reformation.

Economic Exclusion

In many places today throughout Latin America religious thinkers are very critical of Theology of Liberation: I am among them. Theology of Liberation was like a dream. In the first moment, we believed in the transforming power of theology. Theology was considered a tool, an ideological apparel and a platform stating principles and policies for a revolution. We thought that the situation of poverty, misery and oppression in the Third World could only be overcome through a Christian revolution. We were engaged in many socio-political analyses with the help of sociologists and politicians. I remember the time when Gustavo Gutiérrez, Juan Luis Segundo, José Miguez Bonino, Jon Sobrino and others met together in different places in Latin America to debate issues such as popular religion and the idea of the people as subjects of history. I listened to them carefully. It was a kind of romantic movement, idealist and out of the blue. Some Latin American Christians were tempted to look at the communist countries as models for the establishment of the Kingdom of God on earth. In the 1970s, after visiting Warsaw, Prague, Budapest, Kiev, Minsk and Moscow, I was shaken by the many contradictions to be observed. I also visited Berlin when the wall cast a shadow over all our dreams of freedom and equality: West Berlin and East Berlin divided by that huge wall of separation! And I also wandered twice throughout the island of Fidel Castro, eating with the people and testing their dreams and hopes ... hopelessly!

I live in São Paulo, Brazil, one of the biggest cities in the world. This is a place of many exclusions. I do not think we need statistics in order to recognize that. Exclusion is visible all around: economic exclusion. The slogan, 'the poor are getting poorer and the wealthy, wealthier' still applies to our situation here. Theology of Liberation knew this. Our Latin American economic situation touched our hearts and minds. Theology of Liberation was the result of our compassion and powerlessness, written with tears and pain. Because the economic situation was so pressing and overwhelming, we tended to concentrate our efforts around the basic needs of our people: food, clothing, shelter, land, water, health – what else? Then we turned the liturgy into propaganda. We wrote songs of liberation. We encouraged our poets and musicians to express our hopes and dreams. We read the Bible as if it were a commandment. We took it literally: we became fundamentalists. In asking: in your place, what would Jesus do?, we ignored the gap existing between the first century and ours.

But why did Theology of Liberation die? It died because, in the first place, theology is also dying. Because the death of God suddenly became evident. As Heidegger put it so poetically, 'the gods fled from the world and the world became dark' (Heidegger 1975: 188). The result of this is the awareness that we are living the situation called by San Juan de la Cruz the 'dark night of the soul'. Theology of Liberation died but the situation once denounced by it (socio-economic-politic) still persists. And it persists because modernity and globalization are active and well organized in the capitalist world. Neoliberalism, an offspring of capitalism, dominates from the First World, oppressing and manipulating the poor countries of the world. Brazilian society is a society divided among classes. Peasants and indigenous tribes live on the verge of misery. Unemployment and illiteracy are still growing problems around us. Public health and education are not seen as priorities. We are used to corruption and robbery in many levels of our public administration without constraint of right judgement and accountability. The minimum salary in Brazil is still below the equivalent of US$100. In our big cities, besides transportation chaos and filth in parks and streets, there are crowds of homeless adults and children generating criminals of all kinds. This dreadful situation creates a favourable climate for the use of drugs, the practice of prostitution and the degradation of human beings.

The socio-politic-economic situation creates a great mass of excluded people. They are naturally excluded from society at many levels. Let us take the example of our universities. It is true that we have high-level public academic institutions. They are free and, in some cases, offer to their students accommodation and very inexpensive meals. But the poor can hardly complete their secondary school programme because they do not have sufficient time and health to cope with the economic difficulties in their families. They have also to bear the burden of very tiring jobs distant from their homes and from the university.

Churches in general do not have the necessary know-how to address such situations. It is easier, on the other hand, to call the poor to be part of huge Pentecostal assemblies where emotional singing and ecstatic experiences provide some relief and rest to them in the midst of their day-to-day sufferings. Some of these churches preach a theology of prosperity prompting many unemployed people to offer their service and lives in exchange for goods promised by the pastors and guaranteed by a complacent God. The economically excluded find in these churches a place of inclusion, at the cost of losing their freedom and, consequently, themselves. It is, of course, a tragic choice.

Traditional, historical churches have no place for the poor. Generally the congregations are comprised of middle-class people with good will but very small sensibility to open their doors and programmes for the socially different.

Against the background of modernity, there are signs of what has been called postmodernity. What does this term mean? It is not a new epoch in history. It is a tendency or, perhaps, a condition, as Lyotard has described it (Lyotard 1979). It arises from disappointment with the promises of technology, science and democracy. If, on the one hand, the Enlightenment created the century of light, it also opened, on the other, the way to wars, to the dictatorship of the market and to imperialism. The final result of modernity is globalization. The key features of modernity are certainty, dogma, law, reason and order. Postmodern thinking denies the possibility of certainty, the stability of dogmas, the perennial aspect of law and the priority of reason. It defies globalization and proposes fragmentation and the beauty of the small. Against the inclusion promised by globalization, postmodernity believes in another kind of inclusion, the inclusion in the group, in the small community and in the gathering of friends. This is why in the postmodern condition there is no place for 'grand narratives'.

Religious Exclusion

I attended a Eucharistic celebration led by a priest of the Eastern Orthodox Church at the liturgical space provided by the World Council of Churches in Canberra, Australia, as part of the official programme of the 1991 World Assembly of WCC. I was enjoying the beauty of the performance and the fine old traditional music of that Christian tradition, when just before the distribution of the sacramental body and blood of Christ, the celebrant expressed a deep and painful concern, telling us that all non-orthodox Christians were excluded from the heavenly banquet at that most sacred and communal meal. We had been together during this world gathering for many activities, for minor liturgical prayers, some singing, meals at the refectory, chats and smiles, embraces and debates. But when the occasion came to test our commitment to communion (called there by the beautiful Greek term, *koinonia*) there was a stone in the midst of the pathway. We, non-Orthodox Christians, were excluded. At that point I left the place wondering what strange interpretation of the Eucharist was that, when after the consecration of the mystical elements, a particular segment of the so-called Christian Church took possession of something that does not belong to it, retaining it to its particular historical group, as if the Orthodox Church were the only existing Christian Church in the world. This, of course, was not the first experience of exclusion from the 'table of the Lord'. I have passed many times through this unbelievable and ugly atrocity. And each time when this happens I wonder what are they doing, pretending to be the owners of a non-existing copyright. The owner of the Eucharist is the one who supposedly is presiding over it since its first celebration in the Upper Room. And he is always inviting his friends to share his meal with him in joy and love.

I worked for many years, until February of 2004, as an official member of the Anglican/Roman-Catholic International Commission (ARCIC) trying to find ways for implementing the relationship between these two churches. The work of this commission was sponsored by the Vatican and by Canterbury. We produced many convergence documents on doctrinal and practical questions. We even published an official statement about the doctrine of the presence of Christ in the Eucharist in which divergences were erased and agreement was reached. Throughout decades we met annually and spent days and nights together, eating around the same table and worshipping in the same chapels, visiting monasteries, abbeys, cathedrals, convents and historical sites related to the missionary adventures of our churches. We felt accepted one by the other. We developed bonds of affection amongst us: we became friends. But the experience of being included in the same fellowship was not sufficient to give us courage to open our sacramental table one to the other. So, at the Lord's Table we excluded ourselves mutually. And this experience of exclusion made me feel sad and foreign to my self and to the Church.

In my ecumenical experience I learned that we do not need theological agreements in order to get together. We just have to get together. Differences are not to be overcome. Our differences are gifts, divine gifts, to be kept with reverence and awe. We only accept others when we are able to accept their peculiar ways of being and behaving.

Ecumenism has suffered the disease of globalization. There was a time when we dreamed of a unified church universal. I heard many times from ecumenical leaders that we should seek nothing less then the creation of a single, unified and organic church. Some even thought of the World Council of Churches as the embryo of such an organic, one Church. This was also the ideal of modernity. It was linked to the will to power, so sinfully interwoven with our pride and self-sufficiency. Postmodernity has shown the fallacy of all global projects. And because our perceptions are partial and feeble, we Christians discovered that there are so many other fragments of religion around the world and throughout history to be taken into consideration that we, with our separate denominations, are only a tiny portion of the people called by the one we call God to stand in awe and adoration before the mystery of life.

If this is true, we Christians have to deconstruct the great narratives of our past and the complexity of our systems in order to be able to see in the fragments of our institutions and in the partiality of our interpretations, the seeds of a new age of communion in spite of differences.

I mentioned above the proclamation of the death of God. Nietzsche, who was so vehement in transmitting this macabre notice, said that we were the murderers of God. May be he was right for his own time. But today the death of God means the death of a God imprisoned in our systematic theology, in our dogmatics, in our immoral morality and in our idolatrous worship. It seems that looking at the American dollar bill the Almighty and Omnipotent God is ashamed of being the God in whom the Americans trust, as the guarantor of his imperial economy. At this point God prefers to die. The dying God is the same Jesus who was crucified and descended into hell. 'From noon on, darkness came over the whole land until three in the afternoon ... then Jesus cried again with a loud voice and breathed his last. At that moment the curtain of the temple was torn in two, from top to bottom. The earth shook, and the rocks were split' (Mt. 27.45, 50 and 51). We are re-enacting this same story today. Old certainties are shaken and the rocks are split. We have no sure foundation any more. We are living between noon and three o'clock and darkness is over the whole land. We are now like the women who 'were also there, looking on from a distance' (v. 55). This is what Heidegger also means when, speaking about the poets, invites us to 'look from a distance', listening to the words of poetry, waiting for the return of the gods.

In the period of darkness over the land, there is no point in excluding or including. We are all here wandering through the night of the soul. Perhaps it would be good to say that without knowing it we have been included in this waiting by the work of grace.

Sexual Exclusion

We come now to the last type of exclusion, perhaps the most important of all of the four. It is the most important because it touches the centre of our humanity as well as of society. It is cultural, economic and religious. It is cultural because there is no culture without bodies. And bodies are sexual. I wrote a poem some years ago celebrating the beauty of the body, starting with this verse: 'My sex begins in my foot ... it begins also in my hand ... in my eyes ... in my mouth ... it is my body.' Sex is also related to economy in many ways. Are the starving and hungry equally prepared for the sexual pleasures so well performed by healthy and well-nourished people? What is the role of money in the development of bodily relationships? Sex has been interwoven with religion from the beginning. In pagan religions, goddesses and gods had sex and passion. They would never have worried about Sodom and Gomorrah. Only a Puritan god would be able to send his angel to destroy those engaged in sexual acts of pleasure. Our Christian God has been pictured like that. He is a father but has no wife. He has a son but never experimented with an ejaculation. And the Spirit, who is an invisible and disembodied idea, has no body to be caressed or with which to embrace other bodies. This is why in the Book of Common Prayer of the Anglicans, God, Father, Son and Holy Spirit, has no body, no parts and no passions.

The Greeks had the strange idea of separating human beings into two parts: the soul (or mind, or spirit) and the body (or matter, *physis*). For them, spirit or mind were the superior part of humans, contrasting with bodies, fallen matter, inferior and debased. In ancient Greece human beings might suffer a certain accident and fall down into the material world: according to the biblical mythology the same human beings were expelled from Paradise because they ate from the forbidden fruit and discovered that they were naked bodies. Both Greek philosophy and biblical theology, invented the same dichotomy of body and spirit. This turned out to be a sinister Pandora's Box from which emerged all types of disgrace and evil. If our bodies are inferior and are constantly fighting against the spirit, we have the obligation to overcome them for the sake of our spirits. Greek philosophy created the method of intellectual ascesis in order to help us to go back to the blessed world of ideas. Christianity also created ascetic practices, often sacrificial, to help sinners to get rid of their bodies in order to enjoy a perfect 'spiritual life'. This kind of theology, known as Puritanism, was based in the concept of sin and, in spite of transferring human guilt to the crucified Jesus, it forgot the divine grace and stressed good works. Postmodern thinking does not believe in this. Sartre, for instance, stressed the coincidence of existence and essence. We are our body. It is in the body that we are spirit. Paul Tillich said once that Christians never learned to deal with sexuality. Behind this suspicion lies the opposition between body and spirit. The Christian Church tried to tame our instincts. It invented the idea that Christian marriage, for instance, was instituted by God and twisted the narrative of the wedding in Cana (John 2:1–10) to proclaim that Jesus was there to bless the newlyweds. But it seems to be clear that Jesus was there to enjoy the party and to drink wine. Selecting the institution of marriage as the norm, the Church limited the rich possibilities of human sexuality and condemned all practices which did not fit its dogmatic theology.

Sexual exclusion originates from the narrowing of our bodily (and sexual) possibilities. I shall illustrate this with two contemporary cases taken from my experience in the Anglican Communion: the ordination of women and the consecration of a gay bishop. For centuries, only man could be ordained priest in the Church. The history of this adventure is well known. The fight had started officially by the decade of 1940. Throughout the debate it became clear that for centuries women had been excluded from the catholic orders of the Church. It became also clear that the Church had been ruled by a phallocentric hierarchy. At the bottom of this controversy it became also clear that the problem was to have or not to have a penis. If any candidate for holy orders did not have a penis he could not be a priest (no penis, no priest!). Even if this prejudice has been overcome in many Anglican provinces around the world, the issue is still debatable and some so-called believers refuse to take communion from the hands of a woman. The second case is much more revealing. Gays and lesbians have been ignored by the official Church. But they have been around all the time. How many of Jesus' disciples were gays and lesbians? Who knows? How many transgressors (sadomasochist, queer, transvestites, transsexual, onanists, drag queens, eunuchs – why not?) have through the centuries approached the holy altar to receive the body and the blood of Christ in their pure anonymity?

The case of Bishop Gene Robinson is, however, telling. His consecration shook the whole Anglican Communion (some 70 million baptized Christians). Some fundamentalist Provinces are asking for the ex-communion of the American Episcopal Church where the 'blasphemy' was perpetrated. And this was done in the name of the Father, the Son and the Holy Spirit. Most of the debate is based on the Resolution 1.10 of the last Lambeth Conference (1998): 'This Conference ... recognizes that there are among us persons who experience themselves as having a homosexual orientation ... we commit ourselves to listen to the experience of homosexual persons and we wish to assure them that they are loved by God and that all baptized, believing and faithful persons, regardless of sexual orientation, are full members of the Body of Christ ... cannot ... ordaining those involved in same gender unions ...' (9). I have no reason to think that the bishops were not saying what they wanted to say. But if they said this (and they did) they were out of their minds or, still worse, they failed to be honest. If baptized homosexuals are full members of the Body of Christ and if God loves them, why can they not be ordained in the Church of the same loving God? The Anglican Communion has boasted of its inclusiveness. Why, then, exclude these 'loved by God' from the most sacred of its ministries? Were the bishops just playing with words? In the long-lived experience of the Christian Church there is nothing better than to be loved by God. Without any doubt, it is better to be loved by God than to love God. Were the bishops afraid to affirm that homosexuals not only are loved by God but that they also love God? What kind of love were they imagining between homosexuals and God? I do not believe that in the year 1998 the Anglican bishops were aware of 'queer theology'. I wonder how they would behave if they could admit that, after all, God could also be a gay god or a lesbian goddess?

Sexual exclusion is the worst of all exclusions because it denies God's creation, at the centre of which is the human heart. The Church wants to be one. It says daily that it is one. The difference and the different are a threat to the unity of the Church. In order to be one, the Church wants instruments of unity, coercive and patrolling, as in the medieval Church. The Holy Inquisition had the mission to purify the Church from the different. Witches, sorceresses, heretics, homosexuals, adulterers, contenders and unbelievers were burned at the stake. We wonder today if those thus disinherited by the Church were not also 'loved by God'? It is very probable that God forgave them, because he is divine and to forgive is his highest office. If in the place of unity we can see love at the top of the pyramid, things can be different. If the Anglican bishops were able to recognize that homosexuals are loved by God, why should it be so difficult for fundamentalists and conservatives to follow God's example and start loving them right now? And if the bishops had the courage to affirm that they, the homosexuals, are full members of the Body of Christ, does it not mean that those who hate them and reject them, excluding them from the Body of Christ, are against the will and the love of God?

Liberation Theology Beyond Inclusion and Exclusion

The postmodern condition does not give rules nor propose schemes or orientations. The excluded know that they are excluded because they have experienced exclusion in their own lives. What does liturgy mean for them? Do they need a liturgy? This is not a good question. No one needs a liturgy. Liturgy does not belong to the category of the things needed. It is not utilitarian. Liturgy is like art; it is poetry; it is dance; it is painting; it is sculpting; it is theatre; it is cinema, music, opera and play. It is and it is not. It is not poetry; it is not dance; it is not painting; it is not sculpting; it is not theatre; it is not cinema, music, opera or play. It is liturgy. It is the action of the people gathered for experiencing and experimenting with the joy of being alive. It is the bewilderment in face of the abyss and under the threat of the nothing. It is the wonder of standing out of the nothing in the presence of the mystery of being present, the wonder to be in the verge of nothing, but not alone in nothingness.

The Church stands on the verge of the abyss of nothingness. And this is good. And the liturgy contemplating the abyss sees that it is good. And this is good because the abyss, with its darkness and emptiness, empties the Church of its prejudices and dogmas, preparing the way to forgiveness. Jesus said once that we are called to love our enemies. Our enemies are the different. In order to love the enemies we have to face them to let them be 'enemies' which by the grace of God are loved. The binary conception expressed by the words inclusion/exclusion is still fruit of modernity and of the logical way of thinking. But we, Christians, are called to be fools. And only like that we will be able to open our worship to the different without asking them to be literate, to be like us, to have the same tastes we have, to love in the same way we are used to.

How could a liturgy of liberation be the experience of overcoming inclusion/exclusion? There are no prescriptions. The only possible way to be followed is the way of love, and perhaps, queer love.

References

Gadamer, H-G. (1975) *Truth and Method*. London: Sheed and Ward.
Garaudy, R. (1973) *Danser sa Vie*. Paris: Seuil, p. 8.
Gilkey, L. (1996) 'Can Art Fill the Vacuum?', in D. Apostolos-Cappadona (ed.) *Art, Creativity and the Sacred*. New York: Continuum.
Heidegger, M. (1965) *Der Satz von Grund*. Pfullingen: Verlag Günther.
Lyotard, J-F. (1979) *La Condition Postmoderne*. Paris: Les Éditions de Minuit.
Vahanian, G. (1989) *Dieu anonyme*. Paris: Desclée de Brower.
Von Balthasar, H. (1975) *Gloria: Una Estética Teológica*. Milan: Jaka Books.

Chapter 11

Love in Times of Dictatorships: Memoirs from a Gay Minister from Buenos Aires

Roberto González with Norberto D'Amico

Translation from the Spanish by Marcella Althaus-Reid

The Context

During the years 1976 to 1983, I lived through the most terrible period in the history of my country, Argentina. That part of our history, which the military government euphemistically called 'The Process of National Reorganization', left us with 30,000 people disappeared, that is, a whole generation which now is absent. During those years we were all living in a climate of suspicion. Many frightened people used to murmur that the ones who disappeared must 'have disappeared for a reason'. They were guilty of something. As a nation we did not realize that those people, tortured and killed, amongst whom are included the names of many intellectuals, workers, students and youngsters, were searching for human rights and justice in our land.

It was in the midst of the dictatorial regime, in the year 1977, that I started to work with the Argentinian Commission for Refugees (CAREF), related to the United Nations programme for refugees. I was working with people coming from countries near our borders. They were mostly people escaping from countries suffering from dictatorial regimes, and with them I started to learn my first lessons about freedom and human dignity. These were terrible times in my life, times of desolation in the midst of death and a systematic negation of life. It was precisely in this moment that a new theological thinking started to emerge in Buenos Aires, from the ecumenical Evangelical Institute of Theological Studies (ISEDET). It was a thought already initiated in the 1960s, which represented hope for many while at the same time being perceived as a threat by others. I am talking here of Liberation Theology.

Those times were far from easy and ISEDET suffered persecution. Indeed, its library was bombed, destroying many of its valuable and irreplaceable books and manuscripts. Meanwhile, lecturers and students went through a time of harassment in the form of anonymous threatening phone calls. Unfortunately, some threats were carried out: one of its professors, Dr Mauricio López, was kidnapped by paramilitary forces and killed. To make matters worse, to this political persecution another one was added. This was from conservative evangelicals who dismissed the work and seriously questioned the faith of those who dared to mix theology with what they called, 'things of this world', such as politics and economics. They referred to ISEDET as 'The Communist Faculty of Theology' of Buenos Aires, which did not help the situation at all.[1]

I began studying theology in ISEDET in 1980 while the situation was still bad. As students we still received at that time threats and harassing phone calls, so much so that we used to take turns to keep some vigilance during the nights, because we had a good-size community of students living on the campus. But there were exceptional people in ISEDET, such as Professor José Severino Croatto,[2] whom I still remember with love and admiration. He was an erudite biblical scholar and a Liberation Theologian, a coherent human being who taught as he lived, in evangelical poverty and obedience. He taught me that the Bible is not a 'closed book' as if it were a fixed deposit of truth, but rather a book open to all the changes and challenges that a community of believers might need to go through. Severino was a minister and a teacher who help me during those difficult years.

Only a Promise

But who was I during those times, and what was my own theological identity within Liberation Theology? It happened that my life was so full of conflicts that it had become also a battlefield for other struggles with other kinds of dictatorial regimes. Those were personal dictatorial regimes, born of prejudices and a sense of self-negation from my homophobic context. In the same way that Latin America was crying out for freedom, my own body became a symbolic continent in need of liberation, searching for healing and salvation.

In 1985 I separated from my wife and my children, during a very painful period of my life. I could not understand at that time that doors were about to be opened for me, doors of reconciliation, healing and salvation through the opportunity to be, for the first time in my life, myself. Many friends may remember my sufferings at that time. I even remember that Marcella Althaus-Reid, who was a friend and fellow student in my class, suggested that I should start my own gay church. I thought she was outrageous. The point is that at that time the memory of my father was very present to me. When he was dying, and I was 15 years old, he asked me to promise him that I would be 'a man'. He wanted me to marry and to have children, to define my identity as heterosexual, or at least to never make public my homosexuality. It was after he died that I received a call to become a church minister. When I was 19 years old I became a Salvationist, and in the Salvation Army I thought I had found a way to fulfil what I promised to my father, in what I thought was an ideal way. How? I saw many men in the Church struggling also with their sexual identities while praying that God would heal them from the sin of homosexuality. I knew men who concealed their sexual identity and lived in fear and guilt, while making an extra effort to work hard in the Church. So I did the same and also married and had children, a boy and a girl. Was not that the ideal, what my father, my society and my Church wanted me to do?

After many years of hard work, I left the Salvation Army and went to study theology at ISEDET, motivated by a search of an integral Gospel which could address the needs of my country in such difficult political times. Then one year after I separated from my wife, I fell in love with a man, for the first time in my life. Although that relationship did not prosper, it helped me to get closer to God. How? Because it was a time of intense turmoil in my life and I found myself alone, without a minister or counsellor to help me through. Only God was there. I was completing my theological studies while working very hard to pay for my studies. Without a family or a church to support me, I had never felt so fragile in my whole life and yet, paradoxically, I was starting to experience great peace and happiness. I was not feeling sad anymore and I stopped feeling guilty. I found falling in love with a man to be a healing experience and it brought a sense of inner reconciliation with myself. I now needed to deal with God in this matter. What was God thinking now about me? Was God judging or condemning me?

It happened that in order to pay for my studies, I needed to work late as a receptionist at ISEDET. One evening, taking the opportunity when alone, I prayed as I had never done before. It was a special moment and I received the assurance that God had accepted me, loving me as I am and that, as the *Letters to the Romans* says, nothing and no one could ever separate me from the love of God. The significant thing for me was that, for the first time, I used the word 'homosexual' in my prayer. That was the first time that I spoke to God about my sexuality. How was that possible? Why had I never spoken to God about something so personal about myself? What kind of faith had I had that prevented me from speaking to God about myself? I experienced this as deeply challenging, as if I had found God for the first time and spoken with God face to face. It was an experience of conversion.

However, I knew that by coming out I was going to lose the rest of my family, my friends and my place in the church, and consequently the opportunity to fulfil my desire to serve through pastoral work. That sense of lost was immense, but I also felt I was about to gain 'a people'. That was a kind of promise I received from God, that is, that God would allow me to develop my life of faith and my work as a minister. Since then I have always claimed that God fulfils God's promises if we trust in God. I was finishing my theological studies when I came out and many gays and lesbians wanted to talk with me about faith issues. Many heterosexual friends also felt closer to me, as if I was becoming a more sincere, spontaneous person in my life and relationships. However, many others became very critical. Sexuality was not an issue for theological studies, nor an issue for the pastoral work of the churches. The Methodist Church had been supporting my studies up until then, but decided to withdraw this support, just before my exams.[3]

Fortunately, fellow students pressured the authorities of ISEDET to allow me to take my final exams. Yet, it was hard. I remember that when the then dean of ISEDET told me that I was allowed to take my finals he also added: 'I don't know what for ... no church will ever give you any work to do.' I replied to him: 'This is not a problem for you; this is God's own problem.'

'The Faggots Are Inventing a Church'[4]

Those were difficult times for me, full of insecurity and fears for my own future but I had a divine promise. Jesus had accepted me as gay and had renewed his call for a life in the ministry of the Church. I wanted to be a minister for all people. Then I had the blessing to discover the existence of the Metropolitan Community Church (MCC) and I decided to organize a faith community in Buenos Aires. I then made photocopies of something I wrote, inviting people to gay prayer meetings and went distributing them around gay bars and a few streets where gays were starting to move with more freedom after the end of the dictatorial regime. I remember that one night a young man took a leaflet, read it and exclaimed: 'It is incredible! As if the faggots do not know what to invent, they are now inventing a church!' It may have been said with irony, even contempt, but there was some truth in those words. We were about to invent a church; a church where everybody could be welcome; a space for reconciliation with themselves and with God; a place where everyone was going to be invited to the sacred meal.[5] To invent such a church became the aim of my life and one year later (September 1988), Rev. Elder Donald Eastman came to Buenos Aires from the MCC in the USA to ordain me as a minister of our *Iglesia de la Comunidad Metropolitana de Buenos Aires*. A long journey, but God fulfilled God's own promises.

Sunday Worship in a Gay Bar: The First Years

I started the work with tremendous enthusiasm, hope and expectation. At that time we did not have a church building as such, but used to gather in different places. Sometimes we were able to rent a room big enough for worship, at other times we used the living room of one of our members. For a time we used to have worship in a gay bar that gave us its premises for that purpose. The members of our congregation never missed worship, because if they did they would not know where we were going to be next Sunday.

Paradoxically, while we were becoming a striving community, celebrating the Eucharist in bars, other churches that owned large sanctuaries but had very small congregations never offered to give us space for our celebrations. Sometimes we spent months in respectful conversation with a church in order to see if we could use some of their free space once every so often for our worship services, but their responses were usually negative. Then, the conservative fundamentalists (the same people who during the military regime accused ISEDET of communism) called us 'hell's outlet'. They took photographs of our congregation gathering for Sunday worship, publishing them later as part of a condemnatory article about us. This publication created considerable personal problems for many of our members, not only in their family lives but also in their places of work. Then, shortly after that, thieves broke into our worship place, destroying our sacred objects with fire, including communion cups, crosses, Bibles. Finally, a member of our church was barbarically killed in his own house. The dictatorial regime was gone, but not quite yet for us.

Persecutions

Jorge was an active member of our church. I was abroad, participating in a general convention of the MCC in Minnesota when this crime happened. I met him as we in the church worked as volunteers to help with AIDS patients in the hospital of Buenos Aires. At that time nurses refused to hand a clean towel or a cup of soup to an AIDS patient for fear of contagion. Jorge became one of the first AIDS sufferers who spoke openly of his experience in our church. He was killed in his house, but the crime of his murder was never solved. Meanwhile the Argentinian newspapers were full of headlines about 'the assassination of immoral people', attempting to justify such crimes. What had happened, I wondered, to the idea of the dignity of life in this country? Are not these people children of God also? The main churches were silent. The people who were being attacked had been expelled a long time ago from their churches as well as from theological paradigms. I then asked myself: 'Whatever happened to Liberation Theology?' It was so curious. I had worked with human rights issues before in the context of refugees and now many of our activists had experience of working for human rights from the sexual perspective. We needed to do something to oppose the dehumanization and exclusion of many of our people, without any support from any church, liberationist or not. But, what to do and how?

We decided to use the media to let people know of our struggle. I needed to learn to confront a TV camera, that is, to show my face openly and to speak on radio or to be interviewed by newspapers. A friend, Carlos Jáuregui (founder of the Gay and Lesbian Movement of Buenos Aires), taught me to do these things. Sometimes I appeared in the media as a confident and experienced minister, while at other times I was barely intelligible, like a complete beginner. It was a learning process, as I said to myself: in this ministry, I will always be a beginner. And that was true also when I found that the publicity we sought as a tool to defend the sexual human rights of our members produced a backlash even from those same members against our own church. We were going public by showing our faces in the open, but many had their own fears. I discovered then what a poor image they had of themselves and how much they were in need of affirming their own dignity.

Battles with the Roman Catholic Church

The Roman Catholic Church (RCC) is the majority church of our country. Suddenly it decided to become outspoken against gays and transvestites, and even in some cases to promote what their theologians thought was the justified violence from God against a bunch of immoral people. The TV repeated their theological arguments and the claim that according to the Scriptures to kill or to give a good kicking to lesbians or gays was part of God's will. A prominent leader of the RCC spoke on TV and suggested that the government should create a ghetto for gays. It was said then that since gays were defining their own recreational places (special bars or pubs) and even inventing their own church, then they should have their own country in which to live. They suggested the government should give a parcel of land in the Patagonia for a gay ghetto. However, in the midst of my dismay on hearing these things, God manifested Godself once again. As a consequence of the reaction of the RCC, many Argentinians suddenly became outspoken, condemning the killing of homosexuals, questioning the role of church leaders in this. Encouragingly, the Jewish community phoned me to support our human right claims. One of their leaders offered me a space in a radio programme from their community because, as he told me, a long time ago 'first they took the Jews, then the homosexuals ...'.

Those were the years before e-mail, of phoning people all the time. We gathered for public demonstrations of protest at a moment's notice, whenever needed. Sometimes we were in the streets in the intense heat of a summer afternoon, at other times we were out on cold winter nights. In September 1989, I received a call from the National Registry of Religions. They sent me a document containing the following statements:

> The (MCC) Protestant church has been in existence since 1987, performing activities which are considered to be against public order, morality and decency ... It supports homosexuals, transvestites and transsexuals ... and they perform acts of public support and promotion of homosexuality.[6]

Therefore, we were denied official recognition as a church. We were to be an illegal organization.

Praxis: Doing Pastoral Work Amongst Our People

Our work continued though. We did not have a pastoral model yet, but we were working on it. From the beginning, our pastoral work was done by observation, own experiences and a mixture of trial and errors. The pastoral models I studied in ISEDET, which were the pastoral models from Liberation Theology, did not work for us. The basic ecclesial community model was not useful for us because the situation of oppression of our people and their lives was very different to that of the text books of liberationist ecclesiology. Our people were refugees from many churches, who first of all needed to reconcile themselves with their own lives of faith. On the other hand, the pastoral model developed from the MCC was only partly valid. It was not helpful insofar as it was developed on the basis of the United States experience of being gay, lesbian, bisexual or transsexual, but it was useful in terms of the structure of the church. Firstly, it is a more participative and democratic church structure, more so even than in many of the churches that supported Liberation Theology. Secondly, the richness of the MCC is in its people. Those people, rejected and ill-treated by their own churches, have come together now to form a new community. As a community gathered within much more democratic structures they tended to recreate liturgical acts with renewed freshness, while keeping a respect for traditions. Then, there is the fact that our people tend to question and read the Bible with fresh eyes, discussing many theological issues related to their suffering in the community. In this way, we can all grow together, and even I myself grew in faith in knowledge within the community. I am not ashamed to confess that at the beginning of my ministry I rejected transsexuals and transvestites. I did not want them in my church. Then I came to know many of them, as we worked together in the social activities of the church. Many transvestites suffer so much marginalization from society, that I asked myself if Jesus would not be willing to invite them to be part of his fellowship and share communion with us. I sensed that Jesus would support their fight for human dignity and their struggle for liberation from oppression. We discussed these things in community. We read the Bible while they told their experiences, including their cosmetic surgeries and their lives of transgression of the norms of masculinity and femininity of our country. In this way, we became a Christian community.

Compañero, Lover and Friend

My pastoral work had involved the beautiful challenge of supporting gay and lesbian couples wanting to be blessed, to start their lives together. I remember when I 'married' (although not legally) two women in the church. These are liturgical, symbolic acts, which made me think, as a minister, that miracles do happen. For instance, there is the miracle of love happening against all the odds of oppression. I even blessed the union of a heterosexual couple not allowed to marry in their own church because one of them was a divorced person. The Book of Wisdom is clear on this; there is a kind of miracle which happens when we share our work, our difficulties, and even our bed, with a beloved companion of many years. And it happened that after blessing so many couples, and after having been enriched by knowing their struggles for the right to love each other in public, that I wondered about myself. I was alone.

I met Norberto on a Saturday, in a gay bar on the corner of Santa Fe and Uriburu Street in Buenos Aires. That was 15 years ago. I was coming from a pastoral visit to a gay man suffering from HIV and it was late. I was very tired and decided to go to the bar to refresh myself before going home. I met a friend, sat there and chatted: Norberto was sitting at another table. We looked at each other without saying a word as the night wore on. Then he came over to sit at our table and we talked until the morning. When he took a taxi and left, I went home, walking and thinking that so many years of loneliness were about to end. But I had my fears too. I needed to tell him that I was a minister in a gay church, who had been married for 16 years and had two children ... so many things: and Norberto was an atheist. Would he understand me?

He did, but he did not want to become a Christian. Norberto had suffered a lot in the Church, and did not want to be hurt again by Christianity. However, after the first miracle of love between us, other miracles followed. One day he fell ill and as I nursed him, he asked things about my faith. We spoke a lot. He then started to read the Bible, but without understanding very much. I advised him to read the Gospel of Luke first and the Acts. He went straight to the chapter on Pentecost and after finishing it he shouted 'But I understand now!'. Norberto, as many others, was trying to defend himself from the Church as an institution, but now he could see what was the message of Jesus. A month later he was editing our church bulletin and taking communion in the church. With Norberto, I understood the need for a new biblical hermeneutics to accompany our pastoral task in the MCC. A hermeneutic which can have a dialogue with people, responding to their questions and relating to their experiences. I saw the need for a hermeneutic from people's own bodies and their affective relationships. Norberto's conversion was not necessarily crucial for me as such, but it gave a new depth to our relationship and made of us intimate companions in life, including our life of faith.

When Theology Becomes Flesh

Years ago I started to ask myself who were the theologians who had the courage to honestly deal with issue of desire and pleasure. I found very few. And which is the space that the gift of sexuality occupies in theology? Obviously, the space of indecency.

The questions that GLTTB communities present to theology are very challenging for all contemporary praxis and especially for the praxis of Liberation Theology. The theological subject of Liberation Theology has been 'the new man' (sic), that is, the heterosexual man as head of the family, who is part of the masses in need of political and economic liberation. Rubem Alves, the Brazilian theologian, used to say that we exist and live through our bodies, yet the body does not exist in Liberation Theology. It can even be lost at times in many GLTTB theologies. However, divine revelation is a bodily category. It is through our bodies that a more real sense of divine revelation may occur at times, even more relevant than the homophobic readings of the Bible coming from conservative evangelicals. The fact is that so-called 'sexual minorities' have built their sexual identities through a history of struggles and they know that diversity is part of creation. That sense of diversity becomes dangerous for oppressive systems based on processes of systematic normativity, uniformed thinking and taxonomic styles. However, the class analysis of Liberation Theology is useful here, when we ask how it can happen that the homosexual comedian is respected and admired while the lesbian factory worker suffers misogyny and oppression from her own fellow workers? But we need to return to the issue of desire in theology and question how the capitalist system uses sexuality for consumerism and how sexuality becomes regulated according to political needs. For that, the LGTTB theology needs to be familiar with the hermeneutical circle of Liberation Theology, especially in its dialogical element. And what happens then is that Liberation Theology can become indecent, that is, Liberation Theology can liberate itself from it own *machismo* and homophobia. Liberation Theology and LGTTB theologies complement each other and only by doing a common praxis as liberationists and gays will we be able to be a church without barriers of class, race or sexualities. This is at least what we are trying here, in our church community of Buenos Aires, where we continue the task from the Gospel to invent a church of equal and yet different people loving God and working towards the Kingdom of God amongst us.

Notes

1   Ed. note: To be branded as a communist was equivalent to receiving a death sentence in a country under a dictatorial regime that was supposedly at war with communism. 'Communism' though, was a term used for anything and anybody who defied the dictatorship.

2   José Severino Croatto (1930–2004) is considered one of the most important Latin American biblical scholars of the generation forming the first wave of the Liberation Theology. Although a Roman Catholic he worked extensively amongst Protestant churches and teaching centres in Argentina.

3   Ed. Note: In ISEDET, no student could enrol to study Divinity without the support of a church. The degree of Bachelor of Theology and the Master's degree were linked to the future ordination of the student in a church.

4   The Argentinian expression is '*las locas ya no saben que inventar y se inventan una iglesia*'. The word '*loca*' means crazy woman, indecent women (prostitute) and also a homosexual man or transvestite.

5   Instead of Eucharist, we tend to use the term 'sacred meal' (*comida sagrada*) as
    more significant in our own Latin American context.
6   This can be read in the Resolution No. 2050/94 from the Ministry of Foreign
    Relations and Worship, Buenos Aires, dated 2 August 1994.

Index

Abortion 72, 137–8, 144, 154
African Brazilian Religions 22–3, 54, 112, 120, 131
African theologies 20
Agrupación Familiares de Detenidos-Desaparecidos 6
AIDS 22, 68, 96, 133, 183
Ají de Pollo (colectivo) vii
Aleijadinho 65
Althaus-Reid, Marcella viii, 5–18, 30, 46, 48, 67, 69, 82–3, 94, 100, 102, 135, 157, 179, 180
Althusser, Louis 37
Alves, Rubem 19, 64
Anglican Churches 27, 163, 169, 172, 174–6, 185, 198
Aquinas, Thomas 56
ARCIC (Anglican/Roman Catholic International Committee) 172
Argentinian Commission for Refugees (CAREF) 179
Asian theologies 20
Assmann, Hugo 75
Assuar, Raduar 51

Baptist Churches 4, 7, 141
Basic Ecclesial Communities (BECs) 2, 7, 8, 13–14, 19, 21, 28–30, 141, 143, 166
    GLTTB 100, 186
Béjart, Maurice 165
Berkins, Lohana vii
Bisexuality 3, 5–6, 20, 28, 94, 100, 134, 185
Bispo do Rosario 65
Blanchot, Maurice 61
Boff, Leonardo 19, 30, 41–2, 47, 64, 99, 108
Bonino, José Míguez 38, 46, 169
Butler, Judith 37, 46, 101–2, 107

Calvin, 56
Camdessus, Michel 35
Camera, Dom Helder 142
Capitalism 11–13, 44, 46, 71–2, 74,–5, 170, *see also* Market economy
Cardoso Pereira, Nancy ix, 3, 5, 16, 71–80
Caribbean theologies 20
    the Caribbean region 22–3, 30, 138, 153
Carnivals in Latin America 6, 60–62, 66, 126, 130–31, 134, 168
Carvalhaes, Claudio viii, 2, 7, 51–70
Castells, Manuel 45
Castro, Fidel 170
Católicas pelo Dereito de Decidir vii
Chamorro, Graciela vii, 9, 17
Chico Buarque de Hollanda 63, 67–8
Christian Communities 86, 89, 93, 98, *see also* Basic Ecclesial Communities (BECs)
Cold War 6, *see also* Military Dictatorships, Paramilitars
Compton, Roberto 16
Concilio de Lima 111
Consumerism/comsumption patterns 3, 22, 24, 35, 41, 45, 61, 71, 73–9, 124, 134, 164
Cooper, Thia 71
Córdova Quero, M. Hugo ix, 2, 81–110
Croatto, J. Severino 180, 187

D'Amico, Norberto viii, 2–3, 179–88
D'Uva, Mónica vii
Da Vinci Code 83–4
Decency/indecency as dialectic 92, 95, 131, 125, 128–30, 132, 135, *see also* Indecent Theology
Derrida, Jacques 53, 59, 62, 68, 101, 115, 117

Descartes 113
Dietrich, Marlene, *see* Virgin of Dietrich
Duarte, Sandra de Souza vii
Dussel, Enrique 12–14, 17

Ecotheologies 20
Ecumenical Association of Third World
    Theologians (EATWOT) 20
Ellacuría, Ignacio 40, 47
Evangelical Churches in Latin America
    7, 23, 95, 180, 187
    the Evangelicals 10, 42, 56
    and Culture 168

Farajaje, Ibrahim 100, 102
Favelas 53–4, 68
Feminism 12, 25, 76, 91, 107 137, 140–5
    and Liberation Theology 8, 12–5, 138–
        9, 154, *see also* Feminist Theology
    and sexuality 147, 149, 151, 155
Feminist Theology 19, 25–6, 28, 37, 66,
    73, 75–6, 92, 94
    feminist readings 3, 107
Filoramo, Giovanni 91, 106
Foucault, Michel 37, 82, 101–2, 115,
    135
Freire, Paulo 7–8, 27, 107
Freud, Sigmund 37, 66
Fry, Peter 111

Gadamer, Hans 164
Galvão-Pagu, Patricia 65
Garrincha 65
Gay and Lesbian Movement of Buenos
    Aires 183
Gay bars in Latin America 134, 182, 186
Gays 3, 6, 8, 10, 12–24, 20, 27, 125, 142,
    174–5, 179–89, *see also* Gay bars
Gebara, Yvonne 30, 65, 128
George, Susan 45, 71
Gibson-Graham, J. K. 37, 41, 43
Gilkey, Langdom 164
Globalization 34, 36, 42, 44–5, 64,
    170–2
González, Roberto viii, 2–3, 179–88
Gospel of Mary 88, 93, 105
Grace 35, 53, 62, 65, 86, 144, 152, 166,
    168–9, 172–4, 176
Gramsci, Antonio 57

Gutiérrez, Gustavo 15, 19, 30, 41–2, 57,
    99, 169

Hanks, Tomás 30
Haug, W. 74
Hegel, G. W. F. 107, 116, 120–21
Heidegger, Martin 52, 115, 117, 120–21,
    164, 166, 170, 173
Heterosexuality as ideological system 7,
    9, 10, 100–101
    heterosexual Christians 20, 23, 181,
        185
    heterosexual dissidents 6, 13, 11, 17
    as paradigm 123, 131, 134
    see also and economy, Liberation
        Theology and heterosexuality
Hinkelammert, Franz 35, 40, 42, 45, 47
Homophobia 8, 12, 21, 28, 187
Homosexuality 7, 10, 12–13, 28, 111,
    180–81, 185, *see also* Gays/Lesbians

Iglesia de la Comunidad del Centro de
    Buenos Aires 182, *see also*
    Metropolitan Community Church
IMF (International Monetary Fund) 35–
    5
Indecent Theology 81–3, 94–5, 125, 128–
    30, 132, 135, 187
Indigenous theologies 20
Informe de Verdad y Reconciliación 5
    Informe Rettig 16
International Monetary Fund (IMF)
ISEDET (Evangelical Higher Institute of
    Theological Studies) 179, 180–83;
    185, 187

Jáuregui, Carlos 183
Jewish theologies 20; communities in
    Argentina 184

Kant, E. 113
Kid Abelha 61
Kurtz, Robert 71

Lacan, Jacques 37
Latin American Council of Churches
    (CLAI) 155
Latin American Forum 'Inescapable
    bodies' 15, 17

Lemebel, Pedro 6
Lesbians 5, 6, 20, 27–8, 94, 100, 125, 128,
    142, 181–5, 187
Liberation Theology and heterosexuality
    10–11, 15, 67
  and Roman Catholicism 4, 19, 23–5,
    54
  see also Marx, Karl/Marxism
Lispector, Clarice 65
López, Mauricio 179
Lutheran Church 141
Lyotard, J.-F. 61, 122, 171

Machismo 127, 146–7, 159, 187
Madres de Plaza de Mayo 147
Maduro, Otto viii, 2–3, 15, 19–32
Mandrágora vii
Maraschin, Jaci vii, ix, 2, 15–6, 64, 121,
    163–78
Marianism 139, 145–9, 154, 157
  and Roman Catholicism in Latin
    America 145–9
Mariolatry 14
Mariology of Liberation 8, 14, 146;
    orthodox 149, 157–8, *see also* Virgin
    Mary/Mariolatry/Marianism
Market economy 34, 41–5, 63, 68, 71–6,
    83, 85, 95, 161, 166–7
Marx, Karl/ Marxism 1, 3, 11–13, 25, 41,
    47, 57, 66, 74–5, 108, 111–12, 118,
    121, 166
  and Liberation Theology 7, 8, 10, 37
Mary (wife of Clopas) 92
Mary of Magdala 81–110
Methodist Church 27, 142, 181
Metropolitan Community Church viii,
    182
Military Dictatorships 179, 181, 183;
    185, 187
Military Dictatorships in Latin America
    141, 179, 183, 187
Mo Sung, Jung 41, 46, 80
Moravian Churches 141
Moreira Salles Jr, Walter 66
Mothers of the Dissapeared (Argentina)
    6

National Union of Sex Workers in
    Argentina (AMMAR) 96–7, 107–8

Nuñez González, Héctor 6, 16

Orlando y Bravo, Monseñor 137
Orwell, George 54

Palestinian theologies 20
Paramilitars 179, 187
Pastoral Theology and sexuality in Latin
    America 3, 26, 96, 127, 181, 184–6
Paz, Octavio 76–7
Pentecostal Churches 7, 23, 54
Petrella, Ivan ix, 33–51
Pieper Pires, Frederico ix, 111–23
Pinochet Regime 5
Postcolonialism 8, 9, 17, 44–5, 48–9
Postmodernism 51, 58, 64, 118, 163, 166,
    171–2, 174, 176
Prostitution 8, 24, 27, 66, 80, 96–9, 101,
    104–9, 126, 128–9, 134, 147, 170, 186

Queer
  Theory 1, 33–4, 37, 43, 45–6, 58, 67,
    81, 83, 91, 97, 100–2, 122
  Queer Theology 2, 15, 82–3, 22, 67,
    125, 175–6
  Queer (as theological subjects in
    Liberation Theology) 6, 14–15, 94,
    102, 114, 128, 175, *see also* Queer
    Theology/ Indecent Theology

Race/racism 1, 3, 15, 21, 26–7, 54, 100,
    102, 117, 120, 126, 130, 142
Rahner, Karl 56
Ribas, Mario x, 123–36
Ricoeur, Paul 7, 101
Robinson, Gene Bishop 175
Rocco Tedesco, Diana 90–1, 100, 106
Roman Catholicism in Latin America 1,
    9, 13–14, 38–42, 144, 155
  in Argentina 95
  in Brazil 46, 48, 55–6, 65, 120, 123,
    127, 134
  in Costa Rica 174
  in Nicaragua 138
  and sexuality 137, 152, 157–8, 184,
    187
  structure 7, 137, 139
  see also Marianism/Liberation
    Theology

Romero, Archbishop Oscar Arnulfo 57, 142

Salvation Army 180
San Juan de la Cruz 170
Sartre, Jean Paul 174
Saussure, Ferdinand 37
Segundo, Juan Luis 38, 169
Sexual theologies 20
Sierra, Sola 6, 16
Sobrino, Jon 44, 47, 69, 169
Socio-sexual activists 5–6

Taylor, Mark 59, 60, 62, 68–9, 117
The Virtual Queer Liberation Theology
    Group (*La Virtual QTL*) 2
Tillich, Paul 121, 174
Tomita, Luiza vii
Transsexuals 28, 125, 175, 184–5
Transvestites 5, 8, 175, 184–5

Tribalistas 61–2
Trinta, Joãozinho 65
Tupamaros 16

Vahanian, Gabriel 164
Vattimo, Gianni 51, 115, 117–19
Virgin Mary 23, 79, 82, 88, 94, 98, 107,
    123–38, 144–6
  as symbol 147, 160
  Virgin of Dietrich 134
  see also Marianismo
Viturro, Paula vii
Vuola, Elina x, 137–63

Warhol, Andy 126, 135
World Bank 45
World Council of Churches 155,
    171–2
World Forum on Liberation Theology
    16